D0560794

THE MUSICAL

By the same author

SONGWRITING:
A Complete Guide to the Craft

THE
MUSICAL

From the Inside Out

Stephen Citron

Hodder & Stoughton
LONDON SYDNEY AUCKLAND TORONTO

British Library Cataloguing in Publication Data
Citron, Stephen
  The musical: from the inside out.
  1. Musical shows
  I. Title
  782.14

  ISBN 0–340–49657–6

Copyright © Stephen Citron 1991

First published in Great Britain 1991

All rights reserved. No part of this publication may be reproduced or transmitted
in any form or by any means, electronic or mechanical, including photocopying,
recording, or any information storage and retrieval system, without either prior
permission in writing from the publisher or a licence permitting restricted copying.
In the United Kingdom such licences are issued by the Copyright Licensing
Agency, 33–34 Alfred Place, London WC1E 7DP. The right of Stephen Citron
to be identified as the author of this work has been asserted by him in accordance
with the Copyright, Designs and Patents Act 1988.

Published by Hodder and Stoughton,
a division of Hodder and Stoughton Ltd,
Mill Road, Dunton Green, Sevenoaks, Kent TN13 2YA
Editorial Office: 47 Bedford Square, London WC1B 3DP

Photoset and Printed in Great Britain by Butler & Tanner Ltd,
Frome and London.

To the memory of my grandmother, Malke, herself, a one-woman musical.

CONTENTS

ACKNOWLEDGEMENTS

A book such as this, which attempts to show how musicals are conceived, constructed, rewritten, musicalised, rewritten, cast, rewritten and finally produced could never have been achieved without the cooperation of a great number of people. Many of them are friends of long standing, while others, with a generosity that is typical of theatre folk, opened their homes, their recollections and often their files to answer my queries. As in real life, they often disagree with each other, and with human frailty may often be seen to contradict even themselves. But it is from these very differences of opinion that the reader is able to glean one truth – the axiom that makes theatre, and most of all, the musical stage, the most creative art form in the world – that theatre is only consistent in its inconsistencies.

A few, who gave much of their time and cogitation to delve deeply into the almost impenetrable mystery of artistic creation must be singled out. Friends all, I thank them in no particular order: David LeVine, Director of the Dramatists' Guild supplied up to date information on contracts theatre lore and gossip; William Hammerstein, gave me insight into his father Oscar's method of working on lyrics as well as a recounting of his own experiences as stage director and manager; Thomas Z. Shepard was able to clarify the problems of the record producer as well as the quite different ones involved in being a creative composer; Jerome Lawrence elucidated the opposite side, the predicament of the librettist; Luther Henderson answered all questions about arranging, orchestration and conducting. Mitch Douglas gave insight into getting, and working with, an agent, and artist representatives Hilary Rubenstein, Stephen Durbridge and Rod Hall gave invaluable advice on working with an agent in Britain; Sheridan Morley and Mark Steyn are more than fine dramatic critics, they both have an authoritative overview of musical theatre in the United States and Britain, and contrary to reviewers on other journals, rate musical theatre on a par with drama. They both talked with me at length about musical theatrical trends on both sides of the

9

Atlantic. All the Gilfords – a superbly knowledgeable theatrical family – Jack, Madeline, Joe, Lisa and Sam – active in so many forms of musical theatre offered much useful information on producing, acting and directing. Don Black is not only a gifted and successful lyricist, but as President of BASCA (The British Association of Songwriters, Composers and Authors) offered much help in the technical details of getting a show produced.

Since I believe the best way to illustrate the process of creation of a musical is to see what the great creators from the past have produced, this book had to contain a great many examples from the works of the master professionals. My thanks go to all the publishers and estates who so generously opened their catalogues and let me quote from the works they control: The Rodgers and Hammerstein Estate, The Cole Porter Trust, Warner Brothers Music, Chappell Music, Inc., Carlin Music, Hal Leonard Publications, The Really Useful Music Company, Williamson Music, Warner Chappell Music Limited. The credit for the individual numbers they allowed me to quote from will be found on page 323.

My further gratitude goes to all the theatrical artists listed below who talked with me or answered my questionnaires, and to those from whom I have quoted in public round-table discussions at the Dramatists' Guild, The New School for Social Research or Oxford University. They form a veritable Who's Who of the musical. Their names are listed alphabetically below:

George Abbott, Lee Adams, Billie Allen, Peter Allen, Robert Anderson, Danny Apolonar, Howard Ashman, David Aukin, Burt Bacharach, Russell Baker, Michael Bennett, Alan Bergman, Marilyn Bergman, Leonard Bernstein, Jerry Bock, Alain Boubil, Julianne Boyd, Bill Brohn, Theodore Chapin, Martin Charnin, Cy Coleman, Betty Comden, Barbara Cook, Michael Davis, Agnes de Mille, Howard Dietz, Donald Driver, Fred Ebb, Tom Eyen, Ruth Fainlight, Ron Field, Harvey Fierstein, George Firth, Frances Gershwin, William Gibson, Martin Gottfried, Adolph Green, Stanley Green, Marvin Hamlisch, Sheldon Harnick, Wally Harper, Charles Hart, Jerry Herman, Hal Hester, George Hetherington, Evan Hunter, Tom Jones, John Kander, Ed Kleban, Irwin Kostal, Henry Krieger, James Lapine, Arthur Laurents, Alan Jay Lerner, Cameron Mackintosh, Richard Maltby, Jr., Joe Masteroff, Terrence McNally, Thomas Meehan, Mandy

Patinkin, Hal Prince, André Ptaszynski, Sid Ramin, Rex Reed, Tim Rice, Jerome Robbins, Mary Rodgers, Richard Rodgers, Carol Bayer Sager, Harvey Schmidt, Gerard Schonberg, Stephen Schwartz, Stephen Sondheim, Joseph Stein, Michael Stewart, Richard Stilgoe, Peter Stone, Charles Strouse, Jule Styne, Jo Sullivan, Simon Trewin, Jonathan Tunick, Dale Wasserman, Andrew Lloyd Webber, Fran and Barry Weisler, Richard Wilbur, Maury Yeston.

I should also like to thank agents Hilary Rubenstein, Clarissa Rushdie, Ellen Levine and Mitch Douglas for helping with the content and placement of this book. And a special mention goes to my editors: Simone Mauger and Editorial Director Ion Trewin. Ion Trewin's contributions to all kinds of theatre lore in print are not valued nearly enough. He believed in this book from the start, sent me clippings and advice to improve its internationality, and has been able to bring order to the musical theatre – a field famous for its chaos.

Lastly, to my wife, Anne Edwards, goes my love and deep gratitude. Not only have we written two musicals together, but she has often put aside the biography she was currently working on to listen patiently to umpteen musicals – some great, but most of them not so – for we both believe that one learns more from mistakes than successes. Together we analysed them as well as discussed probable future directions of the musical stage. She discussed the contents and scope of the book with me, read and edited my manuscript, proving to me again the wonders of a truly collaborative marriage.

London, Autumn 1990

ILLUSTRATIONS

between pages 192 and 193

Richard Rodgers and Lorenz Hart[1]
First production of *On Your Toes*, 1936
On Your Toes, Palace Theatre London, 1984[2]

Les Misérables, Palace Theatre London, 1985[3]
Cats, New Theatre London, 1981[3]
The Phantom of the Opera, Her Majesty's Theatre London, 1986[2]

Cameron Mackintosh[3]
Gillian Lynne, Hal Prince and Andrew Lloyd Webber[4]

Stephen Sondheim[3]
Follies, Shaftesbury Theatre London, 1987–1989[2]

Aspects of Love, Prince of Wales Theatre London, 1989[2]
Trevor Nunn[3]

Nicholas Hytner, Jonathan Pryce and Lea Salonga[3]
Richard Maltby Junior, Claude-Michel Schönberg, Alain Boubil and David Caddick[3]

Miss Saigon[3]

Cole Porter[5]
First production of *Anything Goes*, Boston 1936
Anything Goes, Prince Edward Theatre London, 1989[2]

The author and publishers should like to thank the following for giving them permission to reproduce copyright material.

[1] The Mander and Mitchenson Theatre Collection
[2] Donald Cooper
[3] Michael le Poer Trench
[4] Clive Barda
[5] Camera Press

A WORD
ABOUT
MUSICALS

MUSICALS! The very word conjures up the most exciting and diverting form of live theatre in the world today. Flashing chorus girls, stunning scenic effects, dashing leading men, solo turns, tap, ballet, orchestra, follow spot, overture to exit music. Two-and-a-half star-struck hours which the movies have given up filming because they've learned this is a unique art form and their screen, no matter how large, is too small to contain all these effects simultaneously. Hollywood, with rare exceptions, has finally come to realise that it can't wrench the intensity out of the musical form that performers bring to it on stage.

And how are all these seemingly impossible pieces fitted together into a seamless theatrical evening? For whether it be Broadway or the West End, today's successful musical must look effortless and inevitable. From genesis through first night, hit or flop, that flow is achieved by a professionality, whether it be one person who creates, directs and produces the show or a team. A musical is not written in fits and starts, but generally in logical order. Following this outline, the reader will embark on an adventure with various professionals as they bring the threads together into the fully fledged theatrical patchquilt of song and dance that is unique in our times.

To the uninitiated, a cautionary word: writing a musical according to this book can no more ensure a hit than reading Barron's Stock Review or the *Financial Times* can guarantee a killing in the stock market, and although most professionals actually do things according to the rules set down in these pages, the number of unsuccessful musicals far outweighs those that succeed. The reason is simple: there is always the first, the groundbreaking idea. And if it is coupled with a score that is fresh, honest, tuneful and intelligent, success usually waits around the corner. But originality is a scarce commodity and on the heels of each fresh idea we are usually bombarded with several carbon copies of the first – the musical we've all seen.

And, incomprehensibly, even the most astute professionals get caught up in these fiascos. Why? Because they are too close to see their 'baby's' faults. And they are hoping all the good numbers might outweigh the problems inherent in casting, book or score. Sometimes they do, and when they do the result is a glorious art form like *Show Boat* which since its debut in 1927 'keeps rolling along', and thrilling audiences young and old in each succeeding generation.

Then there are others. The ones who have an overwhelming sense of originality. The eclectic Stephen Sondheim and Andrew Lloyd Webber who are bored with working on the same kind of property more than once. Schonberg–Boubil who seem to dramatise, almost overdramatise, everything they touch. Kander, Ebb, Coleman, Hamlisch and Styne who have a greasepaint showbiz sound in all their scores. Strouse, Charnin, Russell and Schwartz who have somehow mixed the sound of rock into their theatre songs without commercialising the product. And the older, unique ones; Kern, Rodgers, Coward, Novello, Hart, Hammerstein, Harburg, Stewart, Fields, Lane, Lerner and Loewe among hundreds of others.

Since a musical is more than libretto, music and lyrics – although we must admit that their quality is crucial to its success – there are the brilliant directors, in our time often choreographers – Robbins, Fosse, de Mille, Nunn, and the costumiers and setting designers. For a musical to succeed, every one of them must have a sense of originality. And when they do, the musical theatre becomes truly the greatest show on earth!

Every one of us wonders, however, where the idea that all the creative people listed above come from. It has to be more than, as Michael Stewart, librettist of *Hello, Dolly, Barnum* and *42nd Street* insists, 'the public library'. Certainly the inspiration to musicalise a minor series of poems by T. S. Eliot that resulted in the blockbuster musical *Cats* did not merely come from scouring our local reading room. The idea to create living and developing personalities from the characters Georges Seurat painted or those that the Brothers Grimm invented as in the Lapine–Sondheim *Sunday in the Park with George* and *Into the Woods* respectively, had to have originated from the creative curiosity of 'what if...?' (No idea in this ground-breaking collaboration is too far-fetched to be entertained.) And the outlandish idea that a Scottish village would come alive for one day every hundred years could only have occurred to an inventive musical mind like Alan Jay Lerner's and seen light in his now classic *Brigadoon.*

The keynote, the viability, the thing that makes American and British musicals the best in the world is this very originality. Perhaps the foregoing sounds chauvinistic but outside these two countries, these ideas do not seem to be flourishing anywhere else in the world. Alain Boubil and Gerard Schonberg, the team responsible for *Les Misérables* and *Miss Saigon*, have moved from their native France to Britain so they may better continue their creative work, because, as Monsieur Boubil states, 'France is still back in the old operetta tradition of the 1930s.'

So finally, the successful musical must be infused with the passion to try something that has never been attempted before. Only then can it have the chance of becoming a hit.

The Broadway or West End musical is generally created by a team of professionals. But I don't mean to imply that it is a closed shop, for any art form that does not breathe new life must quickly wither and die. New members who generally have come up through the ranks, are regularly recruited into the team. They might be assistant directors who have learned from their masters and are creative enough to strike out on their own; they could be rehearsal pianists with the imagination to rearrange the tunes in the show into what is called the 'dance music' that will eventually be approved by the composer, or they could be conductors.* Costume and set designers, indeed all the contributors to the multi-million dollar venture that is the modern musical, have their apprentices who will eventually take the place of their masters.

Sometimes a talent inexperienced in the ways of the theatre might be ideal for a particular musical. Then that artist is

---

*Howard Goodall, who has had two musicals produced, *The Hired Man*, and *Girlfriends*, began his career conducting musicals written by others in London's West End orchestra pits.

invited to join and is inculcated into the ways of this particular art form by the group, as when Edward Gorey, the spooky illustrator, was invited to join the team that was producing 'Dracula' and created his first sets.* But more often, this is not the case, for proven success in one art form does not always translate into another. And the specialists who put together a musical have neither the time nor patience to teach even a gifted creator the many tricks of their theatrical trade.

Perhaps the easiest way to understand a new musical's genesis is by following a hypothetical one from conception to première.

I should preface these remarks by saying that what follows is most applicable if the people involved have had hits before, and even in this case the road ahead may not always be as outlined. Theatre is only consistent in its inconsistencies. Most of today's musicals develop in 'workshop'. Producers rarely have the money to gamble on shows. That said, this is the way it *sometimes* is . . .

HOW MUSICALS ARE CREATED

Before the 'new' musical is born, there is the 'old' musical, the one a group of our hypothetical creators is working on. This is happening in rented space, at least one large and several smaller adjacent studios. Our imagined 'new' musical must begin there with the gruelling rehearsals during which many groups are working separately. The large studio will have the dimensions of the theatre stage the show will eventually be playing on blocked out as work space, while the smaller ones will have a piano, barre and mirrors. The cast will not get on to their theatre stage until much later.

On any afternoon, one might find an assistant music director hammering out harmony parts to help a quartet of male voices to keep in tune, while elsewhere the dance captain is rehearsing several girls in a tricky routine. Another music assistant might be rehearsing the lead singer in some difficult passages in what

---

*Harvey Fierstein was the ideal choice of Arthur Laurents and Jerry Herman to write his first libretto; for *La Cage aux Folles*, whose plot revolves around a gay couple who run an elegant drag show nightclub in the South of France. Mr Fierstein's brilliant, and frankly homosexual play, *Torch Song Trilogy* had won the Tony award the previous year.

is hoped to be the hit song of the show (or a new song that is replacing one that seems not to be working), while the director is blocking a scene between the principals. And they may work in groups or sometimes as a total company well into the evening. When all this is over, nerves frayed, everybody seems to want to go out somewhere to relax.

Here is where the musical is born.

For rather than rehash what went on in the studio they've just left, director and choreographer and composer and lyricist might, in camaraderie, discuss what is going on in their heads and expose future projects that intrigue them. Stories they have always wanted to musicalise; concepts they'd like to investigate; favourite plays that have never become musicals; revivals that only need their own, visionary, fresh treatment to attract SRO (Standing Room Only) houses.

And so the nucleus of our hypothetical musical is formed.

Let's imagine our director, D, has always wanted to do a musical version of *Cyrano de Bergerac*. (It's been done and flopped several times but that was because it was never written or directed, let's say, to D's satisfaction.) In these post-rehearsal discussions or telephone conversations, perhaps he* will discover the choreographer, C, has some splendid ideas as to a timely 'Cyrano' production. The composer and lyricist for the present project may be already committed to a succeeding project or they may simply be uninterested in 'Cyrano'. Eventually, C, D, one of the many theatrical columnists or one of the trade papers will spill the beans about the forthcoming 'Cyrano' and someone is sure to suggest a words and music team *and* a librettist for the property.

Inevitably the 'old' show will be produced and go on to resounding success or, as statistics show, more likely fold after a few performances. D and C, along with L who is now set to write the libretto, and W(ords) & M(usic), the team who will be responsible for the score, will meet to discuss their 'new' project. Their first hurdle is to interest a producer who will have to raise the money. Years ago that would be easy since Broadway and West End production costs were reasonable,

---

*The masculine gender is used throughout this book, and has been chosen to obviate the 'he/she' or the even more patronising 'person/people' so often chosen to avoid sexist language. In every case, unless specified both males and females are meant. Many of the theatre's greatest librettists, lyricists, composers and choreographers are women and nowhere is it intended to exclude females from these pages.

but these days, even the simplest musicals cost millions of dollars or pounds. Assuming D wants to interest a creative producer, he will then have to discuss the basic costs of the musical. It may be his notion to present this 'Cyrano' in modern dress, (less costly) and he will have long discussions with L and producer P about the concept – which must lay bare the sickness in a society that prefers physical beauty to spiritual beauty. Once they have agreed on this, and assuming D has had a running hit in the 'old' show (or if he has had a flop, did not exceed his producer's budget and received personal raves for his direction), he can get a vote of confidence from his producer. (The producer, in turn, may interest a large corporation to commit a hefty sum of money to this new and worthwhile project or sell the rights for an original cast recording to a recording company.)*

L, who has to be a prosperous librettist, either with a sum of money from past hits laid by or a hit show presently running, will go off to work on the book. We have to assume his prosperity for his only income for the six or so months it may take him to rewrite Rostand's play may be the $5,000 (against royalties) guaranteed by the standard Dramatist's contract.†

A few parenthetical words must be said about L at this point, for theatre librettists as a whole – although they are the group largely responsible for the success or demise of the show – are rarely permitted visionary ideas.‡ This is not said to demean them, for their contribution is considerable. But they them-

---

* Such teams as Rodgers and Hammerstein who produced as well as wrote musicals were pretty much a sure bet and 'angels' usually clamoured to be allowed to invest in their shows which promised a handsome return on their capital.

† Luther Henderson, who has orchestrated such shows as *Doctor Jazz* (1975) *Rodgers and Hart* (1975) and *Ain't Misbehavin'* (1978) says that Milt Schaffer, who wrote 'a very good show, *Bravo, Giovanni* (1962) (which Mr Henderson also orchestrated) got discouraged and then decided to give up the rat race and teach school.' And according to Mark Steyn, the aforementioned Howard Goodall, one of the bright hopes of the British musical theatre, abandoned the stage after *Girlfriends*, 'which was a terrible flop. Not so much from his point of view, but because he picked the wrong collaborator ... now he makes a nice living doing film and television music.' Mr Steyn continues: 'You know, when you do a television series, even if nobody likes the music, the series still runs and you get paid ... he's figured "who needs it?" ... to write for musicals now, you've really got to *want* to do it, because practically every other outlet in the popular musical idiom is more lucrative and more attractive ... it's terribly sad.'

‡ When Ferenc Molnar was approached by Giacomo Puccini with a request to adapt his great stage success, *Liliom* for the operatic stage, he denied the Italian composer rights to his play. 'I prefer *Liliom* to be remembered as a play by Molnar,' he said, 'rather than as the libretto of an opera by Puccini.' (The rights were later optioned by Oscar Hammerstein, and *Liliom*, transferred to New England, became one of the great standards of the American musical theatre: *Carousel* (1945).)

selves, and the public at large, think of their work as a craft rather than an art. When a playwright completes a play and it is staged, it is essentially the same script that emerged from his typewriter, but this is not so in a musical. Whole scenes will be lifted and replaced for production numbers; the composer and lyricist will musicalise (read rape and revise) many of his best speeches, or a newly written song may make the speech redundant. The librettist must be utterly flexible about his play, for new scenes to smooth the insertion of new songs will have to be written hurriedly when the show is in previews, and some of his most brilliant dialogue may have to be cut while he stands smiling by. It is easy to think that librettists are not artists in the sense of musicians, lyricists, choreographers and even playwrights, although insiders in the theatre are aware of the responsibility and talent necessary to be a successful librettist. To the majority of non-theatrical audiences, they are merely journeymen architects.

Once L has written the script and it has been approved by D and producer, P, and the costs and size of the musical have become clear, set and costume designers will be selected. As I mentioned above, we are assuming this is a professionally crafted musical, and professionals in the theatre usually choose to work with the people they have worked with before. The set designer has a studio where he and assistants design and build scenery, but the costume designer generally has a small studio to design clothes and will select a sympathetic costume 'maker' whose business it is to buy the fabrics and cut and sew the costumes to specification.

Now in our hypothetical musical let us assume that L has written an inspired treatment of the 'Cyrano' story which he will deliver to D. This will be the first draft, and once it is approved by the producer and director, W and M will begin what seems like the never-ending task of inserting the songs. This is called 'spotting', and the word refers merely to spots where it seems words will be insufficient to express the emotion the librettist has been leading towards. These songs probably will not be the ones the audiences will finally hear. Harvey Schmidt and Tom Jones wrote over a hundred songs for their musical *110 In the Shade* (1963) and Richard Rodgers told me he wrote about sixty for *South Pacific* (1949).

M, the composer will probably work as Kern and Hammerstein did, and as most teams prefer to today, when the music will be written first and words added later, although this is not an inflexible rule. It may take them six months to complete their score. Contemporary composers will usually write what is called a piano score in which they will have notated some rudimentary suggestions for the orchestrator. This will give the arranger-orchestrator insight into the composer's music and allow him to begin the enormous job of setting down and copying every note that will be sung or played by every performer.

Then a series of what are called backers' auditions begins. Every producer has a list of possible investors who will be invited to a regal living room, borrowed for the occasion, to hear the librettist read a synopsis of his story as the composer (with the lyricist usually croaking along) sings the main songs. Drinks are served, after which the producer will make a pitch (sometimes announcing who will star in the production), to persuade these possible investors to back his show.* In addition to the cost of mounting the show, many canny producers are trying to raise additional monies as 'overcall' money to keep the show running in case there is a slump in box-office receipts. Although plans for the proposed 'Cyrano' may be going forward they are usually slowed to a snail's pace until the necessary capital is raised. The creators can 'look forward' to many evenings such as these until the required money is forthcoming.

At about this time the composer and lyricist will make a simple tape of the songs, this time sung by professional 'demo' singers and copies will be given to the choreographer, orchestrator, the dance pianist, the sound engineer and even the set and costume designers. These last two will need to know the music in order to create the proper tone for the show. (Imagine *Cabaret* without Boris Aronson's seedy set and Patricia Ziprot's startlingly gross costumes. They have said the whole mood of the show came from their visual creation of what they heard in John Kander's malevolent music.)

A vague idea of the opening dates, rehearsal schedules, stars

---

* Investors who backed the seven million dollar flop, *Rags* in 1988 were able to buy shares at $32,000 each. This entitled them to attend a rehearsal, to meet the stars, two tickets for the opening night and admittance to the post-opening night party (which turned into a wake). Beyond that their total investment was lost. On the other hand, a $1,000 share in *The Fantasticks* (which has been running off-Broadway since 1960) would already have brought an investor almost a million dollars – and still counting!

who might possibly be both suitable and – very importantly – available (certainly for the key roles of Cyrano and Roxanne, maybe even Christian), will be discussed in semi-weekly production meetings. In some seasons, when there is a dearth of musicals it is easy enough to reserve a legitimate theatre, but not (as in 1989–90 on Broadway) when so many forthcoming productions are tumbling on top of each other.* In some years, productions even had to be delayed or made to mark time out of town until a suitable theatre could be found. Successful musicals were sometimes forced to close or move elsewhere when a new production had been booked on to their stage. Space for rehearsal must also be booked and here is where that all important person, the production manager, will come in. He will be responsible for all booking, absences, changes, jockeying of rehearsal and a million other things.

Let's assume the music and lyrics and libretto of 'Cyrano' are satisfactory to the powers that be, (director, choreographer and producer and even the theatre owners – the Shuberts, for example who own most of the theatres on Broadway and Stoll, Moss who are their counterpart in the West End, would not want an obvious turkey booked into any one of their theatres) and it is now early November. The producer has scheduled our play to give its first preview in early April, six months hence. There will be the usual six week rehearsal period and a month of previews before opening night, when the critics are invited.

Orchestrator, musical director and several assistants, 'dance pianist', rehearsal pianist, engineer, will be busy getting started on their work and casting will probably begin now. The stars may have already been slotted in but if not, now is the time they are chosen. And even the most famous have to audition. Once the principals are selected and contracts have been signed (the producer will try for at least a year contract, but big stars like Robert De Niro, Meryl Streep, Jonathan Pryce or Bernadette Peters generally only want to commit themselves to six months), the smaller roles are cast and chorus people (and understudies) will be chosen. Formerly there were singing choruses and dancers; but today all the non-principals must

---

*London has developed an even more imposing theatrical traffic jam, for with the advent of huge musicals whose sets require the theatre to be practically torn apart and reassembled, shows stay put in many of the large musical houses for season after season.

be able to sing, dance and act equally well. (Sometimes there are exceptions as in the casting of a *A Little Night Music* in which case Stephen Sondheim insisted that his chorus must truly be 'singers'; four of the five performers who made up the cast of *Ain't Misbehavin'* were singers, one strong dancer was chosen and the others were worked hard to concentrate on movement.*)

'Cyrano', opening in mid-June, will have a cast of twenty and will be budgeted at seven million dollars. In mid-February, when rehearsals begin, the dance music, or in this case, the ballet, usually a potpourri of songs from the show, will be created on the spot by the choreographer and the rehearsal pianist.† It is a rare composer who will write his own, for most composers are too busy writing new songs to be more than supervisors in creating the dance arrangements. Additionally, they know that the score will be greatly changed before it reaches its final form. Agnes de Mille‡ used to insist that ballets she choreographed be written before the show went into rehearsal, but Bob Fosse§ loved working out the dances with the 'gypsies' on stage.

'Underscoring', music that is played by the orchestra under dialogue, is generally written by the rehearsal pianist as well. It is often suggested by the director, who these days is all-powerful.

By the middle of March, as the cast is ready to leave the studio and rehearse on stage, everyone gets more and more jumpy. Nothing sounds as it did before. Songs that had an

---

*Luther Henderson, who with Richard Maltby, Jr and Murray Horwitt was the guiding force behind *Ain't Misbehavin'*, insists 'the cast was not chosen for their vocal timbre or quality but because their personalities projected.' He adds, 'clowns project, mimes project, and this is the abstractness of projection. That's what the public is expecting on Broadway.'

† Professionals have snidely remarked that the score to *Jerome Robbins' Broadway* which is made up largely of dances he choreographed for three decades of Broadway musicals should be credited to veteran rehearsal pianist, Trude Rittman, who patched together many of the ballets using themes by Rodgers, Bock, Styne, et al.

‡ Although born into a famous American theatrical family, Miss de Mille's first successful choreography was done in London for Cole Porter's *Nymph Errant* (1933). Returning to her native land, she met with little success until she choreographed Aaron Copeland's ballet *Rodeo* (1942). Beause this displayed such a grasp of the Western idiom she was chosen by Rodgers and Hammerstein to stage the story ballets in their first collaboration, *Oklahoma!* (1943). She followed this with a whole series of hits including *Bloomer Girl* (1944) *Carousel* (1945) and *Brigadoon* (1947).

§ Robert Fosse became well known for his choreographic close-knit posturings. He built snapping fingers and vocal shouts into his ballets. It often seemed that the whole show revolved around his loose-bodied, jazzlike conceptions. Starting with *The Pajama Game* (1954) he went on to choreograph *New Girl in Town* (1957), *Redhead* (1959), *Sweet Charity* (1966), *Pippin* (1972), *Chicago* (1975) and a musical built entirely on movement, *Dancin'* (1978).

intimate quality now seem lost in the cavernous (especially when empty) theatre. Voices that seemed big in the studio now seem to whisper, and everybody starts talking about the 'body mike', and 'what does *he* want from me – blood?' And rehearsals get longer and longer. Hanging like the sword of Damocles there is that SEVEN MILLION DOLLARS that everyone feels seems to be riding on one night.

Orchestrations are generally behind schedule; costumes are either gaudy or ill-fitting and may have to be redesigned; a whole new scene may be written and need a new set which has to be hastily assembled; the 'star' may not have enough to do and demand a hit song (as Ethel Merman did when she insisted on singing 'There's No Business Like Show Business' in *Annie Get Your Gun*); and everybody threatens to walk out at least once before 'Cyrano' even gets to the theatre.

And then there are the previews where audiences only snicker at what was supposed to produce a belly laugh. Shuffling of feet and rustling of programmes indicate boredom in the tender song between Cyrano and Roxanne. And worst of all the advance is not building up.*

I am unable to tell you what goes on from then – you may just assume that pandemonium ensues, but since this is hypothetical, let's imagine 'Cyrano' gets rave reviews in the New York press and goes on to become a classic.

THE KINDS OF MUSICALS ON VIEW TODAY

The New York City traffic department has erected a sign, a short way off the Great White Way near 42nd Street, that reads 'Don't Even *Think* of Parking Here!' I would parody the urgent warning for any amateur picking up a copy of this book, that you don't even *think* of writing a musical without knowing the kinds of musical available for your creation, and what classification your particular œuvre will fall into. Your producers and the public will want to know what category of work

---

* The advance box-office receipts are an important factor in a musical's success. Producers have been known to run their offices on the interest from banking the considerable sums the public pays in for tickets to what looks like a hit. As merchandising becomes increasingly important canny producers take full-page ads announcing their show, urging the public to write in or call a credit card number for tickets. All this hype occurs a year to eighteen months in advance of the opening.

they are supporting or attending. Some forms are hard to have produced; others are much in demand. So unless you wish to write your work as a mere exercise – which is something I don't recommend – be aware of your options.

But that does not mean there is nothing to be gained from 'practising' working in the easier forms before attempting a fully fledged musical. A teenage Stephen Sondheim, who asked neighbour Oscar Hammerstein to be his mentor, was requested to cut his teeth by writing no less than four musicals, as exercises. Although Sondheim turned out the four fully fledged musicals, I have always recommended revue, with its short sketches and theatrical songs, as a better way to put one's foot into the musical theatre. One should first learn the craft, and then see some of his work on stage, before tackling a full-length musical which is fraught with so many pitfalls to the unwary. The revue form,* long in disuse, has had a new lease of life today and is generally done with other collaborators. Hopefully one can learn from the collaboration. But Mr Hammerstein's way of dipping his protégé's feet in the theatr. with this enormous solo exercise seems to have done no harm to Mr Sondheim.

The listings below are arranged in order of creative difficulty and not in the chronological order in which they originated. Of course, even the simplest forms must be infused with passion, wit, sensitivity and freshness in order to stand the slightest chance of production, much less going on to become a hit.

Musical Cavalcade or Biography

This is my own term for a kind of revue that is a survey of a particular body of work or the output of a fixed and chosen era. It can be a biography in song of a creator, as *Ain't Misbehavin'* was of Thomas 'Fats' Waller. In that case it used the original songs of the creator with just enough biographical information thrown in to give an idea of the 'times' of the protagonist. Often this kind of theatrical evening is plotless (or at most will have the thinnest wisp of a story). It is not a 'biomusical' with a life story, like *Evita*, *Fiorello* or *Funny Girl*,

*See pages 31–2.

and it generally does not have an original score. It can have the wisp of a plot like *Bubbling Brown Sugar*, whose slight story concerned a group of whites being given a tour of the legendary Harlem nightclubs by several black denizens of the area. This kind of work is generally created by people who have a great admiration (sometimes bordering on fanaticism) for the work of a neglected giant of music or lyrics. The show becomes a labour of love that when infused with wit and wisdom can often open a window that illuminates an artist's life. It is generally less costly to produce this kind of show and the package lends itself easily to touring. But there can be pitfalls. Estates of the non-living artist often make burdensome demands for royalties from creators and producers of the bio-musical.

Much of the success of these shows must be attributed to the fact that they are not merely concerts or musical surveys; those would be better served in an auditorium or on a recording. In each of the cases below, the songs were theatricalised, that is given a point of view, a character to sing to, a fresh or retranslated lyric. This kind of show, while having no libretto to speak of, must have an imaginative director and a choreographer who can approach the songs with theatricalism.

There have been many successful examples of cavalcade or biography. Most of them have been a collection of songs written by a particular composer or lyricist: *Rodgers and Hart* (1975); *Jerry Goes to Hollywood*, a survey of the movie music of Jerome Kern, (1985); *Jacques Brel is Alive and Well and Living in Paris*, translations of Jacques Brel songs, (1968); *A Party With Comden & Green* (1958); *Stardust*, the lyrics of Mitchell Parrish, (1987); *Eubie*, the songs of Eubie Blake, (1979); *Side by Side by Sondheim* (1977); *Nash at Nine*, a collection of poems, verses and songs with lyrics by Ogden Nash, (1973); *Oh, Coward*, Noël Coward's songs and plays, (1972); *Berlin to Broadway with Kurt Weill* (1972); *Ain't Misbehavin'*, the songs of Thomas 'Fats' Waller, (1978); *Sophisticated Ladies*, the songs of Duke Ellington, (1983). *Elvis*, the songs of Elvis Presley, (1988); *Jerome Robbins' Broadway*, the choreography and direction of Jerome Robbins, (1989); *Noël and Gertie*, songs, letters and speeches of Noël Coward and Gertrude Lawrence, (1990); *The Buddy Holly Story*, (1990).

One-Man or One-Woman Show

This is like the musical cavalcade in the respect that it too is not plotted. Since it is generally an evening of encores from a superstar's repertoire, it would seem there is nothing to be written. One would assume it is listed in this section mainly for comprehensiveness, but one should not underestimate the amount of creativity and dramatic story-telling input that must come from a clever librettist and canny director to turn these solo performances into an evening of theatre. To hold a stage for two hours can be exhausting for audiences and artists, and only the greatest who have had a theatrical mind overseeing the selection, balance and pace of the performance have been able to pull it off.

Some famous performers who are, or have been able to hold forth alone because of the interesting repertoire they present, are Beatrice Lillie, *An Evening with Beatrice Lillie* (1952); Victor Borge, *Comedy in Music* (1953); Anna Russell, *Anna Russell's Little Show* (1953); Maurice Chevalier; Josephine Baker, (1967) and (1974); Bette Midler, *Clams on the Half Shell* (1975); Lily Tomlin, (1985); Barbara Cook, *A Concert with Barbara Cook* (1987); Jackie Mason, *The World According to Jackie Mason* (1987); Mandy Patinkin, *In Concert: Dress Casual*, (1989); Patricia Routledge, *One-Woman Show*, (1989).

Vaudeville or Variety

Vaudeville, a series of acts (musical, acrobatic, magic, tumbling, novelty), was a popular entertainment before the days of the movies and somehow survived even until the late thirties. In America it has essentially been dead these last fifty years, but known as variety or music hall it is still quite popular abroad, albeit out of the metropolitan centres. Even in London and Paris, in spite of its role having been largely filled by television, variety since the early sixties lives occasionally when headliners like Yves Montand or Barry Humphries put together a programme of interest to the general public. After the dog acts and the jugglers have warmed up the audience, the headliner will appear and do a forty or fifty minute show.

Old-time vaudevillians Olsen and Johnson revived their

sinking careers with a popular zany hodge-podge called
Helzappoppin (1938) and its sequel *Sons o' Fun* (1941). The
shows that are presented annually at the Radio City Music
Hall and in some of the casinos in Las Vegas, although heavily
overproduced, might be considered as close to vaudeville as
can be seen in the United States. In 1980 Mickey Rooney and
Ann Miller successfully revived a vaudeville-burlesque called
Sugar Babies. I believe their replacements are still touring and
will *still* be playing a split week somewhere well into the next
century.

Burlesque

Burlesque is a form of vaudeville that was always considered
less respectable, but was generally more fun. Pure burlesque
did, of course, have undressing and often went beyond what
censors considered good taste (but not far enough to be closed
down by the police). Theatres that featured burlesque were
often in an unsavoury part of town with audiences who were
predominantly male. Although it would be considered sexist
today and demeaning to women, burlesque was not porno.
Most of its humour was derived from innuendo, and gales of
nervous laughter were heard in burlesque theatres, simply
because the mores of the times made even the mention of sex
taboo.

Much of the art form we call revue derives from the sketch
as it was developed in burlesque. The formula was tried and
true. Skits (performed by some of the best comics who were
later to be successful on more legitimate stages) would be
followed by a striptease. A beautiful girl would spend about
ten minutes artfully removing her clothing, piece by piece
(sometimes tossing it to the audience or to the few men who
comprised the orchestra) while 'dancing' behind a fan, beach-
ball, bubble or whatever gimmick she could dream up. *Ann
Corio's History of Burlesque* made it to Broadway and she fought
and won over the censors by claiming hers was com-
prehensively educational – hence the word 'history' introduced
into the title of the show. Minsky's theatres packed the cus-

tomers in and made stars of Sally Rand, Gypsy Rose Lee* as well as Miss Corio.

Extravaganza

This was a term often used by producers to advertise to the public that they were witnessing an extravagant, costly show. In a way, these shows come closer to elegant burlesque than they do to vaudeville, and are not at all deserving of the title of revue which is often given to them. Florenz Ziegfeld with his *Follies* (1907–31), Earl Carroll with his *Vanities* and *Sketchbooks*, Raymond Hitchcock with his *Hitchy-Koos*, these were some of the annual shows that were on display from the early 1900s to the middle of the century. They all hired long-stemmed beauties by the score and displayed them in lavish and revealing costumes. Since the audience was far enough away and the lighting was generally 'artfully' subdued, showgirls could get by wearing flesh-coloured body stockings while the public thought it was seeing more than it actually was. With the advent of talking pictures that used hundreds of extras, especially as choreographed by Busby Berkeley and others and later with the introduction of Technicolor movies, the public became less impressed with opulence on the stage. This occasioned the birth of the true revue, at first variety and later topical.

Pantomime

Pantomime is the extravagant form of entertainment popular in Britain usually at Christmastime and now most often intended to appeal to children. The word formerly referred to the mimed harlequinade which followed serious productions, its standard characters – Harlequin, the resourceful hero, Colombine, the heroine, Pantaloon, the old fool and so on – copied from the Italian *Commedia dell'arte* style which is several centuries old. Augustus Harris, a Victorian entrepreneur, began

---

* 'Gypsy' Rose Lee's own biography, freely edited, was the basis of one of the most successful and best constructed musicals ever written. Perhaps that was because it afforded a glimpse of the stripteuse, backstage at the burlesque – *Gypsy* (book by Arthur Laurents, music by Jule Styne and lyrics by Stephen Sondheim).

using the stars of his variety shows at Christmastime in a combination of spectacle and knockabout comedy. It was his idea to have the principal boy played by a woman and the dame by a man. For some reason women in men's roles have always made audiences uncomfortable, but men in women's clothes is something the public, especially the British, find hilarious. Although the woman-dressed-as-man was abandoned in these shows, today, no self-respecting pantomime lacks one or possibly two semi-unshaven men in drag.

In the Fifties the comedy was broadened even more to include audience participation. Sandy Powell is credited with pioneeering the technique of getting the audience to shout out 'Look behind you!' as the villain crept up behind him, or warning the hero as someone tried to steal the umbrella he had parked on the side of the stage and had asked the audience to keep an eye on.

Chorus songs, with words flashed on a large screen so that the audience can join in with confidence are part of the fun of going to a panto. Jokes are broad, familiar routines are included and if the villain isn't loudly booed, he is a failure.

Pantomimes are most often based on fairy-tales. But they do leave room in the narration for a totally non-plot-related song or even a poem to be included. Although properly categorised as 'book shows' they are traditional enough to be tucked somewhere between vaudeville and extravaganza. *Cinderella, Peter Pan, Babes in the Wood, Aladdin* and *Puss in Boots* seem to be particular favourites with British audiences.

Revue

Revue which in order to appear racier borrows its spelling from the French, long considered in an ethnic generalisation to be a sexual people, is actually a respectable combination of vaudeville, extravaganza and burlesque, and although it may not be as popular as it once was, is far from dead. Revue certainly was one of the mainstays of the theatre from the early twenties to the sixties, and especially during the thirties and forties was as ubiquitous as operetta or musical comedy, and featured such avant garde theatrical experiences as modern or ethnic dance, political satires, monochromatic lighting and bizarre settings. Often compared in literature to a 'collection of short stories', while the book musical was considered a 'novel', early revues did not need a theme. They were content to use material written especially for the superstars who appeared in them, and became a somewhat artful conglomeration of acts. But as the form developed, some cohesiveness was deemed necessary. In the United States, revues like *Pins and Needles* were directed towards labour; *Working* moved through different professions; In Britain, *Oh, What A Lovely War*, and *Fings Ain't Wot They Used T' Be* dealt sarcastically with war and modern improvements respectively. Even *New Faces*, although themeless had the thread of gifted young debutantes to hold it together.

Some of the legendary revues, many of which were produced in a new edition every season, and dear to the hearts of aficionados are *The Music Box Revues* (mostly with scores by Irving Berlin) *Two on the Aisle, Cochran's Revue, Charlot's Revue* (which introduced Noël Coward and Gertrude Lawrence), Leonard Silman's *New Faces* and the off-Broadway *Shoestring Revues*.

The heyday of the revue was the years between 1925 and 1960. After that, variety shows that were available on TV made the form less sought after. But this type of entertainment always had strong appeal for sophisticated audiences and during those four decades introduced most of the 'standards' of pop music. Revue still seems to be thriving off-Broadway and on the fringe of London's West End. During the writing of this book in 1989, one could attend a revival of *Privates on Parade* (A Military Madcap Revue) *Laughing Matters* (a revue by Martin Charnin), *Oh, Calcutta* (a revue by many collaborators), *Showing Off*. One should mention again what looks like a long-running phenomenon: *Jerome Robbins's Broadway* (already listed as a musical 'biography', for it has all the hallmarks of a dance revue). Yes, even the successful *Black and Blue*, billed as a Broadway musical, is no more than a revue based on the blues.

Operetta

Operetta and its offshoot, the musical play are the two mainstays of today's musical theatre. Far more works in these forms are presented on worldwide stages than all other forms combined. As such they deserve more detailed description of their origins, especially now as we enter the Nineties, when there has been a resurgence of the operetta form led by Britain and France.

Operetta in France

Although we generally assume operetta, with its swirling waltzes and princes and peasants had its origin in Vienna, this is not true. Donizetti had incorporated spoken dialogue into his operas, and these became the rage in Italy in the early nineteenth century. These were called *opera buffa*, and as their vogue spread to France, where they really took hold, were known as *opéra comique* or later *opéra bouffe*. The biggest hit of the Parisian season of 1840 was Donizetti's *The Daughter of the Regiment* which had several show-stopping melodies that would have led the charts, had they existed.

Soon the demand for light works, generally one-acters, was so great that serious composers like François Boieldieu, Daniel Auber, Ferdinand Hérold, Adolphe Adam and eventually Jacques Offenbach were writing short works that filled all the French boulevard theatres. At last, Offenbach decided to attempt a full length work, and *Orphée aux Enfers* or *Orpheus in the Underworld* became the first operetta. This retelling of the classic story, which two centuries earlier had been a serious opera by Gluck, invented many operetta conventions that have remained to this day. Gone were the tragic arias and the high drama; they were replaced by shorter, wittier, less florid songs. Lively dance, (in this particular work, the famous can-can) displaced arty ballet.

Operetta in Vienna

The traditional dance of the Austrian Tyrol is called the *Ländler*. It is in three-quarter time and not particularly graceful, but it was remoulded into the most joyously irresistible dance, the waltz, by Joseph Lanner, a young man from the countryside, recently come to Vienna. Waltzes gushed from Lanner's pen and from those of his contemporaries – especially from one of his closest friends, conductor and composer Johann

Strauss. Strauss was to rule supreme in this swirling city until he was replaced by someone even more talented than himself – his own son.

Johann Strauss II, leading his own orchestra, had already written hundreds of orchestral waltzes until he was persuaded, some say by Offenbach, to try his hand at operetta. His first effort, *Indigo and the Forty Thieves*, although forgotten today, was a howling success and would launch him as the guru of the form. He wrote eleven notable operettas, among them *Die Fledermaus* which Alan Lerner (himself no mean operetta creator) calls 'unquestionably the greatest operetta ever written'.

The success of Strauss's operettas prompted others to jump in the blue Danube. Both Karl Millöcker's *Countess Du Barry* and Karl Ziehrer's *The Kiss Waltz* were successful all over Europe and in America. Victor Herbert, Sigmund Romberg and Rudolph Friml (about whom more will be found under *Operetta in America*), although their careers flourished in the United States, were to continue the tradition of operetta, many of which were translated and performed in Europe as well.

Operetta in Britain

Britain has had a long and noble poetic history dating back to the Middle Ages and flowering in Chaucer, Donne and Shakespeare. This is due not only to the geniuses who happily were born on that sceptred isle, but in part to the enormous richness of the English language, which has a Germanic or Anglo-Saxon word as well as a Latin synonym for practically everything.

By 1840, principally due to a magazine called *Fun* (later named *Punch*) light verse began to proliferate. The subject matter was generally inconsequential, but the rhyming was highly inventive. *Fun* published the original and clever verse of Thomas Ingoldsby, then that of a former barrister by the name of W. S. Gilbert, who had changed professions not only because he had a gift for writing, but because he had none for law. Richard D'Oyly Carte who managed a theatre that had produced a portentous version of *The Tempest* with music by Arthur Sullivan, thought Gilbert would lighten Sullivan's style and right he was. Their collaboration lasted eighteen years, and although there were stormy times (mostly occasioned when Sullivan voiced his objection to being considered merely a 'tunesmith' behind Gilbert's brilliant lyrics), they produced the greatest operettas yet written in the English language. P. G. Wodehouse, Lorenz Hart, Cole Porter, Ira Gershwin, Oscar Hammerstein and their lyrical descendants all owe their creative genesis to Gilbert.

The English language does not translate well, first because, as mentioned above, it has almost double the number of words of any other language. In Gilbert's case, because of his intricate, multiple, internal and original rhyming, these operettas were not successfully presented in the rest of Europe.* But they sailed across the Atlantic Ocean with ease. One other importation from England, *Chu Chin Chow*, written by author-actor-impresario Arthur Ashe, which is considered the first British musical comedy, must be mentioned. Based on the pantomime *Aladdin*, its easily singable songs and an exotic location appealed to an audience eager to get away from the Viennese and unwilling to approach the intellectuality of *The Mikado*. It had a great success and became the longest running British musical until modern times. Chalking up 2,238 performances it heralded the start of the mass-marketed musical with advertising posters on buses and billboards. (All it lacked when compared with the financial success of, say, *The Phantom of the Opera*, were ushers hawking T-shirts and mugs in its intermissions.) It travelled successfully across the Atlantic and ran almost as long in the United States as it did in England.

Operetta in America

The great melting pot that America was to become centred its early theatrical experiences around New York. Newly translated French and Viennese operettas became the major entertainments for a large immigrant population longing to keep ties with its native lands. Because the United States was out of

---

* *The Mikado* which they produced in 1885 was an exception. It was a biting satire on everything British, but set in Japan, and the British public accepted it as Japanese. It ran for over two years in London and was translated into a host of foreign languages. Revived in black and jazz versions, it remains the most popular of all their works.

step with the rest of the world in respect to copyright laws*and because of lax policing of what copyright laws existed, the operettas of Gilbert and Sullivan were easily pirated and available to anyone, so there were at least two companies, always playing and touring the major cities. Operettas satisfied highbrow tastes while extravaganzas, vaudeville and burlesque filled all the remaining theatres with patrons hungry for lighter entertainment. But the public in the smaller municipalities wanted their humour as broad as possible, ad libs as contemporary as possible, interspersed with occasional over-sentimental songs. This grab-bag form of entertainment finally evolved into the minstrel show.†

And down in New Orleans, jazz was being born. All these elements were to have a major effect on the American musical.

But in the large cities, especially New York, Chicago and San Francisco, sophisticated Americans flocked to hear the latest traditional operettas of Lehar, Kalman, Robert Stolz and Oscar Straus – who were all musical descendants of Offenbach and Johann Strauss. Except for George M. Cohan who wrote the librettos for the patriotic comedies he composed, directed, starred and danced in, the major successes were now foreign. Lehar's *The Merry Window,* Kalman's *Countess Maritza* and Oscar Strauss's *The Chocolate Soldier* played everywhere. But soon another name was added to this operetta

---

*The first copyright law was not written until 1887, as a result of a multinational meeting in Berne in Switzerland attended by fourteen countries but not the United States. The European law provided that the author and his heirs controlled the rights to his works for fifty years after the author's death. In the US, the author only had those rights for twenty-eight years and had to renew his option on those rights or the work fell into the public domain. The work then could never retain its copyright protection for more than fifty-six years and sadly, many authors outlived their copyrights. It was not until 1978 that US law was amended to conform with the more protective European one. Britain and France have already proposed laws to extend copyright to the life of the author plus seventy years beyond his death.

† The original minstrel shows consisted of a group of entertainers (banjo players, singers, dancers), seated together in a form bounded by two end men and an interlocutor who sat in the middle. The end men in time came to be called 'Mr Tambo' and 'Mr Bones', and they punctuated their sketches or riddles with music and dance.

In the beginning the shows were performed exclusively by white men. Travelling through the South, these troupes became fascinated with black humour, rhythm, song and dance. The indigenous African dance movement that had evolved into the shuffle and became 'the soft shoe' soon was incorporated into the minstrel show, and eventually the performers themselves began corking up their faces and applying white greasepaint which exaggerated and demeaned their mouths. (After the Civil War, when Abraham Lincoln's Emancipation Proclamation had freed the slaves, black entertainers began to join these touring troupes. But in order to preserve a unity of look, even they had to greasepaint their lips and black up.)

With its tired routines and often heard jokes, the minstrel show fell out of favour early in the century and was only found amusing by amateur groups. Certainly by the Forties the blackface show had become offensive to both blacks and white.

hierarchy – that of an Irishman who had adopted America as his homeland – Victor Herbert. He was to continue his eminent career until the 1920s.

Yet even then other influences were already eroding operetta's stranglehold on Broadway. The minstrel show 'shuffle' had given way to ragtime; the long operetta song was changing to the 32-bar pop tune and the 12-bar blues was coming in from Chicago and New Orleans. Royalty, romance and exotic lands which had always been the themes and venues for operetta now seemed phony and stagy, and no longer held an illusive charm. People desperately wanted to dance, and they wanted to dance to the new ragtime music rather than the old waltz. Although most female singers still employed the soprano or what is now called the 'legit' sound, garden variety or lower-voiced singers were proliferating. They used a normal, natural speaking range, or chest sound (called 'belt' in today's theatre), and the lyrics they sang were no longer full of 'thous' and 'thys' but used the vernacular and were understandable. Who needed the stentorian tenors now that male singers were megaphoned (and later microphoned). They could create an intimate, almost sexual rapport with their audiences. When Irving Berlin wrote 'Alexander's Ragtime Band', he rode on a craze that elevated all the other forms of theatre, especially revue and extravaganza, into the same league as operetta. And this tremendous variety kept the musical theatre, especially as it developed in America, vital for a good fifty years.

In the last decade the operetta has returned in full force, (notably from Britain with the shows *The Phantom of the Opera, A Little Night Music* and *Aspects of Love*) with a semi-rock beat and amplified, to be sure. Because of the enormous risks involved in presenting new works that might lose a total investment of millions, revivals of notable successful operettas have become more common as well.

William Hammerstein, director and producer, believes that operetta never 'went away, and composers and lyricists write in the *métier* of today, using rock as their musical language, just as Lehar and Kalman used waltzes and mazurkas, thus writing in the *métier* of their day'.

Musical Comedy

Of all the terms in musical theatre, musical comedy is the most misunderstood. What today's Americans call 'musical' they formerly called 'musical comedy'. The British *still* call it 'musical comedy' while the French call it 'operette'. Actually, this term is used by the public at large as a generic term for any show with music just as Kleenex is used for any disposable tissue. And the term varies in different countries.

Musical comedy is generally considered to have originated accidentally back in 1866 with *The Black Crook*, a five and a half hour opus that was born when a French ballet company booked into the Academy of Music on New York's 14th Street, and en route on an ocean liner, was left stranded because its theatre burned to the ground. The impresario who had arranged for the French ballerinas prevailed upon William Wheatley, the manager of Niblo's Garden, a large theatre in the vicinity, to incorporate the dancers into a potboiler with a sylvan setting in which the whole company could perform their scantily clad wood nymph dances. Wheatley already had his dreadful melodrama in rehearsal and could smell its failure, so it could not have been difficult to persuade him to add songs, some comedy and of course the dances. The show was a sensation; and although it cost the then enormous sum of $50,000 to mount, it ran for over a year and alerted producers to the vast profits that could be made from an extravagant wedding of song, comedy and dance.

The parameters of musical comedy have not varied much since the days of *The Black Crook*. Then as now, in definition, a musical comedy is a musical play generally with a light plot, its dialogue interspersed with songs and dances. Its language must be of today (although the plot, like *A Connecticut Yankee* can deal with ancient times, but even here contemporaneity is obligatory; witness the show's hit song 'Thou Swell'), and its songs must not be watered down operatic arias. The lyric message of its songs should generally advance the action of the story, but there is time, as in the 'splashing' number sung to 'S'Wonderful' in *My One And Only*, for unadulterated fun and digression. Its dancing is almost always in a lighter vein.

Recent successful examples of this genre are *42nd Street,*

Barnum, Little Shop of Horrors, They're Playing our Song. In late 1989 Cole Porter's gem *Anything Goes* was packing them in on both sides of the Atlantic.

Musical Play*

A musical play, on the other hand, differs from a musical comedy mostly in seriousness of purpose. Songs almost always further the action or reveal character. Dancing tries to be 'realistic', (as in *West Side Story*'s 'Rumble' or its 'Dance at the Gym').† An early example of the pure musical play was *Lady in the Dark*, a story of psychoanalysis with the libretto by serious playwright, Moss Hart. The libretto of a musical play can deal with unpleasantness such as the pre-war Germany of *Cabaret*, a work in which the term musical *comedy* would be inappropriate, death of a major character as in *Man of La Mancha*, murder as in *West Side Story*. It may even tackle contemporary problems in song such as the ill-fated *The Knife* whose subject was a sex-change operation.

Some other recent musical plays include *Woman of the Year, Evita, Merrily We Roll Along, Nine, La Cage Aux Folles, The Rink, Chess, Big River, Les Misérables, Into the Woods, Miss Saigon, Grand Hotel, City of Angels, Falsettoland.*

Concept Musical

The concept musical is a relative newcomer to the musical theatre. Actually it is an offshoot of the topical revue, often done with more seriousness of purpose. It need not have a plot or it may have a slight thread of one. *Company*, one of the first of this genre, examined marriage. Audiences, and the creators, were not concerned whether or not its protagonist, Robert, decided to marry at the final curtain, any more than they are concerned about the fate of all those *Cats*. Dissimilarly in *A Chorus Line*, the concept of getting a job in a musical is the

---

*Although it is generally assumed the first musical play was *Lady in the Dark* (1941), William Hammerstein believes the first musical play or 'billed as a play with music was *Music in the Air*' (1932).

†For two decades, from the early forties to the early sixties, beginning with *Oklahoma!*, classic ballet, as originated by Agnes de Mille, was intruded into the second act of almost every musical. It often slowed the action to a snail's pace. Fortunately the vogue has passed.

very idea which makes the audience care what happens to those kids, and the thread of a plot, practically extraneous, which concerns the director and his relationship to an ex-principal dancer, is merely diversionary.

Other recent successful concept musicals are *1776, Starlight Express, Dreamgirls, Baby, Sunday in the Park With George.*

Theatre Opera

Opera, which was after all the original form from which our lyric theatre arose, has always run in tandem with our musical stage. It has sometimes been more appropriately staged on Broadway or in the West End, and not in the opera house, when it involved works such as translations of *Carmen* (as in *Carmen Jones*) or of *Aïda* (*My Darlin' Aïda*). But more often successful theatre operas have not been mere translations; they were written out of deep feelings and have had strong dramatic books and accessible scores. Although it was not successful at its inception, the greatest theatre opera of all time has been *Porgy and Bess* (which Gershwin timorously called a folk opera). The operas of Gian Carlo Menotti and Benjamin Britten have chalked up extensive runs on Broadway, but they have always been 'opera', not 'theatre opera'. One will never confuse the two if the distinctions is made that *theatre opera is concerned with the song, while opera (like a rock concert), has to do with the singer*. It is Pavarotti's *L'Elisir d'Amore* and Callas's *Lucia* they come to see.

Stephen Sondheim confesses that opera bores him. 'I'm not addicted to the human voice,' he adds. 'What I like about musical theater is the telling of the story, the tension with which it is told. The whole point of opera is to take moments and savor them; to take "good night" and sing if for five minutes. In the musical theater it's "good night", and I want to get on with the next thing that happens.'

Although still advertised as a 'musical play' by their producers, theatre opera no longer intimidates the public. As long as the attendant hoopla and production values are on a grand scale, there seems to be an audience hungry for full-throated singing.

Theatre operas generally have a serious subject similar to the musical play that can be more easily explained by duets, trios and concerted numbers rather than solos. They are generally notoriously lacking in dance.* In all cases, the music and the emotion they carry seem to be more important than the lyrics. And since the music is the creators' paramount intention it is often preferable to 'keep it going'. Running one number into the next seems to make audiences forget about the unnaturalness of actors singing rather than speaking, but it can be dangerous and sound inane in the 'recitativo', the plot connection that runs *between* the numbers.† Although it is a technicality it should be mentioned here that most theatre operas are really *opéra comique* because they usually encompass spoken dialogue.‡

A Note About Categorising Shows

Hal Prince, one of Broadway's and the West End's most prolific and successful producer-directors cautions about labelling musicals and thereby falling into cliché. He says, 'Nothing is dead. Nothing is *not* dead. Book musical [lumping all forms together that are not concept musical] is a label that has no meaning whatsoever.

'More to the point, in the theater we are competing with other media in a way that we never did before. That's reflected in the rejection of certain kinds of musical theater that you can get at home by turning a dial. There's an invitation in the theater to explore what you can *only* get in the theater, what you can *only* get is that relationship between the audience and the live actor; larger-than-life excitement.'

And Stephen Sondheim also agrees that it doesn't matter what you call it. He feels that 'what is new and different in the theater is that there are so many forms it can take. That's what's so wonderful about it.'

The opinions Stephen Sondheim and Hal Prince hold about not 'labelling' any musicals are set forth here to make anyone

---

*Critic Mark Steyn propounds an intriguing précis of musical expression when he says, 'when something has gone beyond the spoken, it develops naturally into song; if it goes even beyond that, it goes into dance.'

†Continual singing of mundane texts led critic Frank Rich to empathise with Andrew Lloyd Webber's onerous task in setting a line like 'Will you have coffee or cappucino?' in his recent œuvre, *Aspects of Love*.

‡*Opéra comique* is not to be confused with comic opera, it merely means any work that has spoken dialogue. The word '*comique*' or '*comédie*' refers to acting. (The Comédie Française is the state-supported acting troupe of France, presenting both comedies and tragedies.)

who wishes to create a musical aware of the freedom necessary within whatever form elected. When asked about what you are creating, choose the subtitle into which most of your work is cast. Then you will understand that the foregoing comments are inserted in this text to free you from the confines of writing within too narrow a framework. No matter what form you elect to cast your musical into, try to be original, and if you are using one of the older forms infuse it with a certain daring. Pure operetta, pure extravaganza, pure revue, etc. are certain to spell pure and certain failure.

1 BASIC TRAINING

FOR THE LIBRETTIST

Introductions, Honesty, Length, Scope, Suspense, Sentiment, Climaxes, Dénouement.

FOR THE LYRICIST

Understanding differences between Popular song and Show song, AABA (Popular Song Form), ABAC (Show Tune Form), Verse Chorus Form, Other Forms, Free Form, Interludes and Extension, Analyses (*My Fair Lady*, *Cabaret*, *The Phantom of the Opera*), The Title, Language, Rhyme, Things to Avoid (Paper Rhymes, Identity, Syllable Length, Contractions and Fillers, Long and Short Syllables, Adjacent Consonants, Alliteration).

FOR THE COMPOSER

Form, Changes of Form, Free Form Song, Work Methods, Phrase Length, Range, Counterpoint, Modulation, Theatricality, Intervals, Word Accentuation.

BASIC TRAINING IN RELATED FIELDS

For the Director.
For the Producer.

A FINAL WORD ABOUT COLLABORATIVE PREPARATION

Before beginning to write a musical, there are several things each contributor to the project must ask himself. Is the project fascinating enough for him to devote to it a long stretch of time?* If so, does he *have* the time to devote to it? And if the answer is still in the affirmative, he must ask the next soul-searching question: Is he equipped to write this work?

We are aware that in every particular area of expertise (some of us have several), those who succeed possess certain essential techniques. They are listed in this chapter. If we don't have them and we still want to write a show we generally go out and seek them. Here then, is what we should know before beginning to write any show. (Further information on each of these three major contributions: libretto, lyrics and music can be obtained from the publications listed in the extensive bibliography in the appendix.)

FOR THE LIBRETTIST†

Today's musical is a very far cry from the properly constructed play that is studied in drama school. The five-act Shakespeare,

---

*Jerry Herman says his show *The Grand Tour* which ran for only sixty-one performances in 1979 was 'my mistake from the start. I really didn't want to do it. I thought it was a lovely play, but not my kind of material. Running from the Nazis just didn't seem to go with Jerry Herman. I wrote it for the wrong reason – because I hadn't found anything else I wanted to do. I *made* myself get excited about it ... It's not my best work by any stretch of the imagination. I don't think the show deserved to be a big hit ... it is a legitimate mistake, but it taught me never to write for the wrong reason.'

†Throughout this book I have used the word 'librettist' to represent the practitioner of the unique, considerable and intricate art which creates the backbone of every musical. Most librettists prefer to be called 'bookwriters' but there are some dissenters. Among them Alan Jay Lerner who writes: 'I am a librettist. However whenever I fill out a form which asks that I identify my profession I do not say I am a librettist. I say playwright-lyricist. One of the reasons I dislike the word librettist is best illustrated by the famous Mrs Malaprop of New York who, years ago, when asked where she had been the night before, said, "To the opera."

the shorter but no less complex works of Restoration comedy, and the well-constructed plays of Ibsen, O'Neill, Wilde, Williams, Coward and Miller are no more like the libretto of a modern musical than a string quartet is like a show tune. But in both cases there are similarities. And the better one understands a string quartet, the closer one's appreciation of a smashing show tune. Additionally, one can gain a deeper understanding of what one needs for an ennobling musical book if the principles of the great classic dramatists are grasped.

DIFFERENCES BETWEEN A PLAY AND A LIBRETTO

Introductions

The author of a straight play can devote most of his first act to acquainting his audience with his characters. In musicals this leisurely pace is taboo. A show must hold the attention from the outset. When we meet Carrie, Julie and Billy (and are told about Mr Snow) at the beginning of *Carousel* we are plunged right into their lives, loves and desires. You've heard the old cliché about a picture being worth a thousand words, well, in a musical not only do we have the stage picture, but the song, (if it is a clear introduction and expression of character) and that is worth a million words. At our first encounter with Mrs Anna in Rodgers and Hammerstein's exotic *The King And I*, we know instantly from her speech and song the kind of woman she is. Strong enough to overcome her forebodings in her first number and brave enough twice to confront the king – at the first act curtain and again in a climactic moment near the middle of the second act. Bobby, the protagonist of the Sondheim-Firth *Company* is fully sketched for us by his friends in their opening number, and Jean Valjean's personality as the hero of *Les Misérables* becomes immediately clear from the very first words he utters, 'Look down!'

Asked what she had seen, she replied, "It was some Italian opera called 'Libretto'." A librettist has always seemed to me someone who associated with opera and operetta and who specialised in unintelligibility and anonymity. Nevertheless that is what I am ... A librettist.'

Honesty

In many contemporary dramas, especially the works of playwrights Tennessee Williams and Arthur Miller, characters are
less than truthful about themselves when we first encounter
them. We, the audience, will gradually come to separate their
lies from the facts through their dialogue or what others say
about them. This is almost never possible in musical theatre,
for our leading character is generally singing about himself. As
we see them in the beginning, so must they truly be. Of course,
they may develop from there, through events in the course of
the play. But a librettist must avoid false clues and make sure
that what is sung introduces his characters as they really are.

One of the great musical directors, Lehman Engel* has said
it most simply: 'One of the chief differences between most
plays and most musicals . . . is that characters in plays are often
not what they seem, in musicals they invariably *must be.*'

Length

The most obvious difference in the realm of the contemporary
lyric stage is that the musical is divided into two acts. The
intermissionless musical tried in *Man of La Mancha*, *1776* and
a few others seems to have fallen by the wayside. David LeVine,
Executive Director of the Dramatists' Guild recalls that even
Man of La Mancha's single act was not a creative decision:

> The original production was done in a theater downtown which was a
> temporary structure while they were building the Beaumont Theater . . .
> it was down on West 4th Street. Originally, *Man of La Mancha* was done
> with an intermission but the traffic patterns in that theater were so bad,
> it took so long to get people back to their seats that they kept going over
> the 11.30 curtain. So purely to get the people out by 11.30 they decided
> to do without intermission. And within a year or two years time critics
> were heralding them as great forerunners because they had done a musical
> without an intermission and it worked so much better . . . that there *was*
> really no place to break . . . which was all a lot of nonsense. The only

---

*Lehman Engel (1909–75) was for half a century Broadway's most sought-after conductor
of musicals. But he is remembered even more fondly as Director of the ASCAP musical
workshop which shepherded many of today's luminaries in the musical theatre on to the Great
White Way.

reason it was done without intermission is that they didn't want to pay the overtime!*

Because of its brevity, as in a lyric, every section of the libretto must count. The book of an average musical runs to about ninety pages (Oscar Hammerstein insisted it should not be over seventy-five), while that of a straight play generally is at least twice that length. Drama can sprawl, but a musical must not overextend its welcome.

In discussing how to telescope all that action into such a brief time, Arthur Laurents (librettist of *West Side Story*, *Gypsy*, *Anyone Can Whistle* and *Do I Hear a Waltz?*) says, 'You have to make every single line count. You have to be very good with a red pencil. You have to do it fast. In musicals there isn't time for chitchat', and Joseph Stein (librettist of *Plain and Fancy*, *Take Me Along* and *Fiddler on the Roof*) mentions that 'it has to *feel* that it is *not* fast. It has to be absolutely comfortable, but there has to be an extreme economy.'

Stephen Sondheim adds, 'To write a good libretto, you have to accomplish everything a play accomplishes in half the time. Of course, songs – if they are sympathetic to the piece – can give you an enormous amount of substance and richness. Nevertheless, the amount of words that Arthur Laurents used in *West Side Story*, which is one of the most highly plotted musicals ever, I think is the second fewest on record for a real book show. I think *Follies* is the shortest book.'

Although *Les Misérables* and *The Phantom of the Opera* run for well over three hours, their librettos are not long; the time is consumed in their musical numbers and stage effects. Yet they are still briefer than many straight plays, notably dramas or picaresque adventures. Eugene O'Neill's *Strange Interlude* lasts five hours and the recent Royal Shakespeare Company's adaptation of Dickens's *Nicholas Nickleby* ran for six hours. This is inconceivable in the musical theatre.†

Perhaps it sounds so predictable as to stymie originality, but musical play construction demands an optimal length. The most successful ones have adopted a time-frame which may

---

* In Britain, single act shows are frowned upon by theatre owners who lose a considerable amount of bar money.

† Opera, however, has always been permitted to move at its own, and admittedly sometimes snail's pace. Most Mozart, Rossini and Verdi opera run over three hours in performance. Wagner holds the record, his operas average four hours. Parsifal, his longest, lasts five and a half hours – not counting intermissions!

have been influenced by the fact that modern audiences don't care to sit for hours in their seats – no matter how interesting the action on stage may be. The first act curtain, which should descend about an hour and a quarter from its rise, ought to leave the plot partially resolved but with its final outcome still in doubt. This is equivalent to the former third act curtain in a classic play or the second act curtain in a contemporary three-acter. After a fifteen minute intermission the play should resume with the second act running forty-five to fifty minutes. The total running time of most musicals should then be about two and a quarter hours; long enough for the audience not to feel cheated because of the astronomical cost of their tickets, and not long enough to become tedious to today's nervous and impatient audiences who consider attending a musical as a 'night out', and are hungry for after-theatre supper or eager to go dancing.

Scope

The scope of a musical is much closer to that of a movie in that it can be 'opened up' by the use of production numbers which would only cause a mêlée in a straight play. When *My Sister Eileen* became *Wonderful Town*, the original setting, a rented Greenwich Village basement apartment Ruth and Eileen, two refugees from a cramped life in Ohio, shared for the entire three acts of the play, was enlarged. Jerome Chodorov and Joseph Fields who had written the original play expanded their libretto to include the street in front of the apartment, an editor's office, a subway, the Brooklyn Navy Yard, a police station and a Village nightclub. Expansion then, is one of the major differences between straight play adaptation and musical libretto.

Expansion may simply be fleshing out the author's intentions. When Alan Lerner working along with Frederick Loewe tried to adapt Shaw's *Pygmalion* in 1954, they decided 'it could not be made into a musical. We just didn't know how to enlarge the play into a big musical without hurting the content. But when we went through the play again ... we had a great surprise. We realized we didn't have to enlarge the plot at all. We just had to add what Shaw had happening offstage.'

William Gibson's intimate, two-character play *Two For the*

Seesaw, which was adapted into a rather glitzy, dancey musical by Michael Bennett, necessarily added new cast members, friends of the couple and a chorus of dancers. And even though the two principals were given thirteen of the sixteen songs in the score, they frequently were joined by the ensemble turning their solos into production numbers. In this way Bennett was able to keep the intimacy and yet adapt it to the motion and colour we have come to expect in a musical. *Two For the Seesaw* and its musicalisation, *Seesaw* make a wonderful study for the librettist wishing to acquire the technique of expansion, one of the major differences between straight play adaptation and musical libretto.

Suspense

Audiences have been sitting on the edges of their seats ever since Manon, a courtesan being chased by the police, returned to her bedroom to sing some exalted music while collecting her beloved jewels. We all know this will lead to her imprisonment and want to yell at the stage: 'Get out before it's too late!' We have similar feelings when attending Verdi's *Il Trovatore*. Manrico, informed that his mother is burning at the stake, starts to rush off to save her, but spends five minutes singing his famous 'Di Quella Pira'. (Sometimes, if the tenor can get away with it, it is sung twice, making us wonder if his mama will be merely charred bones when he comes to her aid.) And Carmen. She has no need to remain at the bullfight which will bring about her death, since she now has her very own bullfighter.

But in every case those opera librettists want us to empathise with their characters; they *mean* our hearts to be in our mouths and our minds to say, 'don't do that', 'don't delay', or 'there's trouble if you go there'.

Librettists of musicals must be equally canny if they want to create suspense – and there is nothing wrong with introducing a song to extend the suspense, as long as the delay is realistic. The best dramatic kind is still the one that will elicit an audience response.

In the last scenes of *West Side Story*, when Tony goes after Chino, we want to warn him to keep away; similarly when Cliff picks a fight with the Nazis in *Cabaret*, we know the outcome will be as grim as Christine's going through the mirror with the *Phantom of the Opera*. Most of this kind of suspense is saved for the ending of the first act, to create a parallel kind of excitement movie audiences get when they watch a car chase or manhunt as a climax to an adventure film.

But there are other kinds of suspense; emotions may pervade the whole plot, and these need not be grim. I refer to comic and romantic suspense. The comic (and rather slim, but somewhat suspenseful) idea of characters being trapped on an ocean liner with the Number One Public Enemy comprises the entire plot of *Anything Goes*. The outcome of the bet to pass off Eliza as a member of society in *My Fair Lady*; the suspense of knowing whether Dolly Levi will land Horace Vandergelder in *Hello, Dolly* or if the Boy and Girl in *The Fantasticks* will fall in love according to their fathers' wishes – all these are on the light side, yet no less suspenseful.

Romantic suspense can be a powerful force – the pull of Anna to the king in *The King and I*, Emile de Beque's attraction to Nellie Forbush in *South Pacific*, Georg and Amalia's love-hate relationship in *She Loves Me* – all create a thread of suspense that tightens and keeps us interested in the plot.

Sentiment

True sentiment is one of the most difficult things to convey in writing without going overboard into the sentimental. Audiences enjoy being moved to tears, and it is every actor-singer's dream to finish a big number to applause, sniffles and eye dabbing.* But first, one must decide where sentiment ends and love begins. Generally what we call sentiment in the theatre is a relationship other than that between man and woman. Love and the attendant love song can easily become bathetic, but sentiment between a father and child or between a much older and a younger person or people from two different worlds (as in Anna and the King of Siam) generally, by its very freshness, will escape becoming mawkish.

Man of la Mancha has a closing scene that comes perilously close to bathos, but Dale Wasserman has crafted his libretto

---

* There is a grain of truth in the remark with which one English actress famous for her acid tongue is often said to have devastated female colleagues: 'If you wept less on stage, your audiences would weep more.'

so carefully that although the audiences may be weeping there seems to be such honesty coming over the footlights that it creates a true emotional catharsis. With the moving music of 'The Impossible Dream' throbbing quietly in the background, Aldonza, the sluttish servant maid who became 'my lady Dulcinea' exhorts a dying Don Quixote not to abandon his heroic ideals. She whispers the words that brought her courage and glory, (a masterful use of *REPRISE* [*see* page 207]) when she says to him, 'but, my lord, they're your own words ... To dream ... the impossible dream ... to fight ... the impossible foe ... to try ... when your arms are too weary ...' This is known by the technical theatrical name of 'recognition scene', and the recognition can be of a person, an ideal or even a concept.

Fanny contains sentiment of the highest order when Marius feels the ironbound devotion to his son. (The warmth between them is intensified because he does not suspect the boy is his child.) And in *Carousel* the moving moment occurs when Billy is allowed to revisit his daughter. The only moment of true sentiment allowed to light-hearted *Mame* is 'My Best Girl', a song sung by her nephew, Patrick, when Auntie Mame, having wrecked the theatrical performance of her 'bosom buddy', actress Vera Charles, is at her nadir.* The librettist must never confuse this kind of sentiment with the lovesong, a powerful, erotic, moving but totally different emotion.

Climaxes

Professional librettists often talk in hard-hearted, rather formulaic terms about the two apexes that should be reached in musicals. The first, they say should be about two-thirds through Act I, and the other they insist must be in the middle of the second act, near the 'eleven o'clock number'.†

---

*Librettists Jerry Lawrence, Robert Lee and composer Jerry Herman realise that Auntie Mame's true sentiment, the reason we are close to tears when she sings lively songs such as 'We Need a Little Christmas', will be created by the theatrical device known as subtext.

† The 'eleven o'clock number' is a carryover from the days when a performance began at eight thirty p.m. A musical's first act, which was then usually longer than it is today, ended near ten o'clock and after a twenty minute intermission, audiences settled down to the second act. Its climax in plot and song had to come as close to eleven o'clock as possible. The hour has changed, the formula exploded, but the tradition and its wisdom lingers on. The essentials of an eleven o'clock number are discussed in WRITING THE LIBRETTO section, page 153–7.

Dénouement

Another drama school stalwart beloved of those who would have us create the 'well-written play', is a gradual tapering off of action near the end of the show. This is known by the technical name of falling action or dénouement. In essence it began as an artistic return to reality, a sort of rounding off somewhat akin to the coda in a symphony, but of course, the musical coda must pull all the foregoing themes together in an exciting fashion, and in the theatre, fashioned after antique Greek and Roman ideals it merely served the purpose of allowing audiences to come down to earth before they faced the unadorned world. It was also a time for the 'message' or moral. Today, although used by some loquacious contemporary dramatists, it has no place in the musical theatre. It becomes an occasion for audiences to slip back into pinching shoes or search for a missing glove. In fact, quite the opposite is demanded as the show draws to its conclusion; it should pick up pace, and even the most leisurely and gentle of musicals must hurl itself towards a strong final curtain.

FOR THE LYRICIST*

Understanding differences between Popular song and Show song

Popular song and theatre song formerly travelled the same road. In the Thirties and Forties songs that made it to the 'Hit Parade', which was the equivalent of today's 'Top 40' were first heard in the theatre. But with the advent of an intimate microphone technique, and then the revival of rhythm and blues and rock, (both of which derived their considerable power from raw feeling, repetition and rhythm – anathema to theatre music) and partially because musicals insisted that their scores be tightly woven into the play, the two roads diverged.

---

*Until a few years ago, it was not proper to call oneself a 'lyricist' because there was no such word in the dictionary. Music in the classical tradition was set (and still continues to be) to poetry. There were only poets and composers. One who wrote light verse that could not be dignified by the name called poetry, or someone who put words to music already written was officially called a 'lyrist'. Popular usage finally defeated tradition and the term lyricist was accepted.

The gulf widened throughout the next three decades until now as we move through the Nineties it seems an impassable one. Heavy amplification causes most words to be lost except on album liner notes, and because of it hard rock lyrics have become more intense, elemental and cliché-ridden. Yet our young people grew up on it and it is hard to keep out of the theatre, or to keep artists successful in the rock field from wanting to make their mark in musical theatre. But most professionals feel they will rarely succeed because they forget that theatre must be a collaborative effort and the songs written for it need to be appropriate to the show and appropriate to the performer. Theodore Chapin, now the Executive Director for the Rodgers and Hammerstein estate, was, at the time of its creation, on the production staff of *Follies*. He recalls:

> Stephen Sondheim wrote 'I'm Still Here' because Yvonne De Carlo had a song she couldn't pull off. He was smart enough to realize that she was the kind of performer who would never understand that the character she was playing was very close to the character, the human being, she was. So he could get away with writing a song which really talked about what Yvonne De Carlo had been through. In another context he wrote 'Send In the Clowns' because Glynis Johns couldn't sustain long passages, which is why it is a little phrase followed by another little phrase.
>
> People who say Paul McCartney or Randy Newman should write for the theater don't understand, first of all, the sheer amount of time it takes to perfect, to shape, to write, to throw out and start all over again. I worked for a director who had a tape of a Paul Simon musical. Well, Paul Simon has said he wants to write for the theater, but I don't know that he understands what the process is.

Paul Simon is certainly a fine songwriter, but he seems to me and to Mark Steyn unlikely to turn out successful theatre songs because, as Mr Steyn puts it:

> Paul Simon writes very elusively, lyrics that require a lot of thinking about. I once asked him about a song of his that begins 'One and one half wandering Jews ...' 'Oh,' he said, 'the reason it's one and one half is because I'm Jewish and my ex-wife, Carrie Fisher is half Jewish. Her father was Eddie Fisher but her mother was Debbie Reynolds ...' You suddenly realize that if Paul Simon ever does write a musical, you're going to have to get to the theater at 11 in the morning to study the program notes.

If lyrics mean a lot less to younger audiences, it's because they have grown up with microphones and amplification and distortion. They are used to referring to album liner notes to find the lyrics they cannot quite comprehend. The sound battle has had opponents and proponents since the early Fifties when microphones were first introduced into musicals. Diehard theatre buffs will tell you that in the pre-amplification days singers and actors projected and audiences, even in the last rows of the third balcony, heard every word. With nothing between singer and audience, an intimacy was created. Mandy Patinkin in his 1989 one-man appearances, *Dress Casual*, tried to recapture just that by performing mikeless in Broadway's intimate Helen Hayes Theater. Luther Henderson says he thinks 'small shows like Mandy's are exceptions. He manages by an extraordinary outpouring of his own personality to bridge the gap. But generally, I think audiences are attuned to the sound which comes by virtue of electric amplification, so that when they don't hear it, they don't feel the message as much.' And a semi-rock approach, a rapprochement, seems to be in the works. This was largely initiated through the theatre works of Andrew Lloyd Webber, some of whose musicals originally appeared on records, developed a following on disc and then drew large and mostly young audiences into the theatre – somewhat akin to a rock superstar packing a stadium with fans who have come to hear again the songs they already know. Rock concerts have to create excitement through light show and audience participation; 'rock operas', as they are sometimes called, achieve the same through lavish sets and costumes.

But whether it be a rock opera, revue or operetta, apart from becoming freer, and with a good director, comprehensible, the theatre lyric has maintained its sense of 'form' over the century. Lyrics have risen in importance as well, blending into or welling out of the libretto, and the public is no longer willing to accept beautiful tunes that mask archaic language and trite rhymes. Since costs have risen so drastically, producers refuse to stage anything that smacks of amateurism. A lyricist intending to write for the theatre had better master the following essentials. Theatre songs are generally built on one of the three forms listed below. An interesting musical will have some songs in each of the three varieties plus the additional use of free or creative form.

AABA (Popular Song Form)

This is still the strongest and most common form in use in the theatre today. In the Thirties it was practically the *only* form in use. AABA is generally a 32-bar* chorus†, with each of its sections falling into 8-bar segments. If you listen to Kern and Hammerstein's 'Can't Help Lovin' dat Man' (*Show Boat* 1927) and contrast it with Webber and Rice's 'I Don't Know How to Love Him' (*Jesus Christ Superstar* 1971) you will notice that although the styles are different, (and even though in the latter, the sections are considerably longer than eight bars), they both sing about a woman's utter devotion to a man, and although separated by almost half a century, *they both use the same form.* In each of them there is a theme, the theme repeated, a new, contrasting theme (called the bridge or release), and a return to the first theme.

And that is no accident. They use this form because it reaffirms one of the strongest artistic principles, a principle so telling and elemental that it is used in painting, sculpture and literature as well: (A) a strong statement, (A) repetition, (B) contrast with a new statement and (A) return to the original statement. Literally thousands of songs, show tunes and pop songs, jazz and rock songs have been written using this form. As far as the contemporary musical theatre is concerned, I have to add that the two current preeminent composers, Sondheim and Webber often prefer other forms. But I have listed below a few well-known songs that come from musicals and you can see that there is a great deal of strength available to the lyricist who chooses this elemental form.

'Ol' Man River' (*Show Boat*)
'Wouldn't It Be Luverly?' (*My Fair Lady*)
'Lover, Come Back to Me' (*New Moon*)

---

* The word 'bar', meaning the metrical period is most commonly used in the United States. 'Measure' is its British equivalent.

† The chorus of an AABA (and an ABAC theatre song discussed next) is most often preceded by a 'verse'. This verse which sets the mood usually does not return and is *not* reprised when succeeding choruses are sung. In early operetta days these verses were long and cumbersome, but by the time the Gershwin brothers and Rodgers and Hart reached their heyday, verses had been shortened to ten lines. (Most often two four-line stanzas and a couplet.) They have changed little over the last fifty years. Although it sounds confusing, do not make the mistake of confounding this non-recurring verse with the verse of a verse-chorus song. In the former the verse (although it needs to be created with care) is merely lead-in material necessary to transport the ear from speech to singing while in the latter it is an *integral* part of the song.

'The Sound of Music' (*The Sound of Music*)
'Tomorrow' (*Annie*)
'What I Did For Love' (*A Chorus Line*)
'Memory' (*Cats*)
'On the Sunny Side of the Street' (*The International Revue*)
'So In Love' (*Kiss Me, Kate*)
'What Did I Have That I Don't Have?' (*On a Clear Day*)
'Some Enchanted Evening' (*South Pacific*)
'Strike Up the Band' (*Strike Up the Band*)
'I Could Have Danced All Night' (*My Fair Lady*)
'If Love Were All' (*Bitter Sweet*)
'Bewitched' (*Pal Joey*)
'If Ever I Would Leave You' (*Camelot*)
'The Lady is a Tramp' (*Girl Crazy*)
'The Man I Love' (*Strike Up the Band*)
'Get Me to the Church on Time' (*My Fair Lady*)
'The Best of Times' (*La Cage Aux Folles*)
'Being Alive' (*Company*)
'Good Thing Going'* (*Merrily We Roll Along*)
'Think of Me' (*The Phantom of the Opera*)
'The Point of No Return' (*The Phantom of the Opera*)

ABAC (Show Tune Form)

This is known as the typical show tune. The form has great strength and somewhat more sophistication than AABA, although it still negotiates the same 32 bars. It is also able to achieve more intensity because its final section can become climactic. Often this type of song seems to 'split down the middle', dividing itself naturally into 16 and 16 bars. Again there are thousands of examples of this form in musicals, a few of which are listed below.

---

*Although both 'Good Thing Going', and 'Being Alive' are written in clear-cut AABA form, Stephen Sondheim when interviewed announced that, 'I seldom use it except when I am doing pastiche. Not many composers use it any more. I think those rules were broken about fifteen years ago. The AABA form is much more common in pop music now than it is in theatre music. Content dictates form, and it's what you have to say that motivates the form of the song. You decide as you go along. If you go down the list of shows on Broadway, even some of the more conventional ones, you will find very free use of song form. AABA is no longer standard.' The reader must be cautioned that Jerry Herman, John Kander and Fred Ebb, Marvin Hamlisch, Jerry Bock and Sheldon Harnick and others disagree.

'But Not For Me' (*Girl Crazy*)
'If They Could See Me Now' (*Sweet Charity*)
'Come Rain or Come Shine' (*St Louis Woman*)
'I Love a Piano' (*Stop! Look! Listen!*)
'Here's That Rainy Day' (*Carnival in Flanders*)
'Limehouse Blues' (*Charlot's Revue*)
'Hey, Look Me Over' (*Wildcat*)
'Hello, Dolly' (*Hello, Dolly*)
'I Still Get Jealous' (*High Button Shoes*)
'Getting To Know You' (*The King and I*)
'I'll See You Again' (*Bitter Sweet*)
'Someday I'll Find You' (*Private Lives*)
'Rock-a-Bye Your Baby' (*Sinbad*)
'Autumn in New York' (*Thumbs Up*)
'Bill' (*Show Boat*)

Verse Chorus Form

This is a very popular form for the theatre, and rightly so for it is able to convey a story that is frequently interrupted with a short chorus or refrain. The verse (which most often is a 'list song') is usually eight lines in length and the chorus which may be an exact repetition each time (or more frequently have a different punch line each time it occurs) should not have more than four lines. I have listed some of my favourites below and an analysis of them will make the form clear. As you can see from scanning the titles below, this form is an excellent choice for comedy songs.

'A Little Tin Box' (*Fiorello*)
'Dear Officer Krupke' (*West Side Story*)
'Meeskite' (*Cabaret*)
'Friendship' (*Dubarry Was a Lady*)
'I Get Carried Away' (*On The Town*)
'Where is the Life That Late I Led' (*Kiss Me Kate*)
'The Ballad of Jennie' (*Lady in the Dark*)
'Look to the Rainbow' (*Brigadoon*)
'Sue Me' (*Guys and Dolls*)
'There is Nothing Like a Dame' (*South Pacific*)
'With a Little Bit of Luck' (*My Fair Lady*)

'Wishing you Were Somehow Here Again' (*Phantom of the Opera*)

Other Forms

Form is not a prison.*It is a tool used by songwriters to create unity and balance. Sometimes a lyrical idea must overflow its boundaries or be pointedly telescoped. Stephen Sondheim's 'Send In the Clowns', sung by the loquacious Desirée in *A Little Night Music* had more to say than could be managed in the AABA form into which it *almost* fits. The songwriter added another A section and the song as performed on stage became an almost Schubertian AABA*A*.† Kander and Ebb's 'Wilkomen' telescopes the AABA form into mere ABA. Since it is a trilingual introduction to the nightclub, sung at the opening of *Cabaret* by the dissolute master of ceremonies, it would naturally have to be briefer and more accessible. ABA seems to have worked well for the Gershwin brothers whose 'Bidin' My Time' from *Girl Crazy* relies upon the form to create a lazy and iconoclastic atmosphere. The same form is used by Toby in *Sweeney Todd* when he sings with timid bravura to Mrs Lovett that nothing will harm her, 'Not While I'm Around'.

Free Form

Most amateurs assume that a song in free form removes all constraints, that the songwriter is free to do anything he likes. Nothing could be further from the truth. For although free form implies the A and B sections as such are abandoned, there must be a compensation in the use of fewer melodic motives.

---

*Stephen Schwartz, composer-lyricist of *Godspell*, *Pippin*, *The Magic Show* cautions that completed music can imprison the lyricist. 'I always get as much of the lyric idea down as possible. I think music is much easier than lyrics, because lyrics are craft, and music is a sort of emotional response to a situation or a particular feeling. So I handle the lyric first. Also, it's important that I get as much of the lyric done as possible right away, because once the music is done, that's it for me. I'm trapped in that form.'

† It is curious that when Barbra Streisand decided to include that song in her 'Broadway Album' she telephoned Mr Sondheim and requested another B section so she could sing the song in what is known commonly and commercially as a 'chorus and a half'. Mr Sondheim then obliged with new and rather simplistic lyrics for the 'bridge' section. (Ms Streisand sings AABA; BA.) The added section has contributed little to the popularity of the song which is now most often performed in its succinct and flowing original form.

Stephen Sondheim's later musicals all make extensive use of free form. Among the many, it would be wise to analyse *Pacific Overtures* and *Into the Woods*, each of which have two outstanding and clear-cut free form songs: 'Someone In A Tree', and 'Pretty Lady' in the former and 'No One Is Alone' and 'No More' in the latter. In every case there is one basic melodic idea, transmogrified and handled in a surprising variety of ways that gives each song its unique and memorable profile. Thus the technique of free form is closer to a classical or symphonic one (a symphony's 'development' section does the same thing with one or two motives), while it is at the same time close to hard rock which explores only one melodic or bass line and creates its culminating effect through repetition.*

Interludes and Extensions

Like the lead-in verse so beloved of theatre lyricists, interludes may often be inserted in theatre music to give a song more pertinence to the play. They are often suggested by the composer for they contribute mightily to creating a well-rounded musical line. Extensions are most often tacked on to create an additional musical climax and are most common in ballads and production numbers. In analysing form remember that neither *extension nor interlude will affect the basic form of the song*.

Analyses

In an effort to clarify the variety of forms used in a musical I have analysed below two classics and one contemporary musical.†

---

*The writer would caution that more than two or three free form songs in a musical can create a sprawling work.

† Lerner and Loewe as well as the Gershwins, Kern, Coward, Hart, Arlen and Hammerstein always have a preponderance of AABA in their shows; younger, perhaps more 'showbiz' creators like Kander and Ebb, Jerry Herman, Adams and Strouse, Jones and Schmidt generally lean towards show tunes which are constructed in ABAC form. Cole Porter, always the master of form, usually came out 50–50 as did Sondheim in his early works. The later ones have employed a great deal more free form. (See page 59), Rock in the pop field and on stage originally used verse chorus form, and perhaps that is why the majority of Andrew Lloyd Webber's output is still in that form.

MY FAIR LADY (Songs by Alan Jay Lerner and Frederick Loewe)

'Why Can't The English'	(Free Form)
'Wouldn't It Be Luverly?'	(AABA)
'I'm an Ordinary Man'	(Verse Chorus)
'With a Little Bit of Luck'	(Verse Chorus)
'Just You Wait'	(AABA)
'The Rain In Spain'	(Free Form Verse; Free Form Chorus)
'I Could Have Danced All Night'	(Lead in Verse; Chorus AABA)
'On the Street Where You Live'	(AABA)
'Ascot Gavotte'	(AABCAA – Classic Gavotte)
'You Did It'	(Free Form)
'Show Me'	(Lead in Verse; Chorus AABA)
'Get Me to the Church'	(AABA with Extension)
'A Hymn to Him'	(Free Form)
'Without You'	(AABA)
'I've Grown Accustomed to Her Face'	(ABAC with Interlude)

CABARET (Songs by John Kander and Fred Ebb)

'Wilkomen'	(ABA)
'So What'	(Verse Chorus)
'Don't Tell Mama'	(Lead in Verse; Chorus AABA)
'Telephone Song'	(Verse Chorus)
'Perfectly Marvellous'	(ABAC)
'Two Ladies'	(Verse Chorus)
'Pineapple Song'	(AABA)
'Tomorrow Belongs to Me'	(4 Line Hymn Stanza)
'Married'	(AABA)
'Meeskite'	(Verse Chorus)
'If You Could See Her'	(ABAC)
'What Would You Do?'	(Verse Chorus)
'Cabaret'	(AABA; Interlude and Extension)

THE PHANTOM OF THE OPERA (Songs by Andrew Lloyd Webber, Charles Hart and Richard Stilgoe)

'Think of Me'	(AABA)
'Angel of Music'	(AABB)
'The Phantom of the Opera'	(AABC)
'The Music of the Night'	(AABC)
'Prima Donna'	(ABAC)
'All I Ask of You'	(Verse: AA; Chorus: ABAC and Extension)

'Masquerade'   (Free)
'Wishing You Were Somehow Here
Again'   (Verse: AA; Chorus: ABAC)
'The Point of No Return'   (AABA)

The Title

Show tune titles must say a great deal, and because of this can
be an enigma to both the lyricist and the composer. When we
think of lengthy titles like 'Bewitched, Bothered and Bewildered', we assume they are overlong for today's taste. But this
kind of thing was and still is, to some extent, necessary. In the
case of 'Bewitched', which had six choruses in *Pal Joey* and
was (in spite of the slow tempo at which it is usually performed
today) originally a sprightly comedy song, the long title was a
'throwaway' that was needed to give the audience the chance
to laugh and not obscure the ensuing joke in the next stanza.*
Though the composer may not always be able to see it coming,
the director and sometimes the lyricist may be able to spot the
laugh. The composer must then adapt his work to the lyric as
Jule Styne did in *Gypsy*. Stephen Sondheim with his uncanny
perception of theatre sensed there was going to be a big laugh
in 'If Mamma Was Married' right after the bridge, and as
Styne puts it 'he convinced me to write two extra bars to give
the audience a chance to laugh ... first time in my life I ever
had a lyric writer say, "Write two extra bars because that's
where we're going to get a laugh." And that's right where we
got the biggest laugh in the show.'

Title placement is one of the most overlooked and most
important aspects of lyric writing because it determines form.
Form is set up when the lyricist chooses where the title will
appear. The two most obvious spots are at the outset and at
the end of the first quatrain. Titles that come at the outset
like 'Hello, Dolly', 'Some People', 'Empty Chairs at Empty
Tables', 'Some Enchanted Evening', or 'I Am What I Am' are
certainly more striking. Those that come at the end of the

---

*Boredom can set in if the title is too long, used too often, or the jokes not funny enough
to sustain laughter. Witness 'The Apple Doesn't Fall Too Far From the Tree' from Kander
and Ebb's *The Rink*. Hammerstein's 'Do I Love You Because You're Beautiful, or Are You
Beautiful Because I Love You' is the longest well-known title. Fortunately the lyricist saved
the song from utter tedium by only using this title once in the entire chorus. It was more than
enough.

first quatrain can be more lyrical and more subtle. Think of 'Wouldn't It Be Luverly', 'This Is All I Ask of You', 'So In Love' and 'Smoke Gets in Your Eyes'.*They can also be comic, a sort of punch line, like 'Doin' What Comes Naturally', 'I Get Carried Away', 'Friendship', 'That's a Good Way to Lose a Man', 'He had Refinement', etc.

In creating a title, the lyricist should define the concept of the situation in the play and take care that the title says it as succinctly as possible.† 'If I Loved You' from *Carousel* tells us clearly about the hopes and projected future of the characters involved. 'Some People' gives us a glimpse of Rose's, (the mother in *Gypsy*), ambitious world as contrasted with all the stay-at-homes, while 'People' tells us what a 'need' Fannie Brice had in *Funny Girl* that made her so dependent on others.

It is desirable, and used to be obligatory, for a musical to have a title song. The raison d'être for this is the hope to get the name of the musical on everybody's lips, for a whistled tune can be a powerful commercial. It is a rather good idea to try for one. When composer and lyricist are inspired, the custom succeeds as in 'Anyone Can Whistle', 'She Loves Me', 'On a Clear Day', 'Oklahoma!'‡ and especially the Jerry Herman musicals *Milk and Honey, Hello, Dolly, Mame, Dear World* and *La Cage aux Folles*. When it is just a dutiful title song as in *Kiss Me Kate, No Strings, On Your Toes, Promises, Promises* and *Silk Stockings*, the song seems as intrusive, annoying and forgettable as a TV commercial.

---

* There are literally hundreds of excellent songs which are exceptions to the norm and don't have their title stated at the outset or appearing at the end of the first quatrain. Among them are 'You'll Never Walk Alone', whose magnificent title emerges only at the end, (although the word 'walk' is used several times throughout the lyric); 'Small World', and 'I Could Write a Book', whose titles are buried within the text; 'Song on the Sand' and 'Dancing On the Ceiling', whose exact titles never appear at all.

† It is an axiom of good lyric writing to avoid unnecessary or redundant words. They must *never* be used in a title. In the title 'Wishing You Were Somehow Here' from *The Phantom of the Opera*, (lyric by Charles Hart), the word 'somehow' adds the final coup de grace to what is a witless and awkward title.

‡ This musical's original title was 'Away We Go', and there was no title song. It was not until late in a tryout run that received so-so reviews in New Haven that this was discarded in favour of 'Oklahoma!' (adding the exclamation mark for further urgency, and perhaps critical insurance).

Language

The librettos of most musicals are written by one person and the lyrics by another and then performed by still another, the character in the play. Since it is hard enough to go from speech into singing, songwriters try to avoid any sense of artificiality here. The lyricist wants to be ever vigilant that there be no gulf between the tone of what is spoken and what is sung. This chasm is often widened into an ocean when archaic language is used in the songs. Even today's most romantic operetta cannot permit itself the mannered lyrics of former times. That is not to say that a period piece must use contemporary speech, merely that bad writing, formerly masked as 'poetic licence' is taboo.*

Imagery, metaphor and simile are all poetic terms that every professional lyricist understands, and certainly are necessary in any song; but perhaps one should counterbalance the short list with 'honesty'. Lyricists are generally clever craftsmen and are often guilty of showing off – sometimes unconsciously. Then audiences lose contact with the character on stage while the lyricist indulges himself. Ira Gershwin often force-fed his pet interests of history or slang to audiences, and Lorenz Hart would abandon the character who was singing on stage and show his erudition by rhyming dizzily, what critic Mark Steyn calls 'ostentatiously, as in "stick to" rhyming with "in flagrante delicto".' Mr Steyn goes on to blame his comperes for 'praising that kind of rhyme that one would have to be a fool not to spot. Critics will praise these at the expense of people who have many more lyrical and less obvious ideas.'

Rhyme

Today's rock makes rhyme less important than popular music did a couple of decades ago, but in the theatre, lyricists still

---

*Sondheim's ear was intrigued by what he calls 'elegantly written language, so thick and rich, without being fruity' in Christopher Bond's play *Sweeney Todd*, and as adapted by Hugh Wheeler the libretto and songs are closely unified. Assuredly this is most easily accomplished when the book *and* lyrics are by the same person. Alan Jay Lerner's book moves into his lyrics seamlessly in *My Fair Lady*, and he is able to choose Arthurean language in *Camelot* which seems archaic, but whose message is thoroughly contemporary. This from 'The Lusty Month of May': 'It's mad! It's gay!/ A libellous display/ Those dreary vows that everyone takes/ Everyone breaks/ Everyone makes divine mistakes/ The lusty month of May.'

count on rhyme to make their songs memorable and graceful. They use it as much as ever before. And despite the precaution of over-rhyming mentioned above, today's lyricist must understand rhyme completely. Rhymes come in many forms, generally called one-rhyme, two-rhyme, three-rhyme and so on. The rhyme derives its name from the spot at the end of the line where the accent falls. One-rhyme *accents* on the last syllable; two-rhyme on the next to last syllable, etc.

An interesting song lyric generally uses more than one kind of rhyme. Songs that stick doggedly to the same kind of rhyme can turn out to be insufferably dull.* (A rundown of the several kinds of rhymes is given below.)

thirst	
worst	**ONE-RHYME**
*thirst*ing	
*burst*ing	**TWO-RHYME**
first of all	
worst of all	**THREE RHYME**
first of the lot	
worst of the lot	**FOUR-RHYME**

But don't let rhyme and cleverness get in the way of meaning. The best lyrics don't look impressive on the page, but when you sing them they have an affecting simplicity. In today's theatre it's *not* the rhyme that matters, but the thought behind it. For example, 'going' and 'growing' is not an especially fresh rhyme, but when attached to a profound thought and used with innovative language, as in Stephen Sondheim's 'Good Thing Going' from *Merrily We Roll Along*, the worn words seem freshly minted:

> *We could have kept on growing*
> *Instead of just kept on,*
> *We had a good thing going . . .*
> *Going . . . gone.*

---

*One-rhymes used to be known as 'masculine' or ultimate rhymes while two-rhymes were designated 'feminine' or penultimate rhymes. Three-rhymes were sometimes called penpenultimate and four-rhymes were pen-pen-penultimate. Fortunately all this sexist and unwieldy nomenclature is now outdated and has been abandoned.

Thus, it is happily no longer necessary to have show off rhymes à la Cole Porter's 'ecstatics' rhyming with 'lymphatics', or Larry Hart's convoluted [I'll call each] 'dude a pest', rhyming with [you like in] 'Budapest'. One should try for natural speech, especially in a contemporary work. Who can keep from smiling at 'you get pneumonia' rhyming with 'he'll never phone ya', from Hal David's memorable lyrics to 'I'll Never Fall In Love Again'. (*Promises, Promises*).

Rhyming, and certainly inner rhyming imply erudition and education, so one should use both carefully unless one wants to create an intellectual atmosphere. I can think of no better way to caution the would-be creator of a musical than to quote from Oscar Hammerstein II's preface to his published lyrics:

> If one has fundamental things to say in a song, the rhyming becomes a question of deft balancing. A rhyme should be unassertive, never standing out too noticeably. It should, on the other hand, not be a rhyme heard in a hundred other popular songs of the time, so familiar that the listener can anticipate it before it is sung. There should not be too many rhymes. In fact a rhyme should appear only where it is absolutely demanded to keep the pattern of the music. If a listener is made rhyme-conscious, his interest may be diverted from the story of the song. If, on the other hand, you keep him waiting for a rhyme, he is more likely to listen to the meaning of the words. A good illustration is 'Ol' Man River'. Consider the first part of the refrain:

> > Ol' Man River,
> > Dat Ol' Man River,
> > He mus' know sumpin'
> > But don't say nuthin'
> > He jes' keeps rollin'
> > He keeps on rollin' along.
> > He don' plant 'taters
> > He don' plant cotton,
> > An' dem dat plants 'em
> > Is soon forgotten.

> 'Cotton' and 'forgotten' are the first two words that rhyme. Other words are repeated for the sake of musical continuity and design. The same idea could be set to the music with many more rhymes. 'River', instead of being repeated in the second line, could have had a rhyme — 'shiver', 'quiver', etc. The next two lines could have rhymed with the first two, the 'iver' sounds continuing, or they could have had two new words rhyming with each other. I do not believe that in this way I could

have commanded the same attention and respect from a listener, nor would be a singer be so likely to concentrate on the meaning of the words.

There are, of course, compensations for the lack of rhyme. I've already mentioned repetition. There is also the trick of matching up words. 'He mus' know sumpin' but don't say nuthin''. 'Sumpin' and 'nuthin'' do not rhyme, but the two words are related. 'He don' plant 'taters, He don' plant cotton'. These two lines also match and complement each other to make up for the lack of rhyme. Here is a song sung by a character who is a rugged and untutored philosopher. It is a song of resignation with a protest implied. Brilliant and frequent rhyming would diminish its importance.

Things to Avoid

It has often been said that a lyric is not a poem. At the risk of boring the reader I must point out once again some of their differences. A lyric must get its message across on first hearing, while we can ruminate through a poem several times to extract its essence.* A poem relies on our eye observing the page and expects our brain to sort out the images, while a lyric depends solely on our ear and our emotion.† A poem *is both* music and lyrics, and as such, a complete work of art. A lyric is only part and awaits the music to be a complete entity. Poems then can use the techniques listed below that won't work in lyrics.

Paper rhymes

The use of words that spell as though they should rhyme, (e.g. *word* rhymes with *bird* and *lord* rhymes with *whored*; however on paper, *word* looks as if it rhymes with *lord*) have been a useful and acceptable tool of poets since pre-Elizabethan times. Other examples of paper rhymes are 'have' and 'save'; 'gone' and 'hone'. Paper rhymes should never be used in a song.

---

*Poetry when immediately accessible (as practised by Edgar Guest, Dorothy Parker or Ogden Nash) is generally denigrated and called 'verse'.

† Stephen Sondheim says 'Exactly what makes lyrics work, which is allowing air and space and music to get in there and enrich what you're saying, is exactly the reverse in poetry. When you read a poem you can take your time and go back over it, but when you sing a song you're at the mercy of the tempo of the music.'

Identity

Identity is another poetic trick that cannot work in any area where the sound of the word must strike the human ear. It implies using the same sound with different meanings (e.g. 'You are so fair, it doesn't seem fair, if I had the fare, etc.). This technique, a favourite of lyricists of the Thirties (especially Lorenz Hart), will always fall flat because one of the things we relish most about rhyme is its ability to pique the ear with the same vowel sound attached to a different consonant. In identical rhyming it is totally absent.

Syllable Length

Syllable length which usually does not vary in a well-made poem – in fact poets try to maintain an even syllable length – is anathema to an interesting lyric. The addition of music can move words with any speed the lyricist chooses. Take for instance Stephen Sondheim's lyric for Jule Styne's 'All I Need is the Girl' from *Gypsy*. A glance at these two stanzas will show you that two bars of music may either be negotiated with a single syllable or a mouthful of words. Here the first section moves at a leisurely pace:

Got my tweed pressed,	(Two Bars)
Got my best vest,	(Two Bars)
All I need now is the	(Two Bars)
Girl!	(Two Bars)

The second section starts out similarly in music and lyric, but moves into a rhythmic explosion because more musical notes have been crammed into the same amount of time, a trick inconceivable, and undesirable, in poetry.

Got my striped tie,	(Two Bars)
Got my hopes high,	(Two Bars)
Got the time and the place and I got rhythm.	(Two Bars)
All I need is the girl to go with 'em.	(Two Bars)

To summarise: today's lyricist avoids slavish use of pentameter, hexameter and the other 'ameters', for nothing can make a lyric sound more 'singsongy'. Yet they are aware of the 'exception to the rule' in an AABA song. Whether aiming for the pop market hit or the show tune hit, in this case, once a section is set up, exact repetition is desired, both in the music and the number of syllables.

Contractions and Fillers

Words like 'o'er', ' 'tis', 'e'en' are to be avoided. They were originally used to fit a two-syllable word into one syllable. This was dictated by the structure of the whole poem. Contemporary lyricists sometimes contract words like 'memory' into 'mem'ry', but that is not so bad as mis-accenting it into 'mem-o-reee'. Inconsistency is more amateurish. For example in *The Phantom of the Opera*, the word 'opera' is sometimes sung in three, sometimes in two syllables betraying a lyric nonchalance that borders on sloppiness.

Throwaway words, words that add nothing to the lyric and are inserted because the lyricist needs extra syllables to fill up a line of music always sound as if the writer did not try hard enough. Words such as 'well', 'dear', 'hon' (the current choices are 'girl' and 'babe') to flesh out the line should never be used. 'Just', is another fill-up word that is to be avoided except, of course, where the meaning is 'honest', or 'exactly', (as in Billy Joel's moving 'Just The Way You Are').

It almost goes without saying that archaisms such as 'thee' and 'thine' (unless the period is historical, or the musical concerns the Amish or Quakers who still use the terms) is totally unprofessional.

Long and Short Syllables

Lyricists are sensitive to the division of music into even-time periods by the use of different note values (i.e. although all eight-notes take the same amount of time to encompass, syllables can vary). If you say words like 'fraught', 'clash', 'scratch', 'grasp' or 'brougham' aloud, you will notice that it takes a lot more time, and lip, tongue and mouth movements to say them than 'a', 'I', or 'me'. And yet these are all words of one syllable and presumably could be fitted to one note. Good lyric writing dictates that a string of long unisyllables be

avoided, for it will sound cluttered, perhaps even incomprehensible in rapid tempo.

Stephen Sondheim recalled: ' "America" [from *West Side
Story*] has twenty-seven words to the square inch. I had this
wonderful quatrain that went, "I like to be in America/ O.K.
by me in America/ Everything free in America/ For a small fee
in America." The "For a small fee" was my little zinger –
except that the "for" is accented and "small fee" is impossible
to say that fast, so it went, "*For* a smaffe in America." Nobody
knew what it meant! especially in fast tempo.'

This writer must add that the main reason for the incom-
prehensibility is the adjacent 'l' and 'f'. In rapid tempo one
cannot take the time to enunciate the word 'small'.

Adjacent consonants

When Nöel Coward wrote his lovely song 'I'll See You Again',
only his unique clipped manner of speech-singing was able to
make the line 'Time may lie heavy between' comprehensible;
today most audiences are puzzled when an operetta tenor (ever
notorious for garbled diction) bellows: 'Tyemay lie heavy
between'. Most of the members of his audience will turn to
each other and ask, 'What's lying heavy between?' Likewise,
in performing Stephen Sondheim's 'Send in the Clowns',
unless the singer comes to a complete stop between the words
'love' and 'farce' in the phrase, 'Don't you love farce?' we
hear, 'Don't you love arce?' Enough said. Adjacent consonants
especially in fast tempo are incomprehensible. And poetic
licence? Merely the bush behind which untalented lyricists
hide.

Alliteration

Alliteration has often been compared to inner rhyme as a trick
of the literate. In a way, this may be true for we certainly have
passed the time when 'show-off' lyrics are acceptable. As with
jalepeno peppers, a little goes a long way. But show tunes
with titles like 'A Ship Without a Sail', 'Till Tomorrow',
'Bewitched, Bothered and Bewildered', 'Bye, Bye, Baby',
'Darn that Dream', 'Toot, Toot, Tootsie' and 'World Weary'
have always been catchy and memorable.

The same, I feel does *not* apply to musicals with clever titles like *The Zulu and the Zayda*, *No, No, Nanette*, (and its sequel *Yes, Yes, Yvette*), *Firebrand of Florence*, *Simple Simon*, *Happy Hunting*, *All American*, *Mack and Mabel*, *Tip-Toes*, *Who's Who*, most of which were flops.* Alliteration is a clever trick that can spark a song but is too artificial to support a whole evening's entertainment.†

FOR THE COMPOSER

How much does a composer of musicals need to know? Orchestration? Arranging? Polyphony? Counterpoint? Atonality? Synthesizers? Modality? Are these essentials?

In the Twenties through to the Fifties some musicals made it to the West End or Broadway simply on the unharmonized tunes their natural but non-conservatory-trained composers presented. These naïve tunes were a reaction against the technically perfect academic sounding scores of Herbert, Lehar, Strauss and Friml. A whole group of 'untrained' composers specialising in the new ragtime, cakewalk and finally jazz, brought fresh air to the musical stage. Certainly, they needed and got help from professional orchestrators and dance arrangers who eventually gave their scores a final glitzy, showbiz sound.

But that kind of show is now old-fashioned and the theatre is looking for fresh voices. Stephen Sondheim often writes polychords and has stated that his favourite chord is 'the 13th'.‡

---

*Cole Porter loved the technique and a long narrative song like 'It's De-Lovely' compiles an alliterative list describing two lovers as 'delicious, delightful, delectable, delirious, dilemma, delimit, de-luxe' in the first chorus. Of their courtship he strings together 'devine, diveen, de-wunderbar, de victory, de vallop, de vinner, de voiks'. Describing their bridal suite, he says 'It's de-reamy, de-rowsy, de-reverie, de-rhapsody, de-regal, de-royal, de-Ritz'. In the last chorus which describes their newborn, Porter switches the alliterative letter from 'd' to a more energetic 'p' as in 'He's appalling, appealing, a pollywog, a paragon, a Popeye, a panic and a pip'. His brilliance made his work an exception to most rules. Even his shows with alliterative titles succeeded. *Silk Stockings* and *Kiss Me, Kate* were hits.

†Stephen Sondheim says, 'As for alliteration, my counterpoint teacher had a phrase, "the refuge of the destitute". Any time you hear alliteration in a lyric, get suspicious. For example, when you hear "I Feel Pretty" and she sings "I feel fizzy and funny and fine", somebody doesn't have something to say.' [Author's note: In spite of the foregoing, two of his finest alliterative songs appear in *Follies*: 'Rain on the Roof' and 'Broadway Baby'.]

‡In our Western system of music, chords are constructed using the seven different members of the scale. (Do, Re, Mi, Fa, Sol, La, Ti.) Because our Western ears find adjacent tones dissonant, we evolved a system of chord construction in what we call a more 'harmonious'

He also does his own arrangements, that is not to say he orchestrates; however Andrew Lloyd Webber and Leonard Bernstein *do* orchestrate their scores. So did Kurt Weill and George Gershwin. Apart from an occasional throwback like *Me and My Girl* the basic musical with simple songs seems a thing of the past.

Today's composers should be able at least to create what is known as a piano-vocal score which uses three staves, the upper one for the vocal line and the two lower staves for the piano. When asked if today's composer needs to know counterpoint and modulation, Luther Henderson, Broadway's preeminent composer-arranger-orchestrator said, 'Oh, absolutely, all of it! This is said notwithstanding the success of rock composers whose meagre repertoire consists of four chords.' Jonathan Tunick, who orchestrated most of Stephen Sondheim's shows feels similarly about the lack of training in today's theatre composers. '[People] look for very simple, even rhythmic phrases ... and very bland harmony that doesn't assault the ear ... Today a person calls himself a composer when he has no more business being called a composer than a person who calls himself a doctor because he knows how to apply a Band-Aid to a cut. Somebody buys a cigar-box guitar and plays a few chords, gets someone to write it down, and he's a composer. That may be an extreme example, but up until recently you were expected to know at least some of the language of musical notation. Can you imagine a novelist who doesn't know how to read or write?'

But it has always been so. The theatre composer has forever lorded it over the Tin Pan Alley tunesmith. There is a story about George Gershwin who enjoyed playing tennis and frequently chose Bert Kalmar, a composer of music for novelty songs as his partner. 'I'm sorry, Bert, I can't play today,' he is reported to have said. 'I've sprained my wrist, and it would be disastrous for me to risk doing further damage to my hand.' Kalmar countered with, 'George, I sprained my wrist last week, and still you insisted we play the game, and so I did.'

---

way, by using *every other member* of the sequence. We can construct simple chords (triads) using Do, Mi, Sol; stronger ones (7ths) by using Do, Mi, Sol, Ti; still more intense ones (9ths) using Do, Mi, Sol, Ti, Re; even more intense ones (11ths) by using Do, Mi, Sol, Ti, Re, Fa; and the most complicated ones, (13ths) using all seven of the scale tones. Of course these tones must be arranged like a ladder, spaced as indicated above, Do, Mi, Sol, Ti, Re, Fa, La. The 13th chord is the end of the line. There is no 15th chord because the next scale member would be the Do, starting the sequence over again.

To which Gershwin shot back: 'Yes, but it's not the same thing, is it?'

Mark Steyn says that the differences between pop and theatre have become amplified as we have moved into the rock era. The composer who has made his name in pop charts may be primarily concerned with creating a powerful musical statement. He continues:

> Most popular music of the kind that makes the top 40 today has no particular interest in lyrical content. It's a question of production. If you go and listen to the way people create these things – even Paul McCartney. They're in the studio, they get a kind of groove on their synthesizers, they lay down the track, and the last consideration, *the very last consideration*, after everything is done, is to put some kind of lyric on it. It's not surprising when the lyric is that much of an afterthought that it boils down to 'Get the Funk Out of My Face', or whatever. You could never use that kind of lyric in the theater. It's simply not dramatic.

It's not actually that these composers are uneducated musically, simply that their expertise is in different areas. Mr Tunick's diatribe against the theatrically untutored doesn't imply that today's theatre composer should avoid all references to rock, he simply wants those who have been successful in the pop field, and who are contemplating doing a musical, to learn enough technique to encompass other aspects of musical creation before they tackle Broadway or the West End. As Mr Henderson explains: 'There should be more composers in the theater who can stretch the flavor of rock into their work without losing the theater quality, somewhat like Andrew Lloyd Webber, who puts a healthy sense of rock into his music. Now, Charlie Strouse did it in *Bye Bye Birdie* and again in *Annie*. Just enough to give a tang without losing the sense of theatre.' Mr Henderson added that 'Stephen Sondheim doesn't [put any sense of rock into his music]. People have to join Sondheim, he doesn't join *them*. And fortunately, or unfortunately, he has the talent to demand it.'

Although a lead sheet* which is a shorthand way of notating a score used to be acceptable, the great theatre composers like George Gershwin, Leonard Bernstein, Richard Rodgers, Noël

---

* A lead sheet (the origin of the word from the 'lead' [usually trumpet or clarinet] line) is merely the tune with names of chords printed above it and the lyrics printed below it. (In the UK the *letter* names of the *chord* are printed below (e.g. G^7, B^b maj^7, $F^{\#m9}$; in France the *musical syllable* names are printed *below*, e.g. Sol mi^7, Re maj^9, La^{13}).

Coward, Harold Arlen, Frederick Loewe, Cole Porter, Jerry Herman, Jerry Bock, Charles Strouse, Burton Lane and many others only used it for sketching (sometimes avoiding it altogether). As technical skills advance, composers want to be able to hear their music exactly as they conceived it. But how can intense sounds like the chords below, constructed in 4ths, and so much a part of the 'American' sound, be indicated on a lead sheet? They can't!

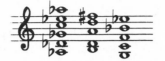

So the obvious answer to the question of how much composers need to know before tackling a musical is **as much as possible**. They read, study, listen to other artists' work, and are always aware of what is contemporary. They see as many shows, musicals and straight plays as they can. If they don't live in a metropolitan area where live theatre is performed, they should visit their local library and study the scores and librettos of all the musicals. Complete piano-vocal scores of most successful musicals are published and available; many orchestral scores are also available. They must take an interest in music of all periods and lands so they will be able to recreate an aura of that time or place if they are to be working on a period musical. And the best of them will remember as they develop the musical, to be true to the book and the characters they are working from.

John Kander who wrote the authentic sounding score for *Cabaret* says he tried to absorb through recordings the German cabaret songs of the Twenties, and he adds:

I listened and listened and listened and then put them away and forgot about them. So when it came to writing the songs I didn't think in terms of writing pastiche or imitations. Somehow or other, the flavor had soaked in just enough.

Some of the reviews were bad for him, although he had anticipated critics saying he had written watered-down Kurt Weill.

I remember telling [Lotte] Lenya, [Kurt Weill's widow, who was starring in the musical] that I never intended to imitate Mr Weill at all. She took my face in her hands and said, 'No, no darling. It is not Weill.

It is not Kurt. When I walk out on stage and sing those songs, it is *Berlin*.' ... And I thought if *she* felt that way, to hell with everybody else.

Form

Every composer should have an understanding of form as it is outlined in the previous section on lyrics.

Composers are aware that the AABA type of song is the easiest of all to write: for a 32-bar song requires the writing of only 16 bars of music. Things are slightly more difficult in the ABAC song since here the composer must create 24 bars of music, and is progressively more strenuous in the verse chorus song which demands at least 32 bars of music.

In the last two decades form has become much freer. AABA and ABAC and verse chorus form often have extraneous sections thrown in. The B section, formerly a bridge, can be doubled or halved. Extensions are added on top of extensions. And the standard 32-bar song is much less frequently found in the contemporary musical.

Changes of Form

The formerly obligatory lead-in verse that paved the way for the chorus has largely disappeared. Composers seem to be able to go directly from dialogue into the heart of the song. If they need explanatory material in the song that will be inserted as an interlude, for audiences no longer have the patience to wait through a long introduction before getting to the heart of a melody.

Free Form Song

The three pitches and four notes listed below form the basis of Stephen Sondheim's magnificent song 'No More' from *Into the Woods*. If you examine the sheet music you will see that the motive has been expanded, condensed, transposed, inverted – indeed, the composer has used all the techniques of conservatory training in creating this musical experience without making the song sound academic. (Since Sondheim writes both lyrics and music, it should be noted that the lyric explores its concept, twisting its images in every conceivable way, and adds to the total experience.)

This then, is the essence of the free form song. Using a melodic motif somewhat like a tone row or a design motif in classic (and even abstract) painting, developing, changing, and always creating unity by returning to the original idea.

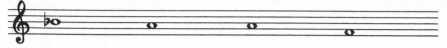

Work Methods

The ever recurring question of which is better (in collaboration and even in solo efforts) – writing the music or the lyrics first – varies with different teams and can even change from project to project. But whether the composer has the lyric before him or not, his method of working on a score should be established. Otherwise he will spend his time staring at blank music staves.

Tim Rice spells an ideal situation for a composer when he says his normal method of working is to 'provide the plot, which my collaborator or collaborators would make comments about and possibly alter. Then they would provide a tune that I hope illustrates the story line I've given them. And then I would write lyrics to the tune. I generally write lyrics to the tune rather than try to write random lyrics.'

Jerome Kern used to write his melodies first, then his lyricists would come along and set the words to his music. So did George Gershwin, Duke Ellington and Richard Rodgers when he was working with Lorenz Hart. Yet from the Fifties onwards, as the excellence of the books of musicals became the factor by which success or failure was judged, the reverse started to become the norm. Jule Styne set the music of *Gypsy* atop Sondheim's words; Rodgers, when he worked with Hammerstein, also wrote his music after the lyricist's words. Often, book and lyrics were by the same person and the composer added his musical line last.

Thomas Z. Shepard, who is working with Sheldon Harnick on *Molette*, a new musical says: 'I never think about musical form, because I feel most of it is dictated by the lyric. Perhaps I feel that way because I almost always work from words first.'

But Mr Harnick usually likes to let the composer write his melodies first. In 1976 he made an exception to that policy when working on *Rex* with Richard Rodgers, (the composer's penultimate show), he wrote lyrics first, for, as he himself admits, he tends 'to fall into AABA, because it's comfortable'. The about face in this instance was occasioned because Rodgers had suffered a stroke and had lost the ability to abstract. 'Rodgers and I had a discussion about something that needed to be written, and he couldn't grasp what I was talking about until I wrote down a dummy* lyric,' Mr Harnick continues. 'Once he saw how everything was supposed to be laid out, he knew how to write the music. It was very strange and difficult, because I wasn't used to writing the lyric first.'

Tim Rice's aforementioned method works well if the playwright is also the lyricist. But a composer who has chosen a section of the libretto that 'inspired' him should begin at once to set it. Sometimes one gets help from the playwright, sometimes not. George Gershwin was greatly assisted by DuBose Heyward and his play *Porgy*. The opening scene in Catfish Row was a crap game, and soon enough Clara with her baby in her arms passes the group crooning the lugubrious lines:

> *'Hush, li'l baby, don' yo cry,*
> *Fadder an' mudder born to die.'*

Of course that gave George Gershwin the inspiration for the now classic 'Summertime', and the scene with its crap game counterpoint. The time of year had not been suggested in the script, but there were enough clues in the stage direction and plot to imply hot weather (geraniums, open shutters, picnics). George invented the melodic line and the title – he often suggested titles to his brother – and Ira created the balance of the lyric.†

It was Gershwin's compositional technique that allowed him to improvise a melody at the keyboard, keep it in his head and then write it away from the piano, but most theatre composers

---

* A dummy lyric, sometimes called 'off the top of the head', will usually have all the syllables of the finished product. It is used to illustrate the rhyming scheme and form. Often improvised by the lyricist in the presence of the composer, it is an expedient crutch employed so as not to stop the composer's creative flow. It will eventually be completed and polished.

† George Gershwin's method in this case was to create a pair of shifting chords (here it was a I chord with added 6th and an inverted V chord) that created an almost palpable heat wave over which he could lay much of this gorgeous lullaby. The form is a simple 32-bar ABAC.

generally make a 'lead sheet', which evolves into a piano vocal score (which may or may not have indications of the orchestration to come).

Phrase Length

Musicals have been more adventuresome in recent years as composers have broken out of the cage of the 32-bar chorus. It is true show tunes are still constructed of four 8-bar sections, but more often, the 8 bars are made up of 5 and 3, instead of the expected 2, 2, 2 and 2 or the ordinary 4 and 4 which has been the norm since Schubert's – the earlier one – time. Stephen Sondheim, Andrew Lloyd Webber, Gerard Schonberg, Stephen Schwartz and Marvin Hamlisch all frequently use uneven phrase lengths. The practice was begun in *Hair* but composers did not emulate it until Burt Bacharach used it so successfully in his semi-rock score for *Promises, Promises*. To their amazement, the public accepted this freedom with open finger-snapping arms.

Range

Time was when sopranos could only work in the chorus of musicals or, if they were lucky and pretty, they might get a featured part in operetta. Our musical world was divided between the 'belters' and the 'legits'; the reigning belters were the likes of Fannie Brice, Ethel Merman, Pearl Bailey and Carol Channing. Even Judy Holliday, Mary Martin and Katharine Hepburn had to learn to use their chest voices. And that did not only apply to women. There were few 'legit' men on Broadway. Singers like Ezio Pinza, Georgio Tozzi, Robert Goulet and Robert Weede who produced pearly tones from their diaphragms were oddities, suitable only for exotic roles. They were never as popular as the natural belters like George M. Cohan, Al Jolson, William Gaxton, Alfred Drake, Anthony Newley, Danny Kaye and Michael Crawford.

The range of the female belter with the chest-produced voice is extremely limited,* but it had to be used by composers and lyricists in order to make the lyric clear. Legitimate singers had been taught (and unfortunately frequently still are taught) that tone takes precedence over words.† Much of that changed in the theatre with the advent of the body microphone. Sopranos did not have to force their tone and distort their diction. And composers who had long been dissatisfied with being confined to writing in the limited range of a belter's octave and a half were free to let their music soar. Many singers developed both ranges, and the mark of a great female show singer was one who could go from head to chest seamlessly.‡ Barbara Cook and a few of her comperes were theatre sopranos who had mastered the art of communicating every single lyric word to their audiences. Those who could easily get jobs had to be able to sing, for example, the coloratura music written for Cunegonde in Leonard Bernstein's *Candide* with its florid line which carries them up to a stratospheric high E flat! Then there developed a new breed of musical singer between the soprano and the belter who was intelligent and clear dictioned. And lo, two decades later comes Sarah Brightman and all those refugees from the concert hall, trilling all sorts of quasi-operatic roulades and scales in *The Phantom of the Opera*. And we can understand the words!

But it has been that way from Mozart's time. Let the composers write the music, expanding technique, making unheard of demands on the singers, let there be demanding stage directors who want to hear every word and a new crop of capable singers will automatically be developed.

Although ranges have expanded in both the West End and on Broadway, a composer or arranger cannot always be as

---

*A good belter can hit C or D an octave above middle C, and go down maybe to F below it. Constantly hitting the top of the range thickens the vocal cords, creates chronic hoarseness and eventually will produce nodes on the cords which require surgery. Many singers in musicals have permanently ruined their voices (especially in the pre-body microphone days) by forcing their top notes into the top of the gallery.

†One has only to hear *Sweeney Todd* or *Porgy and Bess* as performed in one of their opera house incarnations to be truly mystified as to what words are being sung. Contrast that with the original performances under a theatrical director of the calibre of Hal Prince on Broadway or in the West End. Good directors know that the words must be clear and *only then* do they worry about tune and tone.

‡Harvey Schmidt, composer of the score for *The Fantasticks* remembers when he first heard Rita Gardner audition for the part of 'The Girl'. 'What I remember loving about her voice, and the way I had always envisioned the part, was that there was no break between chest and head: there's a lot of coloratura in it, and Rita was one of the few girls we saw at the time who had it.'

altruistic as the foregoing sounds. If a vehicle has a 'star', the composer should write with that star's voice in mind. I quote below some views on 'range' from a question and answer conversation I recently had with Luther Henderson.

C. How do you choose the range when you're writing a show? Do you choose it afterwards, when you're in rehearsal?

H. That depends on the vehicle, for instance, we're working on *Mr Jellylord*. Gregory Hines is at the moment supposed to be the star of the show. We all know Gregory well. He has the regular range of a male voice. I've heard his Sportin' Life in *Porgy and Bess*, so I know he has a good F and G up there. And he can get down and growl. When I write, this is always in my mind. I won't write for a basso who will be comfortable only in the low notes or a tenor whose tessitura is in the stratosphere. I keep the star in mind. If I don't have a star, I invent one and keep the sound of her personality in my mind, and then I'm sure I don't write a melody that requires the talents of a Marilyn Horne.

C. When Leonard Bernstein wrote *West Side Story* he said he wrote the roles as they would be and found singers who could sing them when they did the final casting.

H. Well, knowing Lennie, and his acquaintance with Broadway through his first show, *On The Town*, he must have known the limitations he would have to write for.

C. When you did orchestrations and Wally Harper did the arranging for *So Long, 174th Street*, did you think of the star, Robert Morse's voice?

H. Oh yes, Wally specifically thought of Robert Morse's most unusual voice. In most shows we write for a general voice quality and then, if we get a star early in the run and have to change the range around, we do. Now, *Ain't Misbehavin'* was done for five original voices, and here it comes in a new incarnation and will have a star by the name of Della Reese, who is a female baritone! She's a wonderful performer, but where is she going to fit? When you have a problem like that you give it to the arranger to deal with.

C. Della's voice won't matter too much in the solos; they can always be transposed, but what about the ensembles, the duets and trios?

L. Exactly. The difficulty in that case is you have to decide in whose key you're going to do the number. If the ranges are very disparate and there is a lot of repetition, you could give that voice a harmony part or change key when that person enters. But you better be careful, the latter can make the score sound awkward.

Counterpoint

Counterpoint, which originally was called 'point contra point' (the word *point* being French for note, thus, 'note against note'), has long had a part in the musical theatre, but it was never known by such an erudite name. Was it Mozart or Peter Shaffer who said in *Amadeus*, 'only in opera can you have a lot of people talking at once and make it work. You can't have that in a straight play'?

Musical comedy had its first true counterpoint when, in 1914, Sallie Fisher, singing about how tired she was of the jazzy new rhythms, begged to hear 'A Simple Melody' in Irving Berlin's *Watch Your Step*, while her boyfriend sang a jagged tune against her whose words told us *he* wanted to listen to rag. In those days nobody would use a then pejorative word like 'longhair' to describe the effect. But, in order to be memorable, contrapuntal music should combine two distinctive melodies each of which is good enough to stand alone. Berlin succeeded admirably again in *Call Me Madam* with 'You're Just in Love', where the lyric situation is even more theatrical: a young man complains that he's ill, the all-knowing older woman explains that it's merely the pangs of love.*

In recent years, counterpoint has been used in more intense situations by our more classically oriented composers, but we cannot overlook George Gershwin's exquisite use of the technique in *Porgy and Bess* in 'Summertime', which had Bess's lullaby soaring from one side of the stage, while the chorus sang about the crap game on the other. Leonard Bernstein created tremendous conflict between his two heroines in *West Side Story* in 'A Boy Like That'. Anita, whose vocal line was an attack, was answered by Maria, whose own line was a defence. Like an argument where both quarrellers are talking at once, counterpoint seems an ideal method.†
Recent quasi operatic works like *Evita*, *A Chorus Line*, *Sweeney Todd*, *The Phantom of the Opera*, *Les Misérables* and *Aspects of Love* have made a great deal of this technique, especially now

---

*The counterpoint added to this charming tune was part of the evidence introduced in a celebrated case of copyright infringement brought against Berlin, while *Call Me Madam* was the reigning hit of 1952. The court ruled that this kind of dual melody was often Berlin's trademark and the case against him was dismissed.

† Frank Loesser created a violent musical argument between Tony and his sister in *The Most Happy Fella*. Only counterpoint could have served there.

that the 'don't-stop-the-music' musical has been accepted by the public.

In a theatrically contrapuntal situation many of the words will get lost, so it is often a good idea to have the main thrust of the song sung solo by one voice at the outset, adding the counterpoint later. Where that is not feasible, the loss of lyric is generally more than compensated for by the excitement of battling melodic lines.

One should not confuse true counterpoint with canon or round. (Actually, canon and round are simpler forms of contrapuntal techniques.) In this case one voice starts and another enters *with the same musical line*. The lyrics may be different as was the case in Frank Loesser's 'Fugue For Tinhorns' from *Guys and Dolls*. Here three racetrack touts sang about the merits of the horses they planned to bet on, and their overlapping opinions was not only a musical tour de force but perfectly suitable to the different opinions of horseflesh the argumentative characters held. The dramatic logic is, in short, the only reason for the use of these techniques.

Modulation

Today's composers with their newfound resource, the singer with an extended range, enjoy creating intensity by lifting the key up a half-tone higher. The multi-sharped and flatted keys which were formerly avoided because they were difficult, are now a part of every composer's learning. Composers should not overlook the downward modulation in lyric sections and the *whole tone* and *common tone** modulation which can lead to fresh territory.

Theatricality

Thomas Z. Shepard who has written musicals as well as movie scores, but is perhaps better known as the producer of most of Stephen Sondheim's and some of Andrew Lloyd Webber's

---

*Whole tone modulation creates freshness by being unexpected. The common tone modulation is accomplished simply by making the last melody note of a phrase or chorus the *first melody note of the new section*. This lets the key fall where it may. (It is not feasible when the melody begins and ends on the same pitch.)

show albums, seem to understand best the latter's gift when he says:

> Andrew is very much a product of the rock musical era with his classical training and rock interest. And he has enormous theatricality. He picks subjects that I might not have thought would make great theater, like T. S. Eliot's *Old Possum's Book of Practical Cats*, but he has a nose for it and for what plays on stage. The secret of Andrew is more than one secret. He knows how to write a tune which sticks to you and whether you like it or not, grabs you and holds on to you. It holds on to a lot of people. Another secret is he knows when to bring that tune back,* how to milk his material for maximum musical and theatrical effect, and he creates great superstructures on which to hang these songs.

Intervals

The more sensitive a composer is to his lyrics, the more apt and moving the song will be. But it is no accident that some of the greatest songs have been based on intervals, distances between pitches, that help the lyricist make his point.

The cast dissolved in tears on stage in London during the early rehearsals of *Les Misérables* after Alain Boubil and Claude Michel Schonberg introduced a new song, 'Bring Him Home', which was needed for a climactic moment in the second act. Valjean's beautiful prayer over the wounded body of his soon to be son-in-law begins quietly with the unremarkable words 'Lord above'. But Schonberg clothed them in the interval of an octave skip, thereby sending the protagonist's voice into an almost angelic stratosphere and leaving millions in their audiences ever after with a lump in their throats. Octave skips are difficult because they take a large range, but as in 'Over the Rainbow', whose first word is 'Somewhere', or in 'When You Wish Upon a Star', they can create a celestial emotionalism.

Sometimes intervals alone create a necessary mood. I have always conceived the major third as a walking interval, and indeed listeners seem to sense their absolute rightness in the opening words of 'When You Walk Alone', which begins 'When you walk *through* ...', Augmented fourths are unforgettable and full of wonderment as in the opening pitches of Leonard Bernstein's 'Maria'. Sixths, especially descending

*See Reprises, page 207.

minor ones, are romantic: think of the opening of Francis Lai's 'Love Story'. In short, intervals are one of a composer's basic tools and he should be able to wring emotion or laughter from them as needed.

Word Accentuation

A sensitive composer is one who receives his musical stimulation from the lyric line. Examining the line of Lerner and Loewe's 'I've Grown Accustomed to Her Face', or 'The Party's Over', one will notice an extraordinary wedding of words and music.

I've grown ac - cus-tomed to her face

It is not accidental that the first three pitches rise to the strong syllable 'cus' (coming on a downbeat which always creates an accent), staying on the same pitch as a speaking voice would, and then eventually dropping down resignedly to the important word 'face'. This is Higgins's first admission that he is aware of what Eliza looks like or that she is anything more than a bet to him, and Loewe has created a wisp of a tune that crowns Lerner's moving lyric and follows natural speech patterns.

The par - ty's o - ver

This remarkable motif begins with the strongest force in all musical literature, the sol-do or V-I or dominant – tonic sound. Beginning with a throwaway word like 'the', proceeding to the meat of the phrase which is 'party'. Jule Styne's motif then reaches for what is called an appogiatura, or leaning-note for the syllable 'o', settling down to a resigned resolution on the 'ver' syllable. This appogiatura is especially intense and poignant because Styne has chosen to place it on the fourth of the scale. Of course this song, in *Bells Are Ringing*, is the perfect oblique* torch song and placed where it is, plays with the dramatist's already created mood. These pitches are not chosen

---

*See Oblique Lovesongs. Page 208.

accidentally, but they seem to be the *only* ones possible that can wring out the emotion inherent at this point in the show.

On the other side of the ledger, Mark Steyn, critic for the *Independent*, feels that Andrew Lloyd Webber's lyricists in *Aspects of Love* were 'defeated because of the lack of clear cut structure'. He goes on to point out that at the beginning you have ' "Love Changes Everything", the main song at the beginning, then we're all through. It goes, "News takes time to reach us here, so you'll merit how time flies", then later "Why, why must he spy on us? It was perfect till he came". That is a mistake because I think what made the American musical at its best superior to opera was the union of sung words and music. Once you heard *those* words with *that* tune, they weren't separated. Andrew was enormously impressed . . . as a child by "Some Enchanted Evening". Now, imagine the young Andrew Lloyd Webber sitting in the stalls in the 1950s. Would he have been as impressed by "Some Enchanted Evening" if it had popped up ten minutes later as "Would You Like a Biscuit?" '

RELATED FIELDS

Although the scope of this volume is largely confined to analysis of the contributions of the librettist, lyricist and composer without any one of whom there could *be* no musical, I cannot leave this section without mentioning briefly the two important individuals on whose shoulders the success or failure of any show is dependent. The director and the producer. Without them audiences would *see* no musical!

Today's director works very closely with the creative team. The dialogue, casting, cutting, set changing – actually the entire production – is under his aegis, and although an apt director cannot *write* a hit show, many have put such a strong stamp of originality or freshness on tired musicals so as to make an intriguing evening. Others have been called in at the last minute and frequently have pulled the rabbit out of the hat by turning a so-so evening into a hit. But that never happens on their first show. They also need basic training.

Producers are another matter. Whether they be creative or executive, they need to have a certain vision besides what the public thinks of as merely people who raise the money.

Certainly it is the producer who will sponsor a touring company if the show is a hit or post the closing notice if it is not. They are in a way businessmen, but businessmen with theatrical flair. And again, they need experience and basic training.

FOR THE DIRECTOR

Throughout the first half of this century, directors were hirelings, allowed very little creative input. Their productions were not much more than packages. Even the most successful director's names are forgotten, and the shows they pied-pipered, if recalled at all, are only remembered for their composers and producers. Leading those early extravaganzas to Broadway, it was the legendary Florenz Ziegfeld who decided what would be included in his *Follies*; George White who picked the acts, girls and their scanties for his annual *Scandals*; Raymond Hitchcock who selected sets and skits for every edition of his goo-ily-named series: *Hitchy-Koo*. Similarly, in London's West End, Impresario André Charlot simultaneously chose the stars, supervised the rehearsals and managed each edition of his *Revues*.

Musical plays – those with a modicum of plot – were vehicles for stars. (*Oh, Kay* was written for Gertrude Lawrence, *Sally* for Marilyn Miller, *Lady Be Good* and *Funny Face* had large dance sections tailored for Fred and Adele Astaire.) The director was on the set to see that everything went smoothly for the star. If he also oversaw that no actor bumped into another, entrances and exits were made hastily and through the proper doors, or if he occasionally sat in the far balcony to test whether audiences would be able to hear the play and music, these were dividends. Directors were not much more than glorified stage managers.

Then, somewhere early in the 1940s, when dance became more than a tap interlude, and productions became too involved to be entrusted to the upper office or the ego of performers, the creative director arose. Movement was paramount and names on a markee like Agnes de Mille, Jerome Robbins, Gower Champion, Michael Kidd, Bob Fosse guaranteed it. The public knew it would not be bored at any of their shows.

These choreographer-directors brought their own classical ballet training to the musical. Beginning first with *Oklahoma!*, where Agnes de Mille's contribution was listed simply as choreographer, she came in for more raves than veteran director Rouben Mamoulian. It was inconceivable then that she and the other strong choreographers who followed her would be satisfied with having to obtain approval of their work from the all-over director for long. Choreographers like Jerome Robbins and Helen Tamiris were able to mix balletic and theatrical movement. They had ideas that went far beyond choreographing. Soon there emerged a group of dancer-theatre directors able to take over the concept of an entire production. Others, like Bob Fosse, Gower Champion, Tommy Tune, Michael Bennett and Bob Avian came up through the ranks: passing through the roles of featured dancer, dance captain, assistant choreographer, associate choreographer, choreographer director, to the ultimate 'entire production conceived' halo. Some of them eventually even bypassed the official producer system and went directly to record companies for financing of their projects. Recently it became Michael Bennett's *A Chorus Line* or Bob Fosse's *Dancin'* and, assuring his name as part of the logo and title, *Jerome Robbins' Broadway*.

Now the director became all powerful. Indispensable enough to delay the start of a production until he became available, strong enough to fire a star. Possessing enough clout to order a whole new series of costumes or scenery, he often jettisoned hundreds of thousands of dollars 'for the good of the show'. And he had to be bold and visionary enough to cut lines, songs, lyrics and even 'write out' minor characters in the search for homogeneity. All this power led to the director's name being listed at the bottom of the programme page in letters far bigger than the names of star or writers. ENTIRE PRODUCTION CONCEIVED AND DIRECTED BY BOB FOSSE or HAL PRINCE or JEROME ROBBINS now brings as many people into the theatre and sells an identifiable product to people who, in former years, would have flocked to see a Ziegfeld, Ivor Novello or Cole Porter show or attended the latest Noël Coward or Ethel Merman vehicle.

What would basic training for a director be today? Of course a thorough knowledge of stagecraft, and just as the best conductors are those who have learned their repertoire by playing in orchestras, directors should have spent time on stage. George Abbott, the legendary musical stage director for over half a century, has done the lot. Educated at a Military Academy where he learned to give and take orders, his first jobs in the theatre were as an actor. From there he moved to writing fast-moving farces. Then he began directing them. Cautiously he wet his feet as associate director of a musical and finally took total control. His career is a model for anyone to mould upon. Hal Prince, one of the contemporary musical's leading lights learned at Abbott's knee.

But not every musical relies heavily on dancing. Hal Prince was chosen to do *Evita* because of his way of moving crowds. Likewise Trevor Nunn's background with the Royal Shakespeare Company and his brilliant use of massed forces in Shakespeare histories culminating in his masterful way of maintaining interest throughout the six hours of Dickens' *The Adventures of Nicholas Nickleby*, was ideal preparation for a complicated musical like *Cats*, and even better for his later successes in *Starlight Express*, *Chess* and *Les Misérables*. Michael Blakemore, who handled the split-second timing in the farce *Noises Off*, has an incredible talent – movement. Especially non-dance movement. He was brought over from Britain to direct *City of Angels* whose entire mood depends on the mile-a-minute movement on a split stage.

Then the answer for a would-be director must be: experience. A certain amount of study at a theatre school and then get on stage, offstage out front, backstage. Get experience in acting, singing, writing, understudying. Get to be a disciple of an operating director in the music theatre. And then, *if* you have enough visionary ideas and are bossy enough to get them across – the biggest if of all – when you get a musical librettist, composer and lyricist who believe so strongly in you that they are willing to entrust their 'baby' into your arms, you are well on your way.

FOR THE PRODUCER

The popular image of a producer is of a cigar-chewing, obese and wealthy businessman with a taste for pretty chorines. The layman pictures him in his office high up in the theatre he owns, telephone in hand, feet up on his desk – a man who has risen from lawyer or accountant to theatre manager.

Nothing could be farther from the truth.

Today's producer is generally a hard-working organiser, often a visionary who knows what will work on stage and what will not.*

Yesterday's producers often came from families who owned theatres (like Arthur Hammerstein, uncle of librettist-lyricist Oscar), or like the Shubert brothers or Abe Erlanger, who acquired theatres and chose crowd-pleasing operettas to fill their stages. Usually they made money, but if they did not, they produced one show and were never heard of again. Some were dilettantes like Alfred Bloomingdale whose department store fortune led him to invest heavily in misguided musicals, or more recently British producer Harold Fielding, who had lost several million pounds on his tasteless production of *Ziegfeld* in 1988, and finally had to pack it in after another extravagant flop in 1990.†

But today's producer is totally different. Most have had some theatrical training and generally have served an apprenticeship learning the ins and outs of theatre, for the job needs a vast amount of knowledge in the disparate fields of set and costume design, acting, music, lyrics and staging.

Additionally, producers need to be able to handle publicity and advertising, have a fair acquaintance with accounting. Add to that the psychological temperament to soothe the frayed nerves and fragile egos endemic to theatre people from rehearsal to opening to closing, and you have a long list of attributes that make for success in this field.

Almost more important than these qualities are trust-

---

*Producer David Merrick was the first to realise that Thornton Wilder's 1954 play, *The Matchmaker* could be adapted successfully for the musical stage. He hired Michael Stewart to create the libretto and Jerry Herman to write the score. Together they turned out the smash hit, *Hello, Dolly*.

† According to critic Mark Steyn the production that bankrupted Harold Fielding, *Someone Like You* 'had everything wrong with it, from its colourless title and Civil War setting to its unlikely writing team of Fay Weldon, Petula Clark and Dee Shipman'.

worthiness and personal vision. From Ziegfeld to Merrick to Mackintosh,* these producers have staged a large variety of musicals, but each has had its originator's stamp. As for trustworthiness, a producer has to build up a large list of people confident enough to invest in an unseen product, so reliability is necessary.

Trustworthiness, reliability and vision are uncommon attributes in the theatre. They do not seem to go with greasepaint and creativity. Perhaps that is why there are so few successful producers of musicals today.

A FINAL WORD ABOUT THE THREE MAIN COLLABORATORS

With the technique necessary for today's musical composer, lyricist and librettist it should be clear from the foregoing pages that today's triumvirate is not composed of the same people who keep one foot in the pop field and the other in the theatre. Several decades ago all of our popular music hits were first heard in the theatre; today it is a rare show that produces a song that will make it to the rock charts. Writing a musical becomes a more specialised art form all the time, since the total musical, not the individual songs, will mean the difference between success and failure.

There are, certainly, courses that try to help students learn the major techniques of writing a musical but they are not nearly so specialised as they might be. Unless one enrols in a programme specifically designed for the musical theatre, the budding amateur is sure to have trouble finding professional guidance. This applies to public and private colleges and universities and even to most music conservatories.

---

*Cameron Mackintosh – certainly the British musical's most successful producer – flopped on his first venture; what looked like a sure-fire hit – a revival of Cole Porter's *Anything Goes*. He hadn't yet learned his craft. But his later phenomenal success has been attributed to many things, perhaps most of all is his patience. He seems to allow the show to develop naturally, rather than announcing the project, booking the theatre and then scurrying about to change the project when audiences react negatively. In the twenty odd years he has been producing in the West End he has turned out *Side by Side by Sondheim*, Tim Rice's *Blondel*, Sandy Wilson's *The Boy Friend*, Rodgers and Hammerstein's *Oklahoma!*, Stephen Schwartz's *Godspell*, Julian Slade's *Trelawney*, Lerner and Loewe's *My Fair Lady*, Lionel Bart's *Oliver*, Abba's *Abbacadaba*, Andrew Lloyd Webber's *Cats*, *Phantom of the Opera* and *Song and Dance*, and Schonberg and Boubil's *Les Misérables* and *Miss Saigon*. He recently said he has another project (whose authorship he could not reveal) which has been in the works for four years! He will produce it *when* the show is ready.

Playwriting is part of the curriculum of most liberal arts colleges, but it is a far cry from creating a libretto; poetry is taught and analysed in universities and that too has nothing to do with lyrics; learning to compose string quartets, symphonies and piano sonatas has almost no application except for the by-products of learning harmony and counterpoint in the song-filled world of the musical.

Things are slightly easier for the 'semi-pro'. In the United States ASCAP (American Society of Composers, Authors and Publishers) and BMI (Broadcast Music Incorporated) sponsor musical workshops chaired by estimable professionals in New York, Chicago, San Francisco and other cities where they have offices.* Since both these organisations are only interested in promoting a property and sponsoring a musical collaboration that will be professional and whose members will sign under the aegis of these performing rights societies, the chosen individuals will have to be strong enough and their works powerful enough for them to step directly from those workshops on to the Broadway stage.

Britain has a similar programme, established at St Catherine's College, Oxford, in 1990, through a grant from producer Cameron Mackintosh. Its first Professor of Musical Theatre is Stephen Sondheim who outlined the ground rules of the project, which, it is assumed, succeeding professors will abide by. For his initial session Mr Sondheim chose four composer-lyricist teams and five individuals who write both music and lyrics. Before choosing the thirteen people who make up the group he and his associates listened to ninety entries on tape, the main criterion being 'a search for a personal voice and a voice particular to the theatre not to pop songs'. Because this is a learning project, Mr Sondheim wanted the group to have the advantage of seeing how a show is put together (this coincided with the National Theatre's production of his

---

*Information on colleges, universities, workshops and schools that offer instruction in the musical is to be found in the Appendix. Although admitting to few good ones on the undergraduate level, Ted Chapin gives special mention to the University of Cincinnati and adds: 'What they do there, I have no idea, but every time you sit in on an audition, several of the best candidates are from there. Last year I sat in on auditions for *Show Boat* which has one foot in operetta and one foot in musical theater, and it's very difficult to find people who are right for it.'

Chapin also enthuses about David Craig who trains performers specifically for musicals. Mr Craig, now in New York, has enabled actors of the stature of Alexis Smith to negotiate the wide gap from movies to the stage and into the musical theatre. He is planning to start such a school in California.

Sunday in the Park With George), as well as guiding them through the creation of their own musicals.

So the chosen thirteen journeyed to London, merely an hour away, by day to observe what progress had been made in casting, set construction, costume sewing and the like. Then they returned to Oxford each evening to work on their own projects. Mr Sondheim assigned a different part of the show for all the students to work out each week.*

Stephen Sondheim admits to having no experience in formal teaching, but he hopes that this 'professorship or chair or whatever you want to call it will set some sort of precedent to deal with the writing process in a formal way. I must say that the best possible way of dealing with the writing process in the theatre is to put shows on. And I hope somehow the University will be able to present some of these works or maybe an evening of these works for an audience. So that having said what they planned to say, the authors can find out if what they said came across.'

Courses like the BMI, ASCAP and Oxford are certainly designed for the 'almost-ready'. But every eager amateur can learn a great deal about writing a show from listening to records and studying scores. Most professionals have drunk from the well of inspiration that the classic musicals of the Fifties offered and have studied the changes that appeared with each succeeding year into the Nineties. They have learned what works, and more important, what doesn't work. They know the difference between a success and a *succès d'éstime*, and can even find something to learn from the rare recordings of monumental failures. They know we have outlived the era of the tired businessman show, and that successes have to keep up with issues. And they see every new show to judge its application to the theatre they wish to create.

Attending musicals is a must because those who create them need to live in a specialised theatrical cocoon, but they have to be aware of the issues, vogues, trends and causes that have

---

*For their first assignment Sondheim asked them to write an opening number because he believes the opening to be the most important part of the show. 'It tells the audience what you're going to do.' ['Then, as George Abbott used to say, "you should go ahead and do it in the second act. In the third act you have to tell them you've done it!" '] As they go on through the term writing their musicals, they will learn 'to sustain what they have started to do – what happens as the songs grow. It's not so hard when you have one or two, but when you get five or six songs, you need to be concerned with tone, variety and style.'

always been heard when theatre people raise their unique voices on stage. Even though it may not be used, no aspect of popular culture should be overlooked, for living in a theatrical cocoon is totally different from living in an ivory tower.

2 FINDING THE PROPERTY

What kind of Properties Make Good Musicals? Adapting a Classic Book. The Backstage Musical. The Bio-Musical. The Older Female (and Male). Timeliness. Properties to Avoid. Fantasy. Original Ideas.

WHAT KIND OF PROPERTIES MAKE GOOD MUSICALS?

It may sound simplistic, but perhaps the whole difference between a hit and a flop lies in the choice of material. Anyone could bet that a musical with the unsavoury title of *Sandhog* which was about digging a tunnel under a river, complete with explosions and deaths, would not go on to be a joyous smash hit. Likewise a musical called *Kelly**, whose hero, loosely based on Steve Brody who had no other attribute than that he was the first man to jump from the Brooklyn Bridge, must have been hopeless from the start. And who among us would invest in something called *The Knife*, a musical that sings about castration and sex change? All these shows had understandably brief runs. And yet unlikely subjects like poems about felines (*Cats*) or confessions of theatrical hopefuls (*A Chorus Line*) seem able to run for ever.

---

*Kelly, which opened and closed in a single night in 1965, lost the then unheard of sum of $650,000 in the process. It has since become a camp subject of memorabilia for theatre buffs some of whom founded the *Kelly Club*, an organisation of theatre buffs who enjoy talking about the flops they have attended.

The difference, of course, is upbeat versus down.

This is not to imply that a musical must have a happy ending – *Cabaret, The King and I* and *Fiddler on the Roof* have their share of tears at the final curtain – but simply that downbeat tragedy and hopelessness is best served in straight drama or theatrical opera. A musical, no matter how wistful, tender or moving *must* finally be ennobling.

William Hammerstein who has analysed his father's librettos feels that you have 'to be able to demonstrate that by making this property into a musical, you are *enhancing it artistically*. Making a musical must not be merely adding the music, but the finished product must reveal something different, new, transforming. If you are going to make a musical out of *War and Peace*, be sure that adding music is going to make it more thrilling, more interesting. Too many people don't really examine [the property] carefully before they launch into the project. "Let's make a musical out of *Black Beauty!*" they say. "We'll find a singing horse." People say, "Gee, that would make a good musical" without really thinking about it.'

Carrying the thought one step further, Tom Shepard feels that even a bizarre idea like *Black Beauty* might work. 'If somebody told you,' he says, 'they wanted to make a musical about a barber who slits people's throats while his girlfriend turns them into meat pies, [*Sweeney Todd*] I know you'd say, "Give me a break!" But people forget that there's a great deal of difference between the *idea* and the *development of the idea*. *Oklahoma!* in essence is a bit trivial and naïve! Who will take Laurey to the box-social? But it's a plot upon which a couple of very gifted men constructed the most human of stories. *Oklahoma!* resonates to so much that's inside of us all.'

ADAPTING A CLASSIC BOOK

Michael Stewart, librettist of *Bye Bye Birdie, Carnival, Hello, Dolly* and *Barnum*, always exhorted anyone who wished to write a musical to explore books that had been successful and were now in the public domain. 'It's all there.' he said. 'To become a millionaire, all you have to do is dig it out.'

Yes, Molnar's celebrated *Liliom* became *Carousel*, Shakespeare's *Romeo and Juliet* had a new life as *West Side Story*,

Mark Twain's *Huckleberry Finn* ran several years as *Big River* and the megahit of the 1980s has become the musicalisation of Gaston Leroux's *The Phantom of the Opera*. Certainly Shakespeare, Dickens, Twain, Hugo, Conan Doyle have all had their works adapted into very successful musicals at least several times over, so when anyone is looking for a suitable subject to adapt, classic novelists' and playwrights' properties should not be overlooked.

Plays and movies are much easier to adapt than books as generally the dramatic situations are laid out. Oscar Hammerstein felt that *Green Grow the Lilacs*, by Lynn Riggs, while it was not a success as a play, had elements in it that could be enhanced by adding music. Turning it into the musical *Oklahoma!* was a lot easier than tackling a sprawling novel like Edna Ferber's massive *Show Boat*, a novel that has a span of some forty years and venues from Chicago to the Mississippi to the Show Boat itself,* or a multi-generation story like *Les Misérables*.

THE BACKSTAGE MUSICAL

Since musicals attract a theatrical audience, the backstage goings-on, the casting, the production – both amateur and professional – are constantly fascinating, and in addition to adapted classics form the major part of our musical œuvre. From *Show Boat* to *A Chorus Line*, theatre folk, however outrageous they may be, are believed, even envied by those sitting out front, whose inhibitions would never let them act in such a flamboyant manner.†

Gypsy, one of the enduring classics of the past thirty years, features the quintessential stage mother; Desirée, heroine of *A Little Night Music* is an actress; *Babes in Arms* spawned a thousand spin-offs of the kids who save their parents' homes by putting on a show to raise money; *Mame* dabbles with show

---

*William Hammerstein adds that after the four and a half hour first performances in Washington D.C. the impatient critics dubbed it 'Slow Boat'.

†Although a musical about an actual murderer looked doomed from its outset, the book of '*Legs' Diamond* was made even more unbelievable when it was decided to rewrite the libretto and make Legs a hero who had always wanted to 'get into show business'. The musical which opened in early 1989 took seven million dollars and years of Peter Allen's work down the drain with it.

business; *Guys and Dolls* features Miss Adelaide and the 'Hot Box Girls'; *Man of La Mancha* alternates between a prison trial and theatrical fantasy; *Kiss Me, Kate* concerns an untalented theatrical troupe trying to stage *The Taming of the Shrew.* *Follies* concerns a theatrical reunion; *La Cage aux Folles* opens with the preparations for a drag show in a French boîte. In *42nd Street*, the inexperienced understudy takes over from the incapacitated star and becomes the toast of Broadway – which is not unlike *The Phantom of the Opera* except that in the latter case the lady gets help from the weirdo with the mask.

One could go on and on philosophising as to why a sophisticated public never tires of seeing hopefuls and has-beens in theatrical hot water, but it is more important that the librettist in search of a plot with a touch of 'theatre' in it be aware (perhaps by examining the musicals listed above) that in every case there must be *the non-theatrical foils who play against the ostentatious singing-actors*. The list is long, but I only need to get you started by mentioning *Mame* who opposes her Mr Babcock, *Rose* who loves and loses Herbie, Fred Graham who saves the troupe from thugs in *Kiss Me, Kate* and Desirée who spars with her lawyer-love, Fredrik.

THE BIO-MUSICAL

Actual people as a point of departure for musicals make fascinating fodder. Of course, the rights department is easier to deal with if the subject is deceased (but not always if there is a money-grubbing heir to contend with). Living people the writers must contact before tackling the project;* with the dead, they *must* contact their executors.

Writers are not obliged to stick to their subjects' lives exactly as they lived them – unless they are foolish enough to have given the estate right of approval of script. They will often take a section, a decade or even a year during which the subject had a turning point that might be dramatic and could lead to musicalisation.

---

* Perle Mesta, Washington's 'hostess with the mostess' cooperated eagerly and lent her name and cachet to Irving Berlin's *Call Me Madam.* Mme Mesta had been appointed ambassador to Luxembourg and the script hardly denied it. Lindsay and Crouse who were responsible for the caustic libretto announced in the programme notes that the action was 'laid in two mythical countries. One is called Lichtenburg, the other is the United States of America.'

The paragraph below contains merely a partial listing of subjects whose lives have been given theatrical treatment. There are many more out there in whom the public could be interested.

Fiorello (La Guardia), *George M.* (Cohan), *Funny Girl* (Fannie Brice), *Anastasia* (Dowager Princess of Russia), *Pippin* (King Pépin III), *Ain't Misbehavin'* ('Fats' Waller), *Sophisticated Ladies* (Duke Ellington), *Ben Franklin in Paris, The Rothschilds, Coco* (Chanel), *Mack and Mabel* (Mack Sennett and Mabel Normand), *Song of Norway,* (Edvard Grieg), *Call Me Madam* (Perle Mesta), *Evita* (Eva Perón), *The Unsinkable Molly Brown, The Sound of Music* (The Trapp Family), *Sophie* (Tucker), *The Ragtime Blues* (Scott Joplin), *One More Song* (Judy Garland), *Mayor* (Ed Koch), *Ziegfeld* (Florenz Ziegfeld), *'Legs' Diamond.*

THE OLDER FEMALE (AND MALE)

Another mine of musical plots, although it seems to be running out of steam these days, is to be found in the saga of the older (mostly) woman (but sometimes man). Jerry Herman the chief practitioner of this type of musical says of his work: 'Almost every show – *The Grand Tour* was an exception – has had a larger than life lady on stage. The gimmick is wonderful.'

*Mame, The King And I, Evita, Dear World, Hello, Dolly, Applause, Gypsy,** *Lady in the Dark, Call Me Madam* and *Follies* all feature a mature female or females around whom the show revolves. This kind of musical is often mistaken for the bio-musical. Perhaps it should be retitled the 'female-bio',† for a true bio-musical only exists if the plot is based on a non-fictional character.

---

* This musical is really about Gypsy's mother and adapted from her daughter, Louise's (Gypsy) book. It might more appropriately have been called *Rose*, had 'Gypsy' Rose Lee not insisted it be named after her.

† As hinted above, the older man in the person of *Zorba, Man of La Mancha, Aspects of Love, Les Misérables* and others is no longer immune to musicalisation.

TIMELINESS

There is another aspect of adapting a classic or a bio-musical that must not be overlooked. *Each of these has to be presented at the right time.* For, besides developing story and character, a musical must have a *theme* or *concept*.* And that theme or concept should be close to the public's mind when the show is presented. It's even better if the public is *ready* for a trend that hasn't quite surfaced.

Contrary to the time frame of movies or television, the time between the conception of a musical and its debut on Broadway or the West End is usually several years. Being prescient, spotting a coming trend, sensing what is avant-garde and dealing with emergent issues is always a necessity in choosing a musical project. Musicals that are the last of a trend, or a tired sequel that may have been all the rage when it was begun, will invariably be 'old hat' by the time they get to the stage.

Oklahoma!, Bloomer Girl and *Carousel* opened in the early Forties, when their 'home-made apple pie' quality was needed. Their Americanism at the time of the Second World War and introduction of ballet, which was new to the musical, made their stories, which were not particularly timely, urgent and relevant. *Fiddler on the Roof* whose theme is expressed in its opening song 'Tradition', opened in the mid-sixties, a time of strong self-importance and breakdown of family relationships.† *The Phantom of the Opera* which opened in the late Eighties concerns a relationship that is sexually repellent and inviting at the same time – the 'beauty and the beast' theme which has recently resurfaced in books, magazines and a hit TV series. I am convinced that in spite of the excellence of

---

* The basic concept of a musical implies that it go beyond vogue or fashion. Donald Driver who adapted *Your Own Thing* remembers: 'Hal Hester and Danny Apolonar came to me in the 1960s with the terrific basic idea of adapting *Twelfth Night* the Viola-and-Sebastian comedy where you can't tell the boys from the girls. They had a script outline. I think the title was *The London Look*, having to do with Carnaby Street and all that sort of thing. I told them, "Well, that will only last until the fashions go, but I will do it if I can do a free adaptation." ' Driver then wisely expanded the concept beyond clothing into total personal freedom.

† Family relationships which were crumbling in many countries as well as the United States were most precarious in a rapidly industrialising Japan. Joseph Stein, *Fiddler on the Roof*'s librettist who was in Tokyo for the opening of his play recalls: 'Sheldon [Harnick, the show's lyricist] and I ... thought that the Japanese culture was as remote as we could get from the material in the show. Then at the run-through, the Japanese producer turned to us and said, "Tell me, do they understand this show in America?" I said, "What do you mean?" He said, "It's so Japanese!" '

score and book of each of these musicals, none would have been successful had they been introduced in another era.*

PROPERTIES TO AVOID

'There are no limitations to the subject for a musical, just as there are no limitations to the subject for a play or a novel,' says Joseph Stein, librettist of many hits, with *Fiddler on the Roof* perhaps his best known work. 'The only limitation that I can see is that it has to have an honesty about the relationship of people to each other,' he adds. But James Kirkwood who wrote the libretto for *A Chorus Line* feels the necessity to amplify those remarks and adds that characters need warmth to get through to their audiences. Plays that do not possess that will end up by confusing and eventually losing their audiences.

In addition to 'warmth' and 'larger-than-life characters in larger-than-life situations', characters need to interact. A musical that depends on the 'interior' development of a single character (Blanche Dubois in *A Streetcar Named Desire* is a perfect example) is bound to be static because it depends on 'tone' and those that are talky (*Who's Afraid of Virginia Woolf?*, *Death of A Salesman*) also depend on 'talk' and have little occasion for action and movement.

The plays of O'Neill, Pinter, Chekhov, Ibsen, Strindberg, Anouilh, Ionesco, Albee, Sartre, Stoppard and Fugard all contain strong discussions that are stimulating to the mind but would be difficult to adapt, expand and transform into musical theatre.

The play that is to become a musical should not be too complete, it should have room to open itself out into the musical form. Critic Mark Steyn puts it most succinctly:

Take *Blood Brothers*, now playing up the road [St Martin's Lane, London], most of the critics have praised the dialogue, but I don't like it. And the reason I don't like it is because I think it essentially is a play in which the songs are incidental ... I think it fails the litmus test of

*In adapting the comic strip *Annie* to the musical stage, Thomas Meehan, its librettist, recalls how he consciously tried to find a parallel to make the musical timely: 'Harold Gray [who created the comic cuts] began the strip in 1924 so there was no period per se. We were free to write anything we wanted to. It was my idea to place it in the Depression in New York. In 1972 [when the play was being written] the Vietnam War was continuing and there was a recession ... with feelings of pessimism and downness. The Depression came to mind as an analogous time, with the country very down.'

most musicals because, if you remove all the songs, you'd have a perfectly reasonable play – where *Gypsy* and *West Side Story* would have great unexplained chunks missing.'

Mr Steyn feels the same way about a recent London flop, *High Society*, [a musical version of *The Philadelphia Story*].

You don't need the songs! . . . but there should be a different tempo in a musical. The songs exist on a level of heightened reality, and for that reason each line of dialogue is more weighted than it would be in a play. I don't think book scenes can unwind with the kind of casual languor of your average West End drawing-room play. It just doesn't seem right and it seems an anti-climax after the song.

Farce is another thing that does not work well on the musical stage*. Perhaps it is because the characters are so busy with entrances and exits that we never get to know them, which means they never seem to involve us. Frank Rich, drama critic of *The New York Times* feels that musical farce is 'murder to write', and not without reason has it been almost extinct since Mr Sondheim and his collaborators triumphed in *Forum*.

And as hinted above, the mature female bio-musical, so long a natural, seems a difficult one to bring across in the contemporary theatre musical. Perhaps with the coming and passing of Woman's Lib as an issue, the urgency has waned, or maybe there have just been too many of them in recent years. Yet it does seem to me that there is a natural theatricality waiting to be mined by retelling the lives of our great entertainers, male or female. Anybody who overcomes odds to make a successful life will create that glowingly elevated feeling so necessary at the end of a musical evening.

---

* The one glorious exception seems to be *A Funny Thing Happened on the Way to the Forum*. Its book put together by canny collaborators combined several farces, perhaps the whole gamut of farce and seems to have come up with a distillation of the farcical essence. The songs were done as respites, mostly romantic moments for the audience to be able to massage their ribs aching from the laughter that zaniness on stage provoked.

FANTASY

It would seem that fantasy would be best served in the musical theatre, but that has never been the case. On occasion, there have been memorable shows like *Brigadoon* whose plot involves a village in Scotland that comes alive for one day every hundred years, or *Finian's Rainbow*, so skilfully realised that we actually *believe* the leprechauns. But for the most part, fantasy is a risky business. Certainly situations that are patently impossible can only be realised in the movies. *Superman* as a musical (even with a good score by Adams and Strouse who were to write *Annie* a few years later), *Dream Girl* (about a day-dreaming lady) or *Flahooley* (which concerned a laughing doll) were all failures.

It is unfortunate that one of the greatest opportunities for a fantasy that could outdo all previous fantasies was left undone in the musicalised version of the classic motion picture *Lost Horizon* (rechristened *Shangri-La*, what else?). The stage, lit from below, created merely an eerie effect that made audiences uncomfortable and unable to empathise with the characters.

But most knowledgeable theatre people acknowledge that when fantasy succeeds as in *Finian's Rainbow, Brigadoon*, or Stephen Sondheim's *Into the Woods*, it is unbeatable. William Hammerstein says it's the most delicate theatrical element to deal with 'When it works it's marvelous, but it's like making a Sauce Mornay, it can go badly wrong and you don't know exactly why it curdles and then you have to start all over again.'

ORIGINAL IDEAS

'One of the paradoxes of the musical theater is that in order to experiment, you must be perfect,' says Alan Jay Lerner. Critics and the public always judge musicals with an original plot by a harsher standard,* and since, unfortunately, most of our critics are literary experts rather than musical or lyrical, they

---

* Lerner continues: 'The trouble is you get no A for effort. There is no special consideration that is held out to you if you do attempt to write an original musical. I tried. When I was working with Frederick Loewe, we wrote five musicals in a row, all originals. Only one was successful. I finally thought, "Oh, the hell with it! I'll do an adaptation." I picked *Pygmalion*, and I received much more credit for that than I did with *Brigadoon*.'

are quick to condemn any fault of plot construction or character believability. They write little about the music for it is not their métier; lyrics are another matter, they are quick to praise clever or intellectual rhymes. And because of the enormous power they wield (more on Broadway, for there is only Frank Rich of *The New York Times* whose journalistic opinion counts), I have always urged those beginning in the musical theatre to begin with an adaptation. The book and story are laid out and chances of creating a coherent evening are much greater.

For a young person getting started in musicals the paragraphs above must elicit a confrontational question: why would the public be interested in seeing these old chestnuts again on stage? They've read the book, seen it on stage, watched it 'opened-out' as a movie and perhaps as a TV special. Why in the world would they want to see it again this time gussied up with songs and dances?

I can give you no answer except to say that the public needs insurance and wants to see a transformation of what they already know; what the cloak-and-suiters in New York's garment centre, Seventh Avenue, call 'the same, only different'. Just as children want to be told their favourite stories over and over again, so it seems that grown-up theatregoers want their musicals to have yesterday's theme. And because of that, producers are unwilling to gamble. Professionals rarely option a musical with an original story. There are, of course, shining exceptions like *Bye Bye Birdie, On a Clear Day, Can-Can, Company, A Chorus Line, Finian's Rainbow* and *The Tap Dance Kid*, but beyond these, few fantasies have become gigantic hits and so they remain only that – exceptions.

But no fledgling librettist should go into his work down-hearted. Nor should he feel merely a scribe, or that he is 'grave robbing' when adapting a musical from previously published material. The Greeks used *only* well-known stories for their plays; all of Shakespeare's plots had earlier origins and even Shaw based his *Pygmalion* on an ancient legend. The main 'trick' – and it is an essential one – is to recognise which properties contain the germs of useful ideas and then to realise what needs to be accomplished in conversion.

3 SECURING THE PROPERTY

Working With Material in the Public Domain. Working With Copyright Material. Ascertaining What is Copyright Material. How to Institute a Copyright Search. Taking an Option. Writing on Spec.

WORKING WITH MATERIAL IN THE PUBLIC DOMAIN

There is no way to ensure that while anyone working in the theatre, alone or with collaborators, and spending the two or three required years to get a play, let's say, *The Count of Monte Cristo* or yet another version of *Romeo and Juliet*, into shape for the stage, a parallel team in another part of the country or abroad will not be working on the very same project. Yes, one could copyright songs and script, but that will not prevent competitors from doing the same thing. When I lecture to students, I generally advise them to copyright their libretto, a thoroughly professional move, but warn them to be aware that a competitor may be creating something quite different out of the same material, and unless they can prove that he has had *access* and deliberately stolen their material, they will have no legal case.* No restraining order or exclusivity is possible with material in the public domain.

* Lawsuits sometimes occur over particular songs that sound alike and may have the same or similar lyric. They rarely occur when two teams are working on the same property. In the case of songs they are most often settled out of court, more or less for their nuisance value,

When well-known personalities in the musical theatre are involved in a project there is usually enough press coverage or gossip via the grapevine to make the collaboration known to anyone even vaguely connected with the theatrical community. Perhaps because of this, professionals rarely tread on each other's material.* I suggest to anyone interested in adapting material in the public domain that they keep abreast of as many theatrical journals as possible. But one rarely has to tell people involved in theatrical pursuits anything. They all have a sixth sense about who's doing what and when it will be ready, and the word in the street is 'it's a bomb' or 'it's sure to be a smash'. They all read the various 'bibles' of show business: *Variety, Showbusiness, Backstage, Theatre, Theatrical Index* and *Dramatists' Guild Quarterly*, almost all of which are available in large urban public libraries. *The New York Times* on Sunday (and Friday – Enid Nemy's 'Broadway' column) is a mine of information. In Britain *The Stage*, the London *Evening Standard* and the arts pages of the national daily newspapers are required reading.

WORKING WITH COPYRIGHT MATERIAL

I have mentioned earlier that I do not advise any neophyte working in the musical theatre to adapt plays that are still under copyright.† Yet, for the sake of completeness, and assuming some of the readers of this book have already written musicals in the public domain, or are just hard-headed enough

---

since those with the 'hit' song do not wish a restraining order placed on their material, for by the time the restraining order is removed, the song may have lost its popularity. The law, which is quite vague, states that the plaintiff must show that the works have 'a series of notes (it does not say *how many*) in common and that the defendant had *access* to the material and deliberately or knowingly copied the prior copyrighted material'.

 * The only exception in recent years concerned two musicals called *Marilyn*, based on the life of Marilyn Monroe. Each tried to beat the other to hitdom, and although one opened in London's West End and the other attacked Broadway, neither displayed enough talent to sustain more than a few performances.

 † Although I inveigh against it, many professionals see no harm in a student – and only a student – adapting someone else's work merely as an exercise. This implies never showing the work beyond the classroom and never performing it for profit. William Hammerstein says: 'You could be *sued*!' David LeVine (director of the Dramatists' Guild) adds 'beyond the experience of writing and learning and study, a person dealing with a property they don't own is like walking into someone's living room, removing someone's couch and without their permission being determined to turn it into a chair.'

to plough ahead, here are the procedures to follow for working in that field.

Ascertaining what is copyright material

Many properties that appear to be available for the taking may, without you being aware, still be under copyright. A clever mid-Western American has copyrighted 'Happy Birthday' which most of us assume to be a folk tune, and every time it is performed on radio or TV she is entitled to the attendant royalties. Plays and movies that seemingly were written many years ago, may have had their copyright renewed,* or their author may still be alive. In the case of a collaborative effort, the material is protected until *fifty years*† *after the death of the last living collaborator*. Some material may be revitalised if the author *or someone who is given or sold permission to use those characters* creates a sequel – thus the characters in the prequel and sequel are protected until fifty years after the author's or his delegate's death.

We all know that the works of the great classic authors, Dumas, Austin, Ibsen, Brontë, Dickens, Twain and the like, are there for the taking, and those of contemporary writers like Neil Simon, Tennessee Williams, Arthur Miller, Tom Stoppard are clearly still under copyright. But memory is short, and even many professionals are confused about the availability of the works of Rostand, Shaw, Conan Doyle and the like.‡ In cases such as these, it is obligatory before you begin your project to institute a copyright search.

---

* Some authors have sold their copyrights to others, such as movie companies, and those companies may have neglected to renew the copyright. In that case, even though the author may still be alive or recently dead, the property will be in the public domain.

† In France and West Germany those fifty years do not include the interim of World Wars I and II. Gaston Leroux's novel, *The Phantom of the Opera,* long in the public domain everywhere else, is still protected by copyright in those countries and part of the performance proceeds of Andrew Lloyd Webber's musical would have had to go to the Leroux estate until 1991. For that reason, in spite of public demand, the producers decided not to open a touring edition until the book went into public domain.

‡ When Joseph Stein, Jerry Bock and Sheldon Harnick decided to do *Fiddler on the Roof* they weren't sure whether the stories of Sholom Aleichem from which the plot was derived were still under copyright or in the public domain. It turned out the material was still copyrighted and they had to pay to secure the rights.

How to Institute a Copyright Search

United States copyright is assured and kept on file, as mentioned earlier, for fifty years after the author's or his collaborator's death. In Britain, although the information may not be as easy to obtain,* the copyright protection runs for the same fifty years.

If you wish to find out whether a work is still under copyright in the United States, you will have to write to the Reference and Bibliography section, LM-451, Copyright Office, Library of Congress, Washington, D.C. 20559 giving them all pertinent information about the work and requesting them to institute a copyright search. Or you could telephone them at (202) 287 6850. The more detailed information you can furnish with your request, the less time-consuming and expensive the search will be. Try to provide:

The title of the work with any possible variants.

The names of the authors including possible pseudonyms.

The name of the probable copyright owner which may be the publisher or producer.

The approximate year when the work was published or registered.

The type of work involved (book, play, opera, recording, etc.).

For a work originally published as part of a periodical or collection, the title of the publication and any other information, such as the volume and the issue number to help identify it.

Motion pictures are often based on other works such as book or serialised contribution to periodicals or composite works. Try to list the original work from which your request was derived.

The Copyright Bureau will send you a form indicating that your application has been received and request a fee (usually $10 for an hour's research). They will then send you a certificate outlining the exact status of the work in question. If you wish that certificate certified, that will cost you another $4.

The procedure is similar in Britain, and they too will require

---

*Stationers' Hall, Ave Maria Lane, London EC4M 7DD (071 248 2934) automatically maintains their files for seven years after the work is registered with optional renewal necessary. (Songwriters and librettists generally renew up until the same limit as in the United States.)

all the above identification of the work. For more information, write to BASCA, (the British Academy of Songwriters, Composers and Authors) at 34 Hanway Street, London W1P 9DE or telephone them at 071 436 2261.

Taking an Option

If you are interested in making a musical of a story* that is not in the public domain and under copyright you will have to obtain permission to do so from the copyright owners. On the front page, most works in print will tell you who the copyright owners are, and you can write to the publisher to find out how to contact the author or his manager or agent.

You will then have to propose the project you wish to create and usually the agent will write back specifying a certain fee for a certain length of time. (If you are not sure of your capabilities, collaborators, producer, I'd suggest you take a short – three or six month – option. If you are experienced you might take a year's option – and be *sure* you get an option to renew at an agreed price.)

Optioning copyright material by well-known writers may be prohibitively expensive, and in many cases not available. Most agents, to protect their clients, will deny permission – no matter the money – to petitioners without a proven track record. Ed Kleban who was unknown before writing the outstanding book and lyrics to *A Chorus Line* had written his own adaptation of *A Thousand Clowns*, but Herb Gardner, the author of the play, didn't like it, so it never happened.

And there are even some well-known novelists or play-wrights who do not wish to have their works musicalised under any circumstances.

David LeVine, Director of the Dramatists' Guild tells a funny story about one such author, the late Maurine Watkins

---

*Biographies, if they contain hitherto unrevealed materials may also be under copyright, but generally if you are creating a libretto out of someone's life you will need no approval as long as they are considered a 'public figure' and you are not libelling them or adversely affecting the lives of their heirs. Things are not so simple with biographies of theatre folk, for you may not use their 'creations' at will. Their theatrical personae are considered like a logo or trademark. Chaplin's tramp, Lahr's vibrato, the Marx brothers zany alter egos and the like are protected with or without copyright. The musical *A Day in Hollywood/ A Night in the Ukraine*, after a lengthy court case, had to pay for rights to depict the Marx Brothers in an original farce. Doing so wiped out whatever profit the show had made in its more than two-year run.

who had written the play, *Roxie Hart*, which eventually became the basis of the Kander and Ebb musical success, *Chicago*. In the late sixties when Ms Watkins was deluged with requests that her play be turned into a musical, Mr LeVine says, 'she called me on the phone and asked if the Guild could intercept her mail. "I don't even like opening the letters," she said. So we made an arrangement whereby my secretary opened the letters and if it said anything about making a musical of Roxie Hart, she just put it back in the envelope with a notation "Roxie Hart Musical". Then Ms Watkins could tear it up with impunity and not fear that she was destroying her royalty check [from other works] or an important letter.' Although she was adamant about it throughout her lifetime, after she was dead, her executors gave permission to musicalise her work.

Writing on Spec

Not making sure the property is yours to work on can lead to disastrous results as a recent conversation with Thomas Z. Shepard brings out. Mr Shepard and his collaborators have always secured rights before writing movie scores or operas, but early in his career he was not so careful. His comments on an unproduced work are printed below:

> I took *The Night Kitchen* by Maurice Sendak. I loved that book, I loved the rhythm and I wrote a little mini-cantata. It runs about eight minutes. I played it for him when I was through and he was really very annoyed. He said 'What did you do that for?' It isn't that he disliked the piece, as a matter of fact he even had suggestions for sharpening it up but essentially he felt, especially since I knew him, why didn't I talk to him about it first. Of course, if I talked to him about it first, he probably would have said 'don't do it,' because he is a bit proprietary about his own things, and I *really* wanted to do it. But in the back of my mind I thought he would be so knocked out that he'd fall on the floor. I was really crazy about this piece, and so were all the people I played it for. I had a TV producer who was ready to put it on. But the bottom line was that for whatever reasons, Maurice Sendak didn't want it done.

There are times when songwriters and librettists are so eager to musicalise a property they know is under copyright and so sure that only they can make the material 'come alive' that they begin work without the necessary option. It is a risky business, for the holder of the copyright material may have already contracted with others to work on the project, or be unwilling to option the material for a variety of reasons. As mentioned above, but restated because of its tremendous importance, *so many authors of successful plays or movies are advised by their agents to be wary and are unwilling to take a chance on an unknown, even if they see a sample of the work and think it is brilliant.*

One shouldn't confuse writing on spec with getting paid under scale or being asked to prove oneself in a case where the producer is not sure of an artist's ability to create a certain tone that has already been decided upon for the project.

After Sheldon Harnick had written his first Broadway show (*The Body Beautiful*, a fine musical about prizefighting, unfortunately, tepidly reviewed), he was obliged to write on spec for his next job. Here's how he tells it:

> They liked my work [producers Hal Prince and Robert Griffith], but they weren't sure if I was the right lyricist for a show they wanted to do, *Fiorello!* They were sure about Jerry [Bock]; they hired him right away. Both Bobby and Hal knew my revue stuff, and Jerry told me they felt my work was too sophisticated, too satiric – they wanted warmth from a lyricist. They finally got down to Jerome Weidman, who wanted to do the lyrics. He was the book writer, along with George Abbott. Weidman wrote lyrics on spec, and they wanted him for the book but not, as it turned out, the lyrics. They also wanted Yip Harburg, but Yip, regrettably, had a reputation for being stubborn. They went to Steve Sondheim, Hal's old friend, and Steve, thank God, had reached a point in his own career where he said, 'No, I really want to do words and music now, not just words. So I have to turn this down.' Finally it narrowed down to Marshall Barer, lyricist for *Once Upon a Mattress*, and me. Hal called and he said, 'I'll be honest. I don't think you're the right person for this, but if you're willing to write four songs on speculation – without pay – and prove us wrong, you have the opportunity.' I said, 'I'd love to.' I worked with Jerry and he was so cooperative. They wanted a song that sounded like an Irving Berlin tune from 1927, a waltz for the big going-away party. Jerry went off and wrote four waltzes. He came back and played them and asked me, 'Which one do you like best?' I picked one, and he said, 'Oh, good, I like that one too.' So I had the music and I auditioned for the producers. They liked two out of my four things, and that was enough. I got hired.*

* *Fiorello!* went on to win the Pulitzer Prize among other awards. The waltz Mr Harnick refers to is truly exquisite in *both* words and music. Entitled 'Till Tomorrow', it creates a gentle and moving finale to Act I.

Productions that may be undercapitalised often pay their secondary creators (choreographers, costumers, set designers, arrangers, orchestrators, etc.) less than they would normally. Often these artists have a percentage of the show and they are so confident of the project's upcoming success that they will work for practically nothing, but with an eye to the future.*

I would advise anyone thinking of working on spec to try to harness that energy and those ideas and use them in their current project.

---

*Luther Henderson, arranger and orchestrator of the upcoming *Mr Jellylord* for which, if it is a hit, he will come into a share of profits, told me recently, 'I would call writing the score for a two hour musical for which I'm receiving $1,000, writing on spec.'

4 SECURING THE TEAM

Writing Book, Music and Lyrics Alone. Dual Collaboration. Librettist-Lyricist Working with Composer. Composer-Lyricist Working with Librettist. The Most Common Team: Composer and Lyricist. Finding a Librettist, Composer, Lyricist. Agreements, Contracts, Percentages, Points. Billing.

WRITING BOOK, MUSIC AND LYRICS ALONE

Sandy Wilson did it in *The Boyfriend*, Lionel Bart did it in *Oliver*, Frank Loesser did it in *The Most Happy Fella*, Meredith Wilson did it in *The Music Man* and Noël Coward did it throughout his lifetime. Beyond those few individuals, and except for Mr Coward (for the others were isolated works in long careers), I know no other case in the thousands of shows that have been produced throughout this century, of a successful theatre work where book, music and lyrics have been created by the same person. Perhaps it is rare because it is such an awesome and lonely task with no one's opinion to seek along the way, or maybe because, in this age of specialisation, so few of us have the time to develop the considerable talent of playwriting *and* musical composition *and* lyric writing to the peak necessary to create a professional musical. But when it succeeds as gloriously as in the few masterpieces listed above, an incomparably unified work results.*

The obvious advantages of being a triple threat (besides being able to collect three sets of royalties), are total artistic control of the project and, when it is successful, seamless smoothness. The most apparent disadvantage is the lack of sounding board. Anyone who attempts all three major creative features of a musical must possess strong discipline and have a profound belief in his capabilities.

Although I do not recommend it for a first effort, anyone who has decided to write his own musical must outline the plot first, just as though he were setting up a play, before spotting the moments where there will be songs. Professionals don't go too far into the project before they discuss their work with other theatre people. It is pointless to spend years creating a musical that will finally be unproducible.

DUAL COLLABORATION

Although the triple threat is rare in our age of specialisation, the theatre has often produced those who were able to wear two hats. In the dual role of librettist-lyricist working with a composer, one thinks immediately of Alan Jay Lerner creating *Paint Your Wagon, Brigadoon, On a Clear Day, My Fair Lady*, or Tom Jones who so skilfully manipulated *The Fantasticks*. Currently, Alain Boubil is credited with libretto and lyrics of both *Les Misérables* and *Miss Saigon*. But let us be cautious and not assume wearing these two hats is always successful by remembering Truman Capote who, after he had created a mish-mash plot in *House of Flowers*, completed his hatchet job by deciding to set Harold Arlen's exquisite score to the worst lyrics of the decade.

Yes, libretto-lyricists are not uncommon, but even more plentiful are the cases where someone or a team will write the libretto, while an Irving Berlin, Cole Porter, Jerry Herman, Stephen Schwartz or Stephen Sondheim will be responsible for music and lyrics.

---

* *The Unsinkable Molly Brown*, Meredith Wilson's second Broadway show had a book by Richard Morris. Critic Gerald Boardman expressed the general consensus when he wrote, 'the new work lacked something of the stylish consistency of *The Music Man*'.

The experienced Porter, Berlin and Herman were accepted straightaway as composer-lyricists, but Sondheim had to fight to achieve that position. He wanted to do both music and lyrics for *Gypsy*, and had the approval of the show's librettist, Arthur Laurents who says, 'This was sabotaged by Ethel Merman's agent.' Sondheim adds:

> Mostly Ethel did not want to take a chance on an unknown composer. At that point, all anybody knew me for was a lyricist. I had written the lyrics for *West Side Story*. Well, Ethel had just done a show called *Happy Hunting* written by two untried writers. It had not been a success. I am now second guessing, but I suspect her feeling was: once bitten, twice shy.
>
> Jerome Robbins [the director] had also hesitated about having me do the whole score. I was working on *A Funny Thing Happened on the Way to the Forum* at about that time, and I played him three of the songs from *Forum*. I guess he was impressed enough because he called Leland [Hayward, the producer] and said 'It's O.K. for Sondheim to do the score.'
>
> 'But Ethel said she didn't want to take this chance on me as a composer, then she mentioned Jule [Styne] by name. So Arthur came to me and asked if I would be willing to do lyrics only . . .'

Sondheim, a trained musician felt lyric writing was his 'side-line' and was only persuaded to take the job by his friend and mentor Oscar Hammerstein who told him that the experience of working with these thoroughly professional people and particularly with a star would prove invaluable. As it turned out, Sondheim hasn't 'regretted it for one second. Not only do I love the score, I love the show!'

LIBRETTIST-LYRICIST WORKING WITH COMPOSER

The most obvious advantage of this combination is that the whole literary tone of the musical is unified. Although the librettist-lyricist may be itching to set the lyrics, this part of his personality is usually held in check until a solid book is hammered out. At this point the lyricist's alter ego may surface and begin spotting the moments that are too important or emotional for mere prose. Frank Loesser said, 'when a scene reaches a pitch that is too strong to be spoken, whatever the emotion, then it must be sung.' It is these moments that the lyricist will want to set first. Then enter the composer with whom the book-lyricist will work closely.

In detail, the librettist may choose to replace a book-oriented song with an emotionally oriented one. Tom Jones did just that in the second act of *The Fantasticks*. 'Where "They Were You" is now, we had a song called "I Have Acted Like a Fool", which was very dramatic, but didn't give you much emotionally. We felt a simple touching moment would be better,' Jones recalls. Richard Maltby, Jr in discussing the work noted, 'what has always struck me about that song was that the story hasn't resolved itself when the song begins – an almost irrelevant emotional song – and then when the song is finished, the story has resolved itself.'

Michael Stewart who writes both lyrics and librettos, but only once did both together in *I Love My Wife*, adds to the plus column the ego-satisfying feeling of 'having the enormous pleasure of not passing the ball to that other person who suddenly comes in when you've done all the work and built up to it; and he takes a piece of it and does his little sixteen lines. You hear the applause, and you know it's not for the language used just before the song. [It's for the song itself.] It's wonderful to be able to have that moment for yourself.'

But Alan Lerner finds the difference between writing a libretto and libretto and lyrics, 'Enormous! First of all it takes twice as long.' Lerner doesn't derive the ego satisfaction from hearing the applause his lyrics elicit that Stewart does, and cautions all lyricists, 'never forget for one moment that it is the music that makes the play endure.' He adds: 'If the play is good, it is the music that will place it on the shelf of things that will be done and done again.'

COMPOSER-LYRICIST WORKING WITH LIBRETTIST

One of the most difficult tasks facing a composer-lyricist is to decide what part of the script will be musicalised. Generally we look for the climax to a scene, and as mentioned before, the part that is too important to be said in words. Jerry Herman says: 'In a show like *Mame* the choices were endless because it's such a lyrical piece. I could have written three scores for the character of Auntie Mame, so that choosing the exact moment for her to burst into song was a really important decision. How you make it is impossible to describe simply because you do it from nothing but instinct. My instinct tells me that a certain moment in a scene would be better sung and the "Life is a banquet and most sons of bitches are starving to death," should never be sung.'

But that is not always the case. When Stephen Sondheim was writing *A Funny Thing Happened on the Way to the Forum*, the songs weren't working at all. Burt Shevelove, the librettist, told him there were other ways of writing songs than those that develop people and story. Sondheim recalls, 'Burt said, "You must use songs in a different way than you have used them before, different from the Rodgers and Hammerstein school ... there are songs that just act as respites. That is the way they were used when the Romans used them, and that's the way you should use them." ' But each work is different, *Forum* was farce, and quite another thing from trying to get us to believe an almost impossible story, the task Stephen Schwartz was faced with in *Godspell*.

This is what the composer-lyricist has to say about its musicalisation:

The show was conceived by John-Michael Teblak while he was still at Carnegie Tech. He'd done a version of it at Café La Mama, with songs that didn't really function as musical numbers so much as they gave little respites. Thinking of moving it to off-Broadway, people called me and asked me to provide the score. I worked very closely with John-Michael on that. The notion was to stay very close to the words of St Matthew, or in some cases Episcopal hymns which were interpolated – but to say those words from a different point of view, to make a point the way it was staged and presented.

The actual story was all subtext. The actors were saying lines and telling parables that were presumably familiar to the audience, underneath which was the developing relationship among them. One contribution I think I made to the point of view (and I think maybe it is a useful rule generally) was this: although we were doing 'the greatest story ever told', and everyone knew it, we should pretend that no one had ever heard it before. No one was coming into the theater feeling anything about it, and therefore if we wanted to have a relationship between Jesus and Judas we had better get the audience to care about that relationship. That is what led to a number like 'All for the Best', which was just as you would do it in any musical comedy. We have these two characters, and we want them to be friends and care about each other so we have them do a number together.

A composer-lyricist cannot sit in an ivory tower and expect the rest of the show to revolve around him. Even if he has an obvious hit, he must be concerned with the tone of the total show and care especially how his songs *fit in*. Jerry Herman remembers:

> I threw a song out of *La Cage* that everybody thought was the best in the show. You have to be crazy or brave to do that. It was called 'Have a Nice Day', and at the backers' audition in my home in New York it was the big comedy number, a laundry list of every racial and ethnic slur you can possibly think of. It was sung by the girl's father and everybody just fell apart. In the middle of Act One I have this big comedy gem, I am really in terrific shape. We went into rehearsal, and something kept bothering me every time I got to that number. The cast would laugh – that's always death. I realized that what we had in *La Cage* was a very wholesome show. It is, you know; Harvey [Fierstein, the librettist] says it's about 'Honor thy father and thy mother'. The costume sketches were crisp and pastel, very lovely, very wholesome. The set designs were sky blue and then all of a sudden I had this ugly song – funny, but ugly. I told Arthur Laurents, [the director] 'You are going to throw me out of this theater, but I would like to cut "Have a Nice day".' He said, 'Don't you want to try it in Boston and see what an audience thinks of it?' I said, 'Even if an audience loves it, for me it's out of kilter with what we've done.' So it went.

Sheldon Harnick who writes book, lyrics and music, adds that 'one of the touchiest subjects for a composer-lyricist must be the moment when he says to the librettist, "I'm going to use your joke as a capper for my song"', but Jerry Herman finds the loveliest thing about all book writers I have worked with is they understand the word "collaboration". I asked Mike [Stewart, the librettist of *Hello, Dolly*] for the lines "I put my hand in here, I put my hand in there" [which Stewart had taken directly from Thornton Wilder's play, *The Matchmaker*], and he said "Of course, if it makes a better song, what difference does it make?" Herman adds 'The line "Somewhere between forty and death", describing Vera, was a stage direction in Jerome Lawrence and Robert E. Lee's play *Auntie Mame*. I said "I've got to have it. I know how to use it." They said, "You can do anything you want with it," and I used it as a lyric.'

THE MOST COMMON TEAM: COMPOSER AND LYRICIST

From the legendary ones like Gilbert and Sullivan, Rodgers and Hart or the Gershwins to the great contemporaries like Kander and Ebb, Lloyd Webber and Rice or Bock and Harnick, by far the greatest part of the songs in musicals have been written by composer-lyricist teams.

This always brings up the next question. Which comes first, music or lyrics? Beyond Sammy Cahn's oft-quoted quip, 'Neither. The phone call – then the contract come first,' and Richard Rodgers's one-upmanship response: 'The check,' the answer, which has been rather thoroughly discussed in the preliminary section for composers (See *Work Methods* PAGE 75) is that the method of working varies with the team.

A collaboration is a deep artistic relationship. It need not imply that the individuals like each other, although that helps, but it *must* imply that they *like* each other's work. If they like each other's work habits that is all to the good. Richard Rodgers had little patience for Lorenz Hart's drinking, unpredictability and moodiness and was eventually forced to turn to Oscar Hammerstein as collaborator.* Gilbert and Sullivan couldn't stand each other and collaborated mostly by post.

What should be understood about collaboration is the sensitivity of the working relationship. Artists are touchy people who have to put their own egos aside for a collaboration. Lee Adams who has worked with Charles Strouse on many shows, among them *Bye Bye Birdie*, *All American*, *Golden Boy* and *Applause*, generally writes the lyric first. He says:

> When I come in with a lyric and we go over it, and he criticizes it or suggests changes,† I don't think he's criticizing *me*. He's only criticizing this particular piece of work. It's like raising a child. When a child does something bad you don't criticize him, you criticize what he did, right? One of the essences of composer-lyricist collaboration is intellectual, artistic and creative honesty. This has nothing to do with the underlying relationship, but it's hard on many people's egos. It's hard not to think you're being personally attacked, but it's something you have to learn to live through.

---

* Hammerstein confessed that he used to write his lyrics to tunes in his head – from operas or other songs – and he never told Rodgers what they were.

† Strouse is a lyricist in his own right having written the successful revues *Mayor*, and *By Strouse* among other works.

Tom Eyen, lyricist, and Henry Krieger, composer, who had successes in *The Tap Dance Kid* and *Dreamgirls* work differently from Strouse and Adams. They don't write the genesis of their songs apart and then complete them together; they *start*, and go through the whole process together. Krieger says:

> I know lyricists and tunewriters often work separately, but we work together a lot. Tom and I sit at the piano and we start with a lyric and experiment. I'll say, 'Could you make this slightly shorter?' and he'll make these incredible cuts, very quickly ... or I'll write something, and he'll say, 'It's not building. You're in too low a register. Try it again.' And I'll go up. Because he's hearing ... in his own way.

That utter rapport produced the smash hit song that closed the first act of *Dreamgirls*. But an ideal relationship like that is not easy to find. One often may have to try many partners before coming up with someone with whom one can work comfortably. Proximity, dedication to work, similarity of point of view and equality of technical advancement are all major considerations. A relationship in which one partner is primarily interested in artistic achievement and the other is interested in the box office is doomed to failure from the start.

And one without flexibility is likewise doomed. Concerning his collaboration with Leonard Bernstein on *West Side Story* and the second version of *Candide*, Stephen Sondheim recalls:

> Lennie liked to work together and I like to work apart. I find it difficult to work with anyone about. But sometimes he'd come up with a musical idea or I'd come up with a lyrical one, and we'd develop it together. Certain songs were written differently: there was a song in *Candide* called 'Where Does It Get You In the End?' and I changed it and wrote a lyric to his tune. One night I had an idea for a lyric. I just wrote it out, gave it to him and he set it. It was called 'A Boy Like That'.

Even when the team has finally been formed, a team that may have worked well for a musical, it may have to be dissolved. Composer-lyricist teams used to stay together for their lifetimes, but in today's world divorce is as frequent in the world of the musical as it is in society at large.

Charles Strouse and Lee Adams wrote music and lyrics for many shows together. Of the dissolution of their partnership, Mr Strouse says:

Lee and I have never formally broken up. We are still good friends. It's that our working habits grew different. We'd grown apart. At one time, toward the end of what I'd call our most fruitful period, he moved to the country, and already that was a big change. I'm a New Yorker, and it doesn't mean anything to me to work at eight in the evening; that was not available to me with Lee. Our lives just pulled apart.

The remarkable team of Bock and Harnick broke up after *The Rothschilds* (1970). Here are Mr Harnick's comments on the divorce:

Unfortunately, *The Rothschilds* led to friction between Jerry Bock and me. It had to do with the original director for the show. Derek Goldby. He'd done only straight plays, and there's some mysterious, magical quality in a musical that a dramatic director just can't handle. He wasn't capable of handling a show of that size, I felt, but Jerry thought he was. Jerry felt that Derek had been given a raw deal. He was angry with the rest of us ... and when he was replaced by Michael Kidd, it caused friction. After that Jerry and I kind of drifted apart and never managed to drift back together, which is kind of awful.

The theatregoing public still deplores the dissolution of the Lloyd Webber-Rice team responsible for such gems as *Joseph, Jesus Christ Superstar* and *Evita*. Of course, Andrew Lloyd Webber has gone on to write some very successful shows like *Cats, Starlight Express, Song and Dance, The Phantom of the Opera* and *Aspects of Love* with an assortment of lyricists (Richard Stilgoe, Don Black, Trevor Nunn and Charles Hart among them). Critic Mark Steyn says of the dissolution of that remarkable collaboration: 'Tim Rice is a brilliant lyricist, but everyone knows that Andrew doesn't want to work with people, lyric writers who are his equal.'

FINDING A LIBRETTIST, COMPOSER, LYRICIST

Individuals opt to work with those who are both interested and technically equipped for their particular projects. But finding a partner or several partners for your particular project is not easy.

Mary Rodgers, who, with Martin Charnin wrote *Hot Spot* (1963) a musical about the Peace Corps, when interviewed, told how she met her lyricist-collaborator:

Marty was in the original company of *West Side Story* and he had written some stuff that Steve Sondheim had heard and liked. When I was looking for a collaborator, Steve suggested that Marty and I get together. We worked briefly on the Jackie Gleason show. We also did a show for U.S. Steel and Woody Allen, which was fabulous because U.S. Steel said to BBD&O [the advertising agency], 'We'll give you ten thousand dollars to give to some writers. Let them write an hour TV show, and if we like it, we'll put it on, and if we don't like it, they can keep the money.' So we wrote something insanely iconoclastic and offbeat, figuring we had nothing to lose. We put the songs on tape and performed for all those U.S Steel executives. At the end of our little audition, they said, 'Thank you very much,' and Marty and I collected our ten thousand dollars. The show never got on, but we had a very good time.

Ms Rodgers and Mr Charnin have continued to collaborate on other projects.

Listed below are some other ways of finding partners besides being given the name of a possible collaborator by a friend in the theatrical profession.

1 Contact schools of playwriting and drama in your area. For musical affiliation, contact conservatories such as the Guildhall School of Music and Drama, the Royal Academy, the Trinity School of Music, all in London; the Juilliard School, the Manhattan School of Music and the Mannes School all in New York. There are counterparts of these institutions in most major cities of the world. I know one librettist-lyricist in London who had completed a play with lyrics and, lacking a composer sought and found one studying at the Guildhall School in London. When the music was added to the play, the work went on to win the coveted Vivian Ellis Prize awarded annually for the best new musical.

   Universities' liberal arts departments can be wonderful spawning grounds. Tom Jones and Harvey Schmidt who wrote the book, lyrics and music for *The Fantasticks* began writing together in college. There are theatre groups in every university in Britain and the United States.

2 Contact the British Academy of Songwriters, Composers and Authors (BASCA) at 34 Hanway Street, London W1P 9DE (071 436 2261). Or the American Society of Composers, Authors and Publishers, (ASCAP) at 1

Lincoln Center, New York, NY 10023, or Broadcast Music Incorporated. (B.M.I.) at 40 West 57th Street, New York, NY 10019. They all sponsor songwriting workshops. They can put you in contact with amateurs and professionals in each of their fields.

3 Contact the Association of Professional Composers (071 436 0919) or the Composers' Guild of Great Britain (071 436 0007) both situated at 34 Hanway Street, London W1P 9DE for professional musicians.

4 Contact your local music store. Placing a notice on a bulletin board there might put you in touch with a collaborator. Be specific about what kind of songs you are capable of writing and what kinds of musicals interest you. Include a rundown of how much training you have had and what you expect of your collaborator.

5 Telephone local music teachers and music schools to see if some of the teachers know of a possible collaborator.

6 Advertise in your local paper, especially if there is an alternative paper. In New York, *The Village Voice* lists librettists, lyricists and composers who seek collaborators. *Backstage*, and *Showbusiness*, all have ad columns.

7 Contact performing musicians in your area. They are listed in the Yellow Pages of your telephone directory.

8 Advertise in magazines that are concerned with music. In Britain: *No. 1, One Two Testing, Rolling Stone, Time Out*. In the United States: *Billboard, Keyboard, Musical America, Theatre Arts*.

AGREEMENTS, CONTRACTS, PERCENTAGES, POINTS

As mentioned before, a collaboration must maintain close harmony of ideas and be on the same wavelength in order to be successful. It must also be fair, and above all, discussions among all parties have to be open and honest enough to harbour no resentments. According to a Dramatists' Guild contract the basic distribution of royalties is six per cent. Ideally each of the three major collaborators – librettist, composer and lyricist – receives the same percentage, two per cent, of the gross receipts. But where is it written that life is ideal?* A composer might decide to give up a part of his royalty to win over a particularly suitable orchestrator, or two lyricists might collaborate and split the lyricist's royalty. Then again, sometimes, in order to obtain an especially successful director or star, the collaborators will be asked by the producer to give up a portion of their percentages to 'sweeten the pot' for those glamorous people, who, it is believed, can turn the show into a hit. And frequently, when a show is running at substantially less than capacity, *everyone* will be asked to reduce their royalties so that the production will not be forced to close.

Once the show is more or less completed, and a producer has been obtained, a standard contract in Britain and a Dramatists' Guild contract in the United States will be signed. Before that happens, most collaborators create a simple contract between them. This should be *in writing*, and handled by their theatrical agent, and it is something that professionals rarely neglect. They know that too many handshake agreements turn into bitter brawls when the show is completed, and a black and white contract is the best insurance a creative team can have against the buffets of the star, producer, director and the scores of people who will eventually put the show together and who will all be waiting to demand a piece of the pie they have created.

If there is a percentage of the royalties (called points) to be given away in all of these cases, I believe it always makes for a smoother relationship if all the members of the triumvirate take equal cuts, but that too is generally left to the agent who is certainly better equipped than the artist to argue for his clients.

---

* David LeVine adds, 'the distribution can be 2,2,2 or 1, 2, 3, or 1/2, 1/2, and 5. 2, 2, 2, is used when everybody is of equal prominence or *un*prominence. In the case of *West Side Story*, Stephen Sondheim was just coming into prominence while Arthur Laurents and Leonard Bernstein had a reputation that exceeded his.' Sondheim's contract gave him only one per cent while his collaborators took the lion's share.

BILLING

A musical will become a hit or flop depending on the quality of the book, but what will make it endure beyond a short run is the quality of the music and lyrics. The general public knows nothing of this and will remember only what they read in the advertisements. Thus they read, CAROL CHANNING in *Hello, Dolly*. Few of the audience know or are concerned that the music and lyrics are by Jerry Herman; even fewer are aware or care that the brilliant libretto is the work of Michael Stewart.*

There is a hierarchy, a pecking order, in a programme which is standard form, listing three principals (unless they are well known or have stated otherwise in their contracts).

1 Music and lyrics are listed.
2 Book writer is listed.
3 If the work is based on a previous work, the creator of that work is listed and the work it is derived from is listed.

Most creative artists, especially those who have never seen their work on stage are so delighted and 'honoured' to have a production of their musical that they are not concerned with the immediate monetary return their work will bring them. After all, nobody in the last several decades can have gone into the theatre with a view to making money. The financial rewards in the entertainment business are much more attainable in television, radio, films and records. For composers, lyricists and librettists, the production is generally enough. But fortunately there are clever agents out there to protect their clients (and the more money they make for their artists the more they

---

*The producer, David Merrick, not being specifically contracted to mention Herman's or Stewart's names, usually omitted them. Rodgers and Hammerstein were, on the other hand, superstars, and always put their names above the title. Today, Andrew Lloyd Webber's name alone is similarly almost enough to sell tickets on its own. Critic Mark Steyn deplores the fact that the theatre no longer gives its creators recognition. 'You put in years and years of work and have nothing to show for it. The investment of time compared to, say, writing album tracks for a big pop performer, or the comfortable life of writing in the classical field – you get the worst of both fields in the theatre now ... It always astonishes me when I see reviews of *Les Miz* or *Miss Saigon* that don't mention the lyricist's name ... but it's been the same way since Rodgers and Hart. I guess the public saw little Larry Hart and wondered who he was and why he was clogging up the theatre.'

make for themselves*). Organisations like the Authors' Guild and the Dramatists' Guild will protect these neophytes from themselves and the many unscrupulous producers who may try to take advantage of beginners as well as established professionals.

---

* Agents in the United States generally take anything from ten to fifteen per cent, but the high-powered ones have been known to skim off twenty or twenty-five per cent for their services.

5 SETTING TO WORK

Establishing the Schedule. Establishing the Tone and Period of the Work. Establishing the Cast Size and Cost of the Work.

ESTABLISHING THE SCHEDULE

In the musical theatre, the many artist-contributors often lead such hectic professional lives that establishing a work schedule may be impossible.* The best that can be hoped for is a commitment that the agreed upon property will be the next to be worked on. An approximate target date is usually set and each collaborator appreciates the other's input and works to keep the obligation.

Non-professionals also should fix a target date, for obviously amateurs who need to eat like the rest of us, will have to continue working at a job before they launch their first musical. If a musical is to be written at all, it is necessary that it be *timely*.† Dawdling can be crucial, so approximate dates of

---

On The Town, a landmark hit in 1944, was the first collaboration of Leonard Bernstein, composer, Comden and Green, lyricists with choreographer Jerome Robbins. It was written very quickly because as Robbins recalls 'George Abbott', the director who had been the ideal choice of all the above creators, 'said he would do the show *if* it could be done within a certain time. He had two weeks free – yes, literally – that we could play out of town ... We were all naïve ... We just did it. We didn't worry about it. Lenny and I were out on the coast with *Fancy Free*, [the ballet that was the inspiration for the musical] and so Betty and Adolph came along and we went right ahead developing it out there.'

† *Shenandoah*, whose plot concerned a family's decision to keep itself aloof in the War-Between-the-States, was first presented on Broadway in 1975 and had a long and successful

completion need to be set. Establishing and respecting a projected target date (which, of course, is not written in stone) is the best way to avoid dilettantism. Some collaborators prefer to work together daily, others meet less frequently. Most collaborators meet at least twice a week at the absolute minimum. More is better, for the push, the bouncing off of ideas from one creative person to another is invaluable.*

Tom Shepard working with Sheldon Harnick on *Molette* recalls how it was: 'It was interesting working with Sheldon to see how very methodical and imaginative he is. How after reading the story that we're going to base something on he rereads it and then ruminates on it. Then he draws up a scenario and then he polishes the scenario. Then we talk about it, and then he starts getting more specific within each scene. Only then does he start writing – lines, lyrics, whatever.

'He doesn't simply put a page in his typewriter and write a libretto. He carefully considers the entire piece and where he's going and what he's got to get across. Here was a short story, a mere ten pages. It's interesting how he expanded it and in certain cases contracted it.'

ESTABLISHING THE TONE AND PERIOD OF THE WORK

Tone and period, much misunderstood terms in the theatre, are best illustrated together. For example, the tone of *Gypsy* is backstage sleaze; its period is mostly in the Twenties. *The Boy Friend* is also set in the Twenties but its tone is pastiche and stylisation. *Coco* and *Roberta* also use the same decade as their time-frame and would be considered to belong to the same period as well, but their tone is one of elegant fashion and its world.

The old cliché about consistency being the hobgoblin of

---

run. When revived in mid-1989, most critics felt the era had changed. The critic for *The New York Times* wrote: 'When *Shenandoah* opened on Broadway 14 years ago, it had a historical resonance. America's divided emotions over the Vietnam War were still fresh and its wounds were just beginning to mend. In the new production that resonance is lost.' The revival folded after a few weeks.

*Concerning *On The Town*, Jerome Robbins recalls: 'To start with Betty [Comden] and Adolph [Green] did a very rough outline of the show, and then we collaborated. We spent a lot of time together.' Betty Comden adds, 'Adolph and I meet every day and keep on working. We stare at each other across the room ... We don't quite remember at the end of the day who wrote what. We're just glad there's something there.'

little minds does not apply to a musical. The fragile illusion which is theatre can instantly evaporate when any of the collaborators destroys the consistency, or what is known as 'tone'. The comic strip fantasy world of *Annie*; the exotic world of *The King and I*; the heroic patriotism of *Les Misérables* or the romantic spookiness of *The Phantom of the Opera* must be rigorously maintained throughout the work. In each of these works *all* collaborators (librettist, composer, lyricist, choreographer, costume designer, set designer, orchestrator and director) must be like-minded and view the property with the aim of creating the same tone. No one can slip for even a moment otherwise it will be necessary to rebuild again the fragile 'stage magic'.

It would seem then that a musical set, for example, in a period like the nineteenth century would require a score sounding like Schumann or Mendelssohn, but nothing could be farther from the truth. When Jerome Kern and Oscar Hammerstein II collaborated on *Sweet Adeline* whose period was the 'gay Nineties' they mistakenly decided to use a medley of songs from the 1890s instead of an overture, and audiences chatted all through the overture thinking it was merely 'mood music'. Unable to get the ever important foothold at its opening, the show met with little success.

Today's songwriters are aware that the *tone*, not the period must be recalled. In *Sweeney Todd* it was the malevolence, the screaming of an awakening industrial age, not the 1860s that the music and lyrics elicited; in Sandy Wilson's *The Boy Friend* it was mindless flapperdom; in *Gypsy* it was shabby but ambitious, second-rate show business that Rose personified that was recalled and, to his eternal credit, John Kander's score for *Cabaret*, although it creates a sound more appropriate to the Germany of the late Twenties than the late Thirties (which is the time of the play) acts as a harbinger of the horrors to come better than the 'reedy' music of 1937 ever could. Its tone is sheer terror.

ESTABLISHING THE CAST SIZE AND COST OF THE WORK

It has often been said that Broadway and the West End are going broke, and that they have very little money for the production of new, lavish extravaganzas. But every season we learn that millions are being invested and often lost, with audiences complaining of ill-spent money, mediocre evenings and critics trotting out their most acerbic adjectives to describe these megabuck and megaquid shows.

But clever showmen always seem to find foundations that can be persuaded to invest in what might be considered an arty spectacular; there is always a millionaire lurking in the wings (often with a pretty ingenue who needs backing) willing to get his feet wet in show business, or a seasoned producer with a list of wealthy investors who appreciate the rubbed-off glamour of taking part in a theatrical venture. The wealthy can always use a 'tax loss', and prefer to give it to the cause of 'art' rather than Uncle Sam or the Inland Revenue. Record companies too are willing to invest and underwrite shows by the experienced or ones that feature superstars. Andrew Lloyd Webber's much plugged 'Love Changes Everything', from *Aspects of Love* with a stronger rock beat, added electronic drum machines and heavily miked made it to Number 2 on the British charts.

At the time of this writing, the costumes and scenery for *Ziegfeld* with its outlay of some five million pounds, are lying in limbo in a London warehouse. Earlier fiascos in recent seasons were *Chaplin* (erasing four million and closing in Philadelphia), *Sousa, Roosevelt*. One wonders why producers are willing to risk so much capital when the chance of turning a profit seems to be so small. But, of course, glancing at the sunny side we know that a hit can go on and on for decades. It can become big business and an annuity which spawns its logo on everything from coffee mugs to T-shirts, record albums to music boxes. Then there are the spin-offs: the movie versions, and tapes and residuals to be considered and later on, small theatre productions and revivals.

Nor does the money trickle in. Today's producers do not wait until a show has exhausted its audiences or its publicity in London or New York before taking it on tour. They will open many companies simultaneously. News travels fast and the public is always eager to see a fresh company in the latest rage. Memories are short these days, and the public quickly forgets a show that may have received 'raves' several years ago and is by now old hat. *Nunsense*, a small musical, opened four years ago and now has forty companies performing nightly in cities all round the world. *Cats* and *Les Misérables*, both large and expensive musicals, have almost as many.

But since costs have risen so startlingly, producers of those tremendous musicals are rare and most of them will only take chances on teams whose names are household words. Newcomers to the musical are aware that unless the work is startlingly original, they must keep the cast size to a minimum. That does not mean that the musical need appear skimpy, for if they are able to create an exciting situation with a few singer-actors it is better than a cluttered stage with most of the bodies merely acting as filler. *Baby*, a concept musical (book by Sybelle Pearson, music by David Shire and lyrics by Richard Maltby, Jr) employed the relatively small cast of fifteen. When it is performed in revival or stock, as it frequently is now, it gets by with ten or eleven. *Romance, Romance* is the rock bottom smallest musical, employing a cast of only four. (Actually the orchestra is twice the size of the principals.)

6 WRITING THE LIBRETTO

The Opening. Introducing the Principals. Subplot. The 'Hanging Clue'. The First Act Curtain. The Second Act. Second Act Opening. The 'Eleven O'clock Number'. Production Numbers. Finale. Rewriting – The Second Draft. Humour. Reprise. Length. Balance. Consistency. Particularisation. Timeliness. Emotion. Clean Copy.

The libretto of a musical is rarely written from beginning to end. It is generally created in sections which build one on top of the other, the playwright keeping one eye aware of production numbers, brevity of dialogue, solos, duets, dancing, counterpoint and all the many things that separate a musical from a legitimate play. But even more importantly the librettist-playwright must be aware of and work towards the 'pressure points' of (1) the first act curtain, (2) the opening of the second act, (3) the climax and (4) the finale.

Above all in importance is the opening. Luther Henderson told me, 'if you have an opening – not especially an opening number but an opening sequence that knocks them out of their seats, you can coast for the next twenty minutes. First of all it takes fully ten minutes to get the audience's attention. You have to sledgehammer the whole way. They must be *required* to pay attention and you have to *insist* that they do so! Ask my friend Jule Styne – the overtures he writes are attention-getters. I saw one play [*The Tap Dance Kid*] that started with a domestic scene. The kid was talking, the family was having breakfast, pouring milk on corn flakes and domestic things like that and the audience got bored. It was a preview and I knew the scene was going to be taken out by the end of the week. And it was!'

Revues and extravaganzas all begin with musical numbers, yet contrary to what one might expect, most musical comedies and musical plays – even operettas – start with dialogue and then go into song. Perhaps this is because we have just come from a musical number, the overture, and now it is time to introduce the characters, thereby moving us into the play.

THE OPENING

What should the opening of a musical accomplish? Several things. Period, tone,* character, venue, plot, all must be introduced simultaneously and none of them must be obvious to the audience. The opening of Arthur Laurents's *Gypsy* gives us much more than the harmless children's song 'May We Entertain You?' (which will be brilliantly transformed into Gypsy's strip number at the show's climax and now assertively retitled 'Let Me Entertain You'). Set on stage at a kiddie show in Seattle, the costumes announce the time-frame, the early twenties, and that the venue is a tacky vaudeville theatre. Before any music is played we are introduced to Uncle Jocko, a sleazy monster who runs the show and we hear him insisting that all mothers be shooed out of the theatre. We know from his early lines that he has targeted the kid sister of a buxom vaudevillian he is pursuing to win his talent show.

When Baby June, the star of the act, and Louise, who will later become Gypsy, begin to perform, Rose, the stage mother to end them all, walks down the aisle brassily coaching her daughters. Rose's aisle entrance is a stroke of genius. It not only tells us that Rose is used to breaking rules, but puts us there in Seattle in 1920 with her, for isn't she on the other side of the footlights with us? The curtain has been up barely two minutes, but her lines are written not only to infuriate Jocko,

---

* In discussing the opening of *A Funny Thing Happened on the Way to the Forum*, Stephen Sondheim recalls how he came to write 'Comedy Tonight'. 'It was a late substitute for another number, "Love Is in the Air", which was very charming, but left the audience with the wrong idea of what kind of show it was going to be. When Jerome Robbins came down to Washington to help out he said the opening number ought to catalogue exactly what was going to take place so that the audience really would be oriented. So I wrote a list song, "Comedy Tonight", saying "this is what you're going to see." '

but *to make us sense* she favours June and criticises Louise. Through her audacious questions to Jocko, she soon discovers the kiddie show is fixed. Then, subtly threatening to expose the hoax, she has Jocko's favourite disqualified, thus placing her own daughters in the limelight. It's monster against monster, and of course Rose wins. During this brief scene, she also bosses the conductor, drummer, spotlight operator and stage manager, so we see what a steamroller Rose is. Through it all, Arthur Laurents is a clever enough librettist to maintain our sympathy for Rose while we marvel that she gets away with such brashness. (And he sustains that – no easy feat – throughout the play.) With the music going under, interspersed with dialogue, this kind of scene could only happen in a musical, and as such it fulfils all the needs of a musical opening.

The Phantom of the Opera opens with the provocative sound of a gavel striking an auctioneer's block while the musty curtains and turn-of-the-century costumes establish place and time. 'Sold', the auctioneer shouts, 'a papier-mâché musical box in the shape of a barrel organ. Attached, the figure of a monkey in Persian robes playing the cymbals.' This first sentence as well as the item on the auction block have an exotic sound.* And when the monkey is purchased by the now aged Vicomte de Chagny, whom we will meet shortly as the young hero, he sings sotto voce and philosophically, wondering if the music box will play on after we are dead. The mystery and foreignness are at once apparent. Who is this man, we ask? Why are they all here? Then the auctioneer opens the bidding on the Opera's famous chandelier, saying that it figured in the famous disaster. He explains that it has been restored and 'fitted with the new† electric light so that we may get a hint of what it may look like when reassembled.' Then, as the chandelier slowly rises to the very top of the auditorium and he mentions frightening away the ghosts of so many years ago, the organ and orchestra launch fortissimo into the overture. By that time the audience have already met one of the leading characters, gathered that there will be disaster, are wondering what ghosts will be frightened and feel the threat of that massive antique chandelier suspended above, which indeed

---

* 'papier mâché'; 'musical box' rather than music box; 'Persian robes'; 'barrel organ,' all bespeak an earlier era. The language is not chosen lightly.

† A simple word like 'new' here sets the time of the action as the turn of the century when electric light first came into use. This is typical of a good librettist's economy.

seems to move them back into the nineteenth century and change the theatre into the Paris Opéra.

I don't mean to imply that every musical play must begin with dialogue or even use it to set the scene, merely to assure you that tone, time and place must be obvious from the outset. *Wonderful Town* with libretto by Comden and Green, begins with a long production number introducing the two unsuspecting sisters from Ohio to Greenwich Village. The song is called 'Christopher Street',* and it is frequently interrupted by dialogue. By the time it is ended we have a good idea of the lifestyle of Ruth, Eileen, Wreck, Helen, Appopolus and all the denizens of Manhattan's bohemian quarter who will be important in the play.

Joseph Stein's libretto for *Fiddler on the Roof* does a similar thing, this time introducing us to Anatevka, the Russian-Jewish village locale, its characters, its rabbi and Tevye, our long-suffering hero, his wife and his five daughters. At the same time it introduces the concept of the play. Tradition. Whenever possible, it is extremely desirable to lay out the concept of the musical at the start.

Company, with libretto by George Firth, succeeds in doing just that. Setting the scene at the apartment of the cast's only bachelor, Bobby, the show's quasi-hero, we discover the guests assembled, all couples, waiting for his entrance, preparing to surprise him on his arrival. In these few musical minutes we learn much about them and a great deal about Bobby through their particular views of him.

INTRODUCING THE PRINCIPALS

Our former great ladies of the theatre like Katherine Cornell, Wendy Hiller, Helen Hayes and especially Tallulah Bankhead always objected to plays in which they were given the opening lines. They much preferred to have their audiences 'warmed up' before they were greeted with an ovation when they came on stage. This kind of vanity does not apply to musicals. The

---

* Of the writing of that splendid number, Betty Comden recalls: 'I think openings always give trouble – many shows have more than one opening number before the right one is arrived at ... we first had a number about 3.2 beer which came in that year, then one about self-expression because our show took place in Greenwich Village ... before we came to the final one.'

audiences are usually warmed up by the overture after which there is inevitably a pause to seat latecomers.

Musicals don't have room in their books to allow chit-chat, nor is there room for vanity by allowing the leading lady to make a grand entrance. Whether or not the principals are introduced at once, the mood of the play must be apparent. 'Summertime' sets the mood for *Porgy and Bess*; 'Fugue For Tinhorns', although sung by minor race-track touts, introduces us to the flamboyant world of *Guys and Dolls*. Those librettos that begin with the introduction of principals must do so without dawdling. At curtain rise Curley, the hero of *Oklahoma!*, comes on stage singing 'Oh, What a Beautiful Morning'; Cliff, the main love interest in *Cabaret* is discovered en route to Berlin at the very opening; Dolly in *Hello, Dolly*, sings about her philosophy at the very outset; in *Fiddler On the Roof*, Tevye and family sing about 'Tradition' as soon as the curtain is up, giving the total concept of the musical in the first five minutes; Albin, who dominates *La Cage Aux Folles*, changes to Zaza before our eyes as he sings 'I Put a Little More Mascara On' which, as in most musicals, must accomplish several things at once. In this case it introduces the leading character as well as telling us we are going to be for the next two hours in the world of the female impersonator. This provides a splendid opening at the same time as leading the audience quickly into the play.

But not every opening needs to be flamboyant. Mark Steyn believes 'a musical can open low-key'. He continues: '*My Fair Lady* opens with lots of dialogue but then that opening number, "Why Can't the English Teach Their Children How to Speak?" I mean, what else is the show about? It's a perfect opener.' Then he goes on to criticise the opening of *Aspects of Love*. 'You have "Love Changes Everything". Well, maybe. But after you've spent a couple of hours in the company of these people, you realise – love changes nothing! I think that's a failure of playwriting, they don't seem to know what they're supposed to be setting up . . . they don't know what their show's about.'

As for the attendant introduction of leading characters, Mr Steyn feels what is most important is that the librettist does not confuse or mislead the audience.

The best possible example I can give you is from *High Society* where Richard Eyre, an artistic director of the National Theatre, was given carte blanche to scour the Cole Porter catalogue for whatever he needed. Now he decided, looking at [the play from which he adapted his libretto], *The Philadelphia Story*, that he was going to be looking for a song that was vaguely connected with journalism and came up with a number called 'How Do You Spell Ambassador?' which is basically saying that hack journalists are so stupid they can't spell, and know nothing of what they are writing about. Now, apart from the fact that it's not a very good song, it's misleading . . . because the two people we identify with are the photographer and the journalist. They are where our sympathy lies, so Richard Eyre's choice of opening number was . . . worse than useless in that it misled us. It made us think we were in for a musical of, let's say, *The Front Page*, which is about how rotten journalists are. The show limped along for about 40 minutes until it hit a song called 'Who Wants to be a Millionaire', which defines the philosophy of the leading character.

In a concept musical such as *A Chorus Line, Baby, Company* or *The Rink*, a group number will best serve to introduce the characters and each of these gives a necessary glimpse into the several personalities who will make up the play.*

SUBPLOT

Secondary characters have been a part of musical theatre since the days of opera and operetta. When we think of subplots in the old-fashioned sense, we think of contrast, usually laughable; the comics who gave release to the main action; the timid parent who becomes aggressive just before the final curtain; the kid sister who comes on with her football hero for a last bow. These all serve to release the tension the author purposely builds into his plot while manipulating the hero and heroine.

Although it is an axiomatic technique of 'serious' drama, subplot lends itself even more gloriously to the musical theatre, for here the byword is entertainment. Musicals can stop now and then for a song or dance as long as the diversion is in keeping with the general outline of the play. Formerly this was done in front of the 'traveller', a curtain that moved sideways

---

* This is one area where the musical form is superior to straight drama, for the playwright must go through a long exposition to let us see the persona of each of his creations while we can view them all almost simultaneously in song.

across the stage behind which the set could be changed for a production number while chorus and principals were slipping into new costumes. And although it sounds like an expedient device it is much more than that, for by laying aside the main business of the evening, subplot creates suspense.

Even while the audience are diverted with a musical number there is still that nagging question: what are the hero and heroine up to now?

Subplots are easy to create; what is difficult is to manipulate their characters to fit neatly into the action and jibe with the main story.

Multiple Subplots

Show Boat an early Kern-Hammerstein classic is an example of many story threads or subplots unfolding simultaneously. Adapting Edna Ferber's sprawling novel of life on the Mississippi, Hammerstein chose to centre the action on the love story of a riverboat owner's daughter, Magnolia, and the gambler, Gaylord Ravenal, with whom she falls in love. Since this is a generational story, we are in on their courtship, marriage, parenthood, separation and final reconciliation. But we are constantly being diverted by the squabbles of Capt'n Andy and his shrewish wife, Julie, the show boat's leading actress (a mulatto who is passing for white and is married to a white man) and her threatened exposure; the travels of dance team Frank and Ellie, and the domestic problems of Queenie and her stereotypic indolent husband, Joe. Without these rich diversions and their attendant songs, the romance of Magnolia and Ravenal melts into saccharine operetta. With them moving in and out of the love story, Hammerstein achieves a multifaceted libretto, incorporating a panoply from all walks of Mississippi riverboat life that makes this work, even now, some sixty years after its creation a vital, viable and much performed musical.

Hello, Dolly, Michael Stewart's libretto that critic Martin Gottfried calls 'one of the best our musical theater has ever produced' is another example of multiple plots.* Here there

* Not only has American critic Martin Gottfried championed *Hello, Dolly*'s libretto, British critic Mark Steyn too is lavish with his praise for Michael Stewart's book: 'If they ever did a university course on the great musical, they should start with this one. It's so good it's

are two couples, a situation which affords so many possibilities for ensemble numbers. We are introduced, almost at the outset to Dolly Levi, the widowed matchmaker and Horace Vandergelder, Yonkers' self-styled 'half a millionaire'. Shortly afterwards we meet Horace's two clerks, Cornelius and Barnaby and we learn of their plan to take the day off to go to New York, and then we immediately meet the female part of the subplot quartet, Irene Molloy, a modiste and her assistant Molly. We know, almost straightaway, that at the final curtain Cornelius will end up with Irene, and Barnaby will be paired off with Molly, but we are constantly being shifted back to the main plot, and we never lose sight of it: Dolly's manipulation of Horace and her plans to get him to the altar. The two couples of the subplot are responsible for most of the farce and animation that keep the plot entertaining.

Singular Subplots

A good musical can have many interesting characters that surround the main protagonists, but more often one couple will stand out. They will be known as the 'Second leads', meaning they are the subplot.*

In *Oklahoma!* the subplot concerns the not-too-bright, easily bedded Ado Annie and the rug seller, as well as the semi-sophisticated farmhand, who are both wooing her. This is in tremendous contrast to the virginal Laurey and the presumably clean minded Curley. I personally feel, however, that the secondary relationship has little bearing on the story and this has always prevented me from enjoying this musical. It seems to me that any sophisticated theatregoer can see through this creaking device. But there is a wonderful freshness about its score and one can only sit in the theatre amazed that Agnes de

---

unobtrusive. When you come away from a musical and you remember brilliant lines of dialogue, in a way that means there's something wrong, because the best books are unobtrusive.'

  * Although he understood the importance of the romantic subplot, Oscar Hammerstein was disinterested in this diversion from the main thrust of the story. William Hammerstein recalls: 'I was standing in the back of the Majestic theater with him one day, and the young couple come on [in *The King and I*] and sing 'We Kiss in a Shadow', and so he turned around and walked into the lobby, and I followed him. He smiled and said, "That's the Chesterfield Hour" [a schmaltzy radio programme of overly romantic songs] ... He didn't like to watch that part, although he wrote subplots probably better than anyone and he and Rodgers as well as Jerry Kern wrote wonderful songs for them ... they bored him.'

Mille was able to combine ballet and Broadway dancing in a never-seen-before way.

Hammerstein's subplot works better in *Carousel*. The clever librettist knew the value of contrast and was always struggling to portray the forces of good against evil or compliance against rebellion. Here Carrie and Mr Snow, although clearly subplot, come to represent respectability in contrast to Julie's and especially Billy Bigelow's nonconformism. This is wisely brought home as the story moves into the second act ballet.

The King and I finds Hammerstein in peak form. Early on, we see the leading lady Anna Leonowens, who is schoolteacher to the King of Siam's children, become an accomplice of Tup-Tim and her lover Lun Tha in their clandestine affair. This gives Mrs Anna the chance to sing the wistful 'Hello, Young Lovers' that merges the subplot with the main plot. Late in the second act, after Lun Tha has been executed at the king's command, this barbarous act causes a rift between Mrs Anna and the king. Tup-Tim's insubordination is even woven into the inventively exotic ballet – this time the work of Jerome Robbins.

Cabaret (which in its stage version differed greatly from its treatment in the cinema), had a traditional subplot involving the romance between a mature German landlady, Frau Schneider, and her elderly Jewish tenant, Herr Schultz. Although the score of the musical allowed these unlikely lovers some charming solos and duets, their romance was clearly a stage device. The subplot was shifted in the film which seems to have taken the stage play one giant step further towards realism. Now the romance is between a wealthy Jewess and a young Jewish fortune hunter who has woven a web of lies to hide his religion from the Nazis. They both come to the hero for English lessons which establishes a connection with the main plot.

This important change was not so much occasioned by the search for truth as by a determination in the cinema version to confine the musical numbers to what could be done on the stage of the cabaret.* The creators of the film believed that

* Ron Field, *Cabaret*'s choreographer, remembers the run-through before the company opened in Boston to which Hal Prince, the show's director, invited and sought out the opinion of his friend Jerome Robbins: 'I was nervous about him seeing my work. Naturally. Jerry thought the show was wonderful, but his strong suggestion was that any dancing that didn't take place as part of the performance at the Kit Kat Klub be cut from the show. In other words, his suggestion was that we cut the telephone number and cut the engagement party

landladies and fruiterers do not burst into song in their bed-
rooms and did not oblige the subplot characters to sing.
Realism, I believe, makes for successful musical movies. It is
not essential to the stage. *Cabaret* is perhaps the only musical
whose stage version *and* cinema versions differ substantially.
Yet they are equally successful and each is true to its medium.

Other shows with interesting subplots are *La Cage aux Folles*
(The son and Anne); *She Loves Me* (Kodaly and Ilona); *Kiss
Me Kate* (Bill and Lois) and *South Pacific* (Lieutenant Cable
and Liat).

I don't mean to imply by the foregoing, that every book
musical needs a subplot. The concept musical will work very
well without it. *The Fantasticks, Company, A Chorus Line,
Pacific Overtures, Sunday in the Park With George* have no
need of any intrusion to divert the audience from their stories.
And musicals based on a single protagonist generally have
enough characters acting as forces around them to make the
use of subplot unnecessary. Think of *Gypsy, Mame, Man of
La Mancha, Fiorello.*

Sometimes the subplot or its performers can be so interesting
that they steal the show away from the principals. Critics
believed the failure of *A Tree Grows in Brooklyn*, in which
Shirley Booth played the role of Aunt Cissy, made the main
love story seem like a wait between her appearances. In spite
of excellent score and book, it was obvious that Aunt Cissy had
the most interesting part, and audiences fidgeted whenever the
gravel-voiced Shirley was offstage. Lisa Kirk did the same in
Allegro.

THE 'HANGING CLUE'

The 'Hanging Clue' is my own term for a dramatic device long
known in the theatre. It is sometimes referred to as the 'plant'
and consists simply of a bit of seemingly harmless information
lightly dropped which will become crucial to the plot. The

---

dance that Lenya did with the sailors ... Hal just overruled it, a decision I will always be
grateful for.' [Author's Note: The realism attained in the movie version of *Cabaret* was
precisely due to a decision that all musical numbers be performed on the Kit Kat Klub's
stage, so one can say Jerome Robbins's uncanny visionary theatricalism was responsible for
making the film so splendid.]

'clue' cannot be innocuous or false as in so many second-rate detective stories, for in that case the audience will feel cheated and misled, but well handled, it should make everyone gasp, 'But of course! It was there all the time.'

Perhaps the simplest example of a hanging clue is found in the myriad melodramas of the past. Seeing a revolver placed in a drawer, or even a line of dialogue referring to the presence of one (this usually happens in the first act) would inform any seasoned theatregoer that the gun would be used some time before the final curtain. This creaky device occurs even in a masterpiece like *Hedda Gabler*. When we see Hedda clean her gun, we *know* it is not extraneous, it will be used for murder or, in this case, suicide.

Musicals often need the hanging clue as well, for the kind of suspense and gnawing malaise it affords is essential to ensure that audiences return for the second act. The best clues are those that fit smoothly into the story and because of their presence transform the plot. A few examples will illustrate how clever librettists manage to manipulate this.

Beginning with one of the most obvious examples of this genre, *Annie*, follow Thomas Meehan's libretto: Annie's main desire in the comic strip and in the stage musical is to be reunited with her parents. She wears half a locket, a memento she has had since her pre-orphanage days. When the comically mean Miss Hannegan who runs the orphanage discovers that Annie has been befriended by rich Daddy Warbucks, she comes forth with an accomplice and the other half of the locket. Producing the trinket, they swear they are the waif's mother and father. Of course the bogus parents are discredited by the end of the show, but what suspense there is in the plot has been enhanced by the missing half of the locket.

Using an object such as a locket, gun, handkerchief or the like is something of a cliché, but since the tone of *Annie* is derived from and tries to emulate a comic strip, it seems acceptable. Much more subtle and common is the use of crucial information that is dropped early in the show, and upon which the plot will hinge.

Sweeney Todd is almost totally the work of Stephen Sondheim, but its plot device and hanging clue are in the brilliant libretto. When, early in the first act, Sweeney is approached by a demented, sex-starved hag who asks, 'Hey, mister, don't I know you?' the audience becomes uneasy, not for the woman, but for Sweeney who we have already suspected of trying to hide his past. It is only at the very end of the musical, after the hag has got in his way and his fears of exposure lead him to slit her throat (as he has done to so many others before) that we learn she is his beloved wife, Lucy, now driven to whoredom and finally to madness by the corrupt, villainous judge on whom anti-hero Sweeney has wreaked his revenge. Now the echo of the hanging clue, 'don't I know you?' takes on a pathetic an unforgettable irony, for we realise the crazed Lucy has uttered it not as a threat but with an honest hope for recognition from a loved one.

A hanging clue may be benevolent as the villainous Bill Sykes's dog in *Oliver* that eventually leads the police to his master, or it may be as abstract as the preoccupation with the sea that propels Marius in the musical *Fanny* to leave his adored. We learn early of his fixation with the ocean and sailing, and when Marius finally bids Fanny goodbye, as set in Harold Rome's exquisite title song with the moving lines 'Here's a boy with no heart to give, it was given to the sea long ago', few of the audience can remain unmoved.

The King and I also uses song to expose the suspenseful clue. When Tup-Tim who has been sent as a 'gift' to the king drops a hint in her first song: 'He'll never know I love another man', we can be sure there is trouble ahead, and in this somewhat threatening atmosphere we sense the danger. Late in the second act, with the death of Tup-Tim's love, Lun Tha, we are given a reflection of the whole play's concept: an emerging nation and its monarch's move from barbarianism (as represented by the king) to polite 'civilisation' (as represented by the 'and I'.) Thus, the hanging clue is more than that, it encompasses the play's total message.

A similar situation pertains in *Song of Norway* when we are shown Edvard Grieg's love of the fjords and the music of his country. Here, in a much less subtle fashion than in *Fanny* or *The King and I*, we know that by the final curtain he will put aside love affairs and sunny Italy and hurry home to write Norway's immortal music.

Although the libretto of *Show Boat* is half a century old, its hanging clues do not seem dated. There are two of them, and we learn of them early on. The first, that Gaylord Ravenal is a riverboat gambler, will not affect the plot until the second act. The other one, that Julie has a secret, (that she is mulatto) will be exposed and act as the climax to Act I.

Other musicals that feature this device are *Cabaret*, (Ernst returns from Paris and at the border substitutes his satchel for Cliff's. We know he will turn into the heavy in Act II); *Kiss Me Kate*, (the IOU signed so lightly by the dancer, Bill, with hero Fred Graham's name, turns out to be the thing that holds the plot – and the company-together.)

In *My Fair Lady* it is the bet that Higgins can transform Eliza into a 'lady' and in *Funny Girl*, Fanny Brice's love of clowning and her decision *not* to try to be beautiful (which is dropped in early in the first act) pays off when she enters dressed as the pregnant bride to become the hit of the Ziegfeld Follies.

It should be clear from these instances that this device is only effective when used carefully and subtly. It seems to me that the pattern used in *Show Boat* where a pair of clues are solved, one at the end of Act I and the other at the end of Act II works wonderfully. Not every musical needs the hanging clue, but wherever it is used, and made to seem incidental, it adds interest to a libretto.

THE FIRST ACT CURTAIN

Every professional in the theatre is aware of the main 'pressure points' peculiar to musicals that do not necessarily exist in non-musical theatre. Some librettists have even gone so far as to say that if these are taken care of, it doesn't matter about the rest of the evening. Of course that is stretching it too far, but these spots must be interesting, involving, clear and 'inspired'. They are:

THE OPENING
THE FIRST ACT CURTAIN
THE OPENING OF THE SECOND ACT
THE ELEVEN O'CLOCK NUMBER
THE FINALE

The opening of a straight play, as we have seen, can be murky, talky and atmospheric. Audiences have come to expect that it will 'take them a while to get into the swing' of it. But that must not happen in a musical. Beginning often with a bit of dialogue, the audience are then plunged headlong into a musical number. Almost as important is the first act curtain, for here some of the plot must be resolved while leaving hanging threads that will be tied up at the finale. This is especially important in the musical as we know it today, with its lengthy first act and somewhat foreshortened second.

The bio-musical often cannot be plotted to lend itself to a strong closing first act because one can't arbitrarily set up a mid-life crisis for the protagonist.*

In addition to the uncompleted plot there is another important aesthetic that must be attained when the curtain falls on Act I. It's what I call 'the need for air'. Tom Shepard who produced and recorded the legendary Lincoln Center gala benefit of *Follies* recalls:

> When we did the concert version, Steve really wanted to play it without an intermission, and I pleaded for an intermission for some very practical reasons. I said, 'I have no other way to check what I've recorded on the tape, I really need a chance to see what I've got.' I really wanted an intermission. I wanted the audience to be able to talk and buzz. It wasn't that it was so long, in truth, the whole show fit on two LP's – but it was so rich. It was a very high calorie meal. I used the excuse of checking the equipment, which was true and necessary. But Sondheim's point was well taken, he felt from the plot point there was no place to break. Yet the emotional intensity of the audience was such and the songs and performances were so intense, you needed to get out of your seat for a while.

If it is a dramatic musical, the audience should feel they have been put through a wringer, and need to go out and have a drink or a smoke. This means the moment of greatest intensity must come at this point. If this point can be put over to the audience through dance, or better yet, song, then there is an even stronger emotion; as Al Capp said, 'a double-whammie'.

One of the great first act finales is to be found in *Dreamgirls*, the Krieger and Eyen score which was shepherded into a Broadway smash by Michael Bennett. The manager of the Dreams, a Supremes-type group, informs Effie, the overweight gospel-voiced leader of the group that she is being replaced,

---

* This was an inherent problem in the musicalisation of the life of *Ziegfeld* in London (1988). Someone must have said 'Well, the first act should be an hour and twenty minutes, so we'll chop it there.' And the curtain comes down from nowhere.

on the stage and in his bed, by a more glamorous substitute. This provokes the heart-rending song that closes the act, 'And I'm Telling You I'm Not Going'. The mere title explains its concept. The song and its placement were a triumph for the show and made a star of newcomer Jennifer Holliday. Audiences gave her a standing ovation nightly. And the situation did everything a first act finale should: left the audience in doubt, prepared them for the second act (the fall and eventual comeback of this star,) and made them so emotional – since they were already standing and applauding – that they had to make their way to the theatre bar for a drink.

These hanging threads and utter tension before an audience goes out for a breather are important in all musicals, and although one would not think so, essential and achievable even in the concept musical.

Look at *Company* whose first act ends with a scene on Amy's wedding day. Although she and Paul, the bridegroom, have been living together for several years, she is terrified of the rite of marriage because she has seen all the official marriages of her friends turn bitter. Paul, who has assured her his love will see them through, and Bobby, the play's leading character and best man, are having breakfast with Amy before they all go to the ceremony. The newspaper has predicted rain and Amy has decided she's just not ready to get married. Paul refuses to accept her decision until finally she tells him she doesn't love him. Wounded, he exits, at which point Bobby offers to marry her.

Then we get the concept of the play in a nutshell from Amy.

AMY: Isn't this some world? I'm afraid to get married, and you're afraid *not* to. Thank you, Robert, I'm really . . . It's just that you have to want to marry *some*body, not just some*body*. (SHE *hugs him*)

(THUNDER *outside, it begins to rain*)

Oh, would you look at that . . . he went off without an umbrella or anything.

(SHE *puts on a raincoat and grabs another coat and umbrella for Paul*)

He'll get pneumonia. I've got to catch him. Oh . . .and he's so good. Isn't he? So good!

(SHE *exits as* BOBBY *tosses her the wedding bouquet*)

I'm the next bride.

(*The lights come up on* ROBERT'S *apartment. All the birthday guests are looking at him as in* ACT I, SCENE I. ROBERT *stares at* AMY *as* SHE *enters with the cake and the music builds*.)

CURTAIN

One has only to listen to Amy's rapid-fire song 'Getting Married Today', one of Stephen Sondheim's most intense, and read George Furth's magnificent dialogue which leads to the ending printed above, to feel like a squeezed-out sponge. Additionally there is the suspense; for we don't know if Amy and Paul *did* marry, or even if they are still together. And will Bobby accept some 'healthy' ideas about marriage, or will he grope blindly for that some*body* in the second act. The suspense is not unlike the awful suspense we feel in *A Chorus Line* which has no intermission, but while we sit in our seats we wonder all through the second half of the show which of these likeable kids will be chosen.

Many audiences were critical of the first act ending of the Sondheim-Lapine *Sunday in the Park With George*. The concept is the artist's creation and the opinion that a visionary rearranges reality. Just before the intermission, Georges Seurat has gloriously completed his canvas, and the audience feels no urge, except for the considerable beauty of the score, to go back into the theatre for Act II. The theme – how an artist rearranges life or even creates life – has been satisfied. The librettist had to work very hard, and unfortunately he did not succeed in transforming the concept, actually a spin-off of the original one. This time it is that nothing is permanent in this world except for 'children and art'. One might sense the same thing in *Into the Woods* where everything seems wrapped up in happily-ever-after before the intermission. But perhaps, because it *is* a Sondheim-Lapine confection, we suspect things will not remain so rosy, that the happinesses will become unglued in the second half.

Gypsy, which has been called an almost perfect book, falls somewhere between a concept and conventional musical. The difficulty encountered in its first act closing happens because it is a biographical musical and no matter how we'd like to, we cannot manipulate life. (The same difficulty was apparent in *Fiorello*, and for the same reasons.) However, *Gypsy*'s main story thrust is Rose's determination, and in the great song

'Everything's Coming Up Roses', which ends the act, we witness Rose trying to inveigle her daughter Louise, (after Baby June has left her) into helping Mama find her dream. 'You can do it,' she implores, 'all you need is the chance. Mama is gonna see to it!' Finally she pleads, 'Everything's coming up roses for me and for you.' (Notice the 'me' gets the first consideration.) Putting this small scene directly before the first act curtain is the essence of creating drama, sending the audience out at the intermission with the worry, 'Can Rose pull it off this time?'

Gypsy and its superb plot manipulation at the end of Act I prompted Mark Steyn to say:

> One of the most difficult things for a librettist to do is to convince people by the end of Act I that you are not just spending time with these people. You're not just passing the hours until you come outside and find that the last tube's gone and your car's been clamped, but you are *actually involved with them*. Speaking of *Gypsy*, one of the things I hate is self-pity, because I don't think it's very interesting. At the end of Act I when the mother's world is crumbling, today, Charles Hart, the lyricist of *Phantom* would have written 'Oh, God, my life is miserable!' And Andrew would have written a tune for it. But Styne and Sondheim found a different way. She turns around and says 'You're going to be a star!' In the context of the show, it's a woman going off the rails. It's so startling even that late in the first act that it makes us gasp. It's an unpredictable reaction to what was maybe a predictable plot twist. That's the essence of the musical. Very few themes – instead, what counts is the variations.

Perhaps it is easier to understand the importance of the first act curtain if one sees how it works in a fantasy like *Brigadoon*. The 'secret' of Brigadoon is exposed to the audience late in Act I. We are told that if one of the villagers leaves, the town will disappear into the mists of Scotland for ever. It is, agreed, a rather contrived plot device, but it works. The hero, Tommy, stumbles into this town at the beginning of the musical, meets and is charmed by the simplicity of Fiona, the heroine. It is the wedding day of Fiona's sister, Jean, and throughout the act we witness the hero and heroine falling ever more deeply in love.

At the end of Act I, a spurned suitor, Harry, interrupts the postnuptial celebration. He leads a Sword Dance, which in itself creates tension and a feeling of danger. At its culmination, Harry asks the new bride to dance with him. The music reaches new heights whereupon Harry kisses Jean violently. Of course a fight breaks out in which the new husband is disarmed. Tommy, the American hero, saves the day. Here is how Alan Jay Lerner wrote it:

FIONA: Tommy! Tommy!

(TOMMY, *his eyes fixed on* HARRY *doesn't turn to reply to her.* HARRY *slowly rises and looks at* JEAN.)

HARRY: All I've done is to want ye too much.
(HE *walks slowly to the side of the stage and then suddenly turns back to the crowd. They all hold their positions as if not knowing what he is going to do next.*)

I'm leavin' Brigadoon, and 'tis the end of all of us. The miracle is over!

(HE *runs off. There is a sudden stunned moment, then everyone realises the import of his leaving and springs into action. Cries of 'we mus' stop 'im' fill the stage and all the men surge forward to run after him.*)

The suspense inherent in this fine first act curtain is obvious.* Coupled as it is with the romance, the exciting Sword Dance and the violence of the spurned lover, we need a breather. We also want to come back to see if Brigadoon will have disappeared into the mists.†

The most gut-wrenching ending of Act I I know occurs in *West Side Story*, when Tony stands over the bodies of Bernardo and Riff, as Romeo did over Tybalt and Mercutio, but perhaps because this scene is so contemporary we become more involved than we are in Shakespeare's play. Tony utters an anguished cry that at once signals his need for help and his realisation of loss. 'MARIA!' There is no further dialogue, and it is not necessary because we have Leonard Bernstein's magnificent score, now ruminating, now rumbling. All we need

---

* We are satisfied at least through the first act curtain, but at the end of the second act Alan Lerner seems to have become stuck for a solution to the plot and reopens the gates of Brigadoon through the power of love.

† On the subject of first act suspense, Luther Henderson has this to say: 'I learned a lot from being married to a director. [Mr Henderson is married to director Billie Allen.] The first act curtain should end with a cliffhanger. It should come to something. They're going to shoot him if they ever catch him tap dancing, and he's snuck away and is doing great in this nightclub. At the end of the act they open the stage curtain and – bam – there are his mother and father. The curtain comes down and the audience says, "What's going to happen?" What I'm saying is overkill, but you understand. It doesn't have to be that literal, but it has to build to something that will be solved in a good deal less time than the first act took.'

is a description of the dramatic action on stage. Here's what Arthur Laurents wrote to bring the curtain down:

> (*Another police whistle closer now, but he doesn't move. From the shadow,* ANYBODYS *appears. She scurries to* TONY *and tugs at his arm. A siren, another whistle, then a searchlight cuts across the playground.* ANYBODYS' *insistent tugging brings* TONY *to the realization of the danger. He crouches, starts to run with her to one escapeway. She reaches it first, goes out – but the searchlight hits him just as he would go through. He stops, runs the other way. He darts here, there and finally gets away as a distant clock begins to boom.*)

THE CURTAIN FALLS

The same kind of chill, with a bit less melodrama is in the air in *Cabaret*'s first act closing. This occurs at the engagement party given by Herr Schultz and Frau Schneider. The elderly couple (she is his German landlady and he a Jewish fruit merchant who rents a room in her apartment) have invited all their friends to the festivities. After Herr Schultz sings 'Meeskite', a Yiddish-type song, most of the party guests pull away and give their host the cold shoulder. Frau Schneider pleads for tolerance when one of the guests asks, 'You, a German, will marry this man?' 'But he's German as well, he was born here,' she insists. 'He's a Jew. He's not a German,' comes the icy retort. And he leads the guests in an innocuous-sounding patriotic hymn. Soon we see swastika armbands and the hymn crescendoes into a Nazi chorus, 'Tomorrow Belongs To Me', with which the act ends. This subtle and quite chilling Aryan outpouring follows all the essentials for a good first act ending.

THE SECOND ACT

When critics zero in for the kill on a musical, they usually attack the second act. Even the greatest classics have come in for their share of post-intermission brickbats. It seems endemic to the form. Or is it that after all the hoop-la of the exposition, author, critics and public alike are unable to sustain the momentum, and the letdown is inevitable? No one seems to know the answer, but mention 'second-act-itis' and any theatre person will understand the diagnosis. Even though straight dramas usually reach their peaks of intensity in the second act, musical theatre seems much more vulnerable. So we are left with a theatrical enigma; one that the lay public cannot seem to understand. They have no idea of the difficulties inherent in concluding a show. 'What problems come in that were not apparent in the exposition? After all,' the layman will query, 'isn't the second act generally much shorter than the first?'

Brevity has nothing to do with it. The audience has to do more than be interested in how the story will turn out. It has to care about the characters. As the critic Mark Steyn says:

> In Act I you've got to set up the characters, you can have lots of jokes because it's a way for people to get interested in the characters ... but you've got to rein that in by the start of Act II ... Arthur Laurents did a great job with this in *Gypsy* ... he went through the second act *taking out the laughs!*. The laughs distracted from the audience's emotional involvement with the characters. And the characters must be interesting. Of course, the best jokes in the world won't compensate the audience for an uninteresting character.

Even though it seems that the inherent interest in the character would be observed from the outset, and the librettist should be able to change it, this is easier said than accomplished. It has already been mentioned that even though his work is the first to be crucified by the critics, the librettist and his product seem to come lowest on the creative totem pole and have the least clout. The script is usually hammered out and stays fairly close to its accepted design *before the show goes into rehearsal*. Somehow in the months of previewing which precede the Broadway or West End debut, it always seems more urgent to add a new number here, shorten a production number there, change the set, add some lines for scene change, alter the keys, underscore or modulate. The script, and especially its second act is often twisted like taffy with no thought of how it will ever be rolled out flat. Common excuses are: (1) 'We have to tie it all up with a ribbon.' (2) 'No one will notice that it doesn't make sense.' (3) 'We grabbed them in the first act and we can coast on through.' (4) 'This is musical comedy; who says it has to be believable?'

In amateur companies, due to the rush to get all the musical pieces together for a gala first night, the script is never changed, but an over eager director may look for what he considers a 'perfect' first act and rehearsal time on the crucial second act may be short-changed. But take heart, a clever and experienced director will allot the proper amount of rehearsal time to this most important and vulnerable aspect of any musical. He will see that the second act does what it must – create the high point of tension to climax the show. Directors and librettists working closely together have given shows like *My Fair Lady, Fiddler on the Roof, Lady in the Dark, Brigadoon, Oklahoma!, She Loves Me*, and a great many others a warmth and growth to their second acts that, in my estimation, outshines their brilliant first acts. For in each of the above cases, by the time the second act is under way, we have become so fond of the characters we are reluctant to see the second act end.

What The Second Act Must Accomplish

Obviously in a plotted musical the loose threads of the previous act will be tied together. In an unplotted musical, (revue) sketches must be longer, subjects should be broader, sarcasm more trenchant and whatever production numbers there are more animated and perhaps more lavish.

Tension in the plotted musical will be increased. The love interest will reach some sort of struggle and come to a resolution* and a satisfactory musical climax will be reached.

THE OPENING OF THE SECOND ACT

It is many years since we have outgrown the habit of ringing down the first act curtain in mid-song or mid-dance only to have it rise fifteen minutes later on the same group in the same

---

* The bio-musical may have problems in treating its love interest because it needs to maintain at least some similarity to the subject's real life. *Fiorello* (with libretto by Jerome Weidman and George Abbott and score by Sheldon Harnick and Jerry Bock) had to deal with two love interests since the first Mrs La Guardia died during the time span of the musical. A heroine who doesn't appear in the second act is difficult to rationalise in any plot, especially in a musical, but the librettists solved it cleverly by focusing strongly on the character of the man and having his secretary who would become the second Mrs La Guardia, (and dominate the second act) always present in the background. *Gypsy*, as noted earlier, which also focuses strongly on the character of Rose, solves similar problems in like fashion.

place, but by this time a whole lot wearier.* This type of first act non-ending makes audiences feel there was actually no reason to have an intermission, but it was inserted because the public began to cough, rustle programmes and grow restless from sitting too long without a break.† Today's librettists are aware that even if something is going to happen in Act II at the 'dance at the gym, the palace ball, the swanky nightclub' they must let it finish before the act is over – and they always insert some loose threads to manipulate and tie up in the second act.

A plot device, once established can be a powerful and yet comfortable way to get the second act started. *Fiddler on the Roof* uses a device Joseph Stein, the librettist, set up at the beginning of the musical – Tevye's monologue, – this time to God. It is amusing, character revealing and shows the protagonist's acceptance of his fate. It is also a good way to inform the audience of what has happened in the time between the acts. In this case, since the first act ended so dramatically with the wedding of his daughter Tzeitel and the tailor Motel, during which there was a pogrom, we are grateful for this gentle opening. Here is the prologue that leads to the first scene.

PROLOGUE

The exterior of TEVYE'S *house.* TEVYE *is sitting on a bench.*

TEVYE: (*To heaven*) That was quite a dowry You gave my daughter Tzeitel at her wedding. Was that necessary? Anyway, Tzeitel and Motel have been married almost two months now. They work very hard, they are as poor as squirrels in winter. But they are both so happy they don't know how miserable they are. Motel

---

* Shamefully hiding behind the name of 'nostalgia' this type of entr'acte was inserted into the British musical, *Me and My Girl*, with the entire cast 'Lambeth Walking' off stage and through the auditorium at Act I's close, returning and dancing back onto the stage to begin the proceedings of Act II. Although it is a creaky device and the bane of critics, audiences seemed to love it and it afforded the tunesmiths another chance to plug the only hit song in the show.

† The intermission of *Kiss Me, Kate* was handled smartly and given a then contemporary feeling which contrasted strongly with the two themes of the musical (backstage intrigue and Elizabethan travesty) by having the musicians 'jam' the 'Too Darn Hot' number outside the stage door (although I have never known instrumentalists or dancers to spend those valuable, reviving fifteen minutes performing). *Cabaret* used its intermission time cleverly by having the Kit Kat Klub orchestra play a raucous medley of tunes from the show while the audience milled out and in. The device seemed realistic in this case and, although it served to reprise the tunes, it did prepare us for the second act opening which beings with an ominous cymbal call to attention on the stage of the cabaret.

keeps talking about a sewing machine.* I know You're very busy –
wars, revolutions, floods, plagues, all those little things that bring
people to You – couldn't you take a second away from Your
catastrophes to get it for him? How much trouble would it be?
Oh, and while you're in the neighborhood, my horse's left leg –
Am I bothering You too much? I'm sorry. As the Good Book
says – Why should I tell You what the Good Book says?
(EXIT)

A second act must always be a consequence of the first.† You
may know what is going to happen. The pleasure comes from
watching *how* it happens. Perhaps the most classically perfect
unravelling of the Act I consequences I know is to be found in
Hugh Wheeler and Stephen Sondheim's *A Little Night Music*.
Its opening creates a delicious excitement which is a direct
repercussion of the first act. That act has been working towards
plot entanglements or convoluted liaisons and ends with each
of the principals deciding to accept an invitation to an explosive
'Weekend in the Country'. We expect mayhem, and we are not
disappointed. We hope, since this is operetta, that after the
mayhem everyone will end up with a proper partner. The
second act opening, of course, brings them all to Mme Arm-
feldt's country house, some armed with venom, some with
naïvety, and all ready for the plot to unfold and climax.

Porgy and Bess, with libretto by Du Bose Heyward, is
another masterpiece of second act tension. By the end of Act
I, Porgy has established a tender living relationship with Bess
(climaxed in the moving duet 'Bess, You is My Woman Now'.
All the residents of Catfish Row except the crippled Porgy –
who insists Bess should go with them – are leaving for the
annual picnic on Kittiwah Island as the curtain falls on the
first act. We know that Sportin' Life, Bess's former pusher is

* First heralded as the 'new arrival at Motel's house', the unveiling and blessing of the
sewing machine is one of the charming highlights to come in Act II.

† Mark Steyn deplores the inexperienced composer-lyricist, frequently a convert from the
pop or rock field who, when working in the musical theatre will not have developed a sense
of consistency. Here are some comments: 'In *Time* which ran a couple of years here [in
London], there was this intergalactic space judge, and he talked like all judges, in a very
formal, cold, pedantic manner. Then suddenly in Act Two he bursts into song. "Bursts" is
the operative word, because suddenly this cold, formal character sings "Hey! I said, Hey!" It
was ludicrous. It was as if in *The Sound of Music*, Sister Maria sang, "I'm Jist a Girl Who
Caint Say No". It's laziness. Somehow these people believe they are writing in a field which
owes nothing to what has gone before ... that's a terrible thing about rock ... people boast
about how they are doing something terribly new ... dragging theatre into the 21st Century,
when actually they're pushing it back into the 19th where you had all those glaring gulfs
between book and lyrics.'

going to the outing as well and that the brutish Crown, Bess's previous lover is hiding on the island. Will Bess succumb to dope or sex, or will she remain true to Porgy? Of course this means enormous tension ahead, since our programme informs us that Act II begins on Kittiwah Island.

Perhaps even more anxiety grips the audience at the first act curtain of Alan Jay Lerner's libretto for *Camelot*. Lancelot and Guinevere have confessed their love shortly before Arthur enters and announces that he wants to invest Lancelot with a knighthood. Writing a subtle speech, in which subtext is more important than the words that are spoken, Lerner has Arthur sense their love and resolve at curtain's fall, in a moving spoken soliloquy, to do what no king before him has done, to forgive them. We know this must eventually lead to calamity in the second act and we are touched but not mollified when, at the curtain rise Lancelot sings the romantic 'If Ever I Would Leave You' to Guinevere.

But I don't mean to imply that tension is the only way to begin a second act. The unbearable tension with which Arthur Laurents's libretto for *West Side Story* left us at the end of its first act dissolves into sunlight and joy in the opening of the second. We discover Maria and her friends trying on wedding clothes, and after a bit of chit-chat she sings 'I Feel Pretty'.*

Agnes de Mille's 'Chase Ballet' at the beginning of the second act of *Brigadoon* works on many different levels. For after an almost static first act anchored in the marketplace, the chase after the spurned suitor bent on destroying the village gives us some movement and opens up the entire musical.

THE 'ELEVEN O'CLOCK NUMBER'

World theatre has always chosen different times to raise the curtain.† The French, preferring to dine before the play, opt

---

* Although Arthur Laurents loves 'I Feel Pretty', it is one of Stephen Sondheim's least favourite lyrics. 'I wanted to show that I could do inner rhymes . . . so I had this uneducated Puerto Rican girl singing, "It's alarming how charming I feel",' he chides himself, and adds 'You *know* she would not have been unwelcome in Noël Coward's living room . . . I asked Sheldon Harnick after the show what he thought . . . I went back and wrote a simplified version of the lyric which nobody connected with the show would accept.'

† Cabaret, of course, begins much later than theatre. Sometimes when the latter tries to imitate the former in a theatrical setting, a later hour may be chosen. *Nash at Nine* and *The 9:15 Revue* are typical examples. Occasionally producers whose shows are just hanging on by

for 8.30 p.m.; in Madrid, because of the siesta, theatre does not begin before 10 p.m.; Broadway in search of unanimity elects 8 p.m.;* the British, traditionally determining their starting hour from the length of the play begin anywhere from 7.15 to 8.30. But formerly all theatres everywhere began at 8.30.† Yet even more important than the hour of beginning in years past was the time when the curtain descended. No matter what time it first went up, it usually rang down on Broadway at 11.15. Theatre, being an élitist affair, was mainly a privilege of the wealthy who had no worries about babysitters, late subway or underground travel, or getting to a job the next morning. In keeping with the gala spirit, it was usually followed by supper and dancing.

Because of that 8.30 starting hour, a musical's first act rarely ended before 10 p.m. Adding a twenty minute intermission and entr'acte music – long since abolished – tradition demanded that the second act curtain should rise near 10.25 p.m. This meant that the climax point of the second act, the spot where the plot resolved itself and led to the big production number, happened near 11 p.m. Times have changed and critics have said that the eleven o'clock number is an old-fashioned device (it does not happen in the later Sondheim shows although there are *four* of them, one for each of the principals in *Follies*). Now the eleven o'clock number on Broadway, if it occurs at all, usually is at about 10.15, but the phrase has stuck.‡

---

their fingernails will set a later time to raise the curtain hoping to catch some stragglers eager to see any kind of show and who may have dawdled or been unable to buy seats for their first choices. David Merrick, the famous Broadway producer did just that during the last years of *42nd Street* (to the consternation of his producer rivals) when he *advertised* that he was holding the curtain of that show until 8.15, while every other show on Broadway began at 8.00.

* Twenty years ago, when attendance was falling off on Broadway, the league of New York theatres decided to try an experiment and raise their curtains at 7.00, hoping to inveigle business people in the city into having dinner, attend a show and get home at an early hour. The experiment failed miserably, for many of the dyed-in-the-wool theatregoers stayed away, and the 8.00 curtain was restored except for opening nights. New Yorkers seem unable to make up their minds about the quality of a theatrical offering without reading what the critics of *The Post* and especially *The New York Times* think. In order to have their reviews published the next day (Broadway *insists* theatrical reviews be published the very next day; Chicago, San Francisco and London seem to publish a day or so later. Los Angeles generally waits a few extra days), critics must get them to their editors no later than 10 p.m. This necessitates that curtains rise obligatorily at 6.30 on opening nights.

† Noël Coward immortalised that item of magic excitement in a series of nine short plays collectively entitled *Tonight At 8.30*.

‡ Mitch Douglas librettist-lyricist of *The Ragtime Blues* feels, 'the 11 o'clock number works the same way a confrontation scene works in drama. It's the peak where the antagonist and the protagonist clash violently. It must be about somebody confronting something big. The

What must that eleven o'clock number contain? Two things. It must climax the play and state the concept as well. If it can be a showstopper* without taking away from our emotional involvement with the characters – even a production number – that is all to the good.

The title song in *Cabaret* crowns Joe Masteroff's remarkable libretto in the second act's fifth scene. (There are seven in the act.) Although sung as a solo, it takes place at the Kit Kat Klub and qualifies as a semi-production number.† The number states Sally Bowles's philosophy about breezing through the brevity of life, and does so with memorable showstopping music and lyrics. As such it qualifies as the ultimate eleven o'clock number.

Both of *Gypsy*'s eleven o'clock numbers, 'Let Me Entertain You', and 'Rose's Turn', work on all counts and in a similar fashion, for indeed we have been pelted with the songs through-out the evening. The latter is the emotional climax to the play, but the former has been around since its inception, but never accompanied by strongly accented second and fourth beats, the hallmark of raunchy burlesque. As climax to the plot, we now see plain-Jane Louise transformed into a dazzling woman and neophyte stripper. Throughout the few minutes of the number we watch her gain confidence and work her way up to the top of her profession. Then, on top of Gypsy's success, we are witness to Rose coming apart at the seams.

Lady in the Dark in which Moss Hart used his own Freudian analysis to illustrate the heroine's problem of being unable to decide on a lover, presented 'The Saga of Jenny' as the eleven o'clock number – pure production number which deals with a woman who rashly made up her mind and all the attendant problems the decision brought her. It is the last defence of the heroine, a heroic attempt to hide behind the mask of a career which will be stripped away in the final number, 'My Ship'.

---

soliloquy in *My Fair Lady*, beginning with "I've Grown Accustomed to Her Face", is a good example.'

* William Hammerstein recalls staging *Oklahoma!* in Oklahoma City. The eleven o'clock number is, of course, 'Oklahoma'. 'It's a very exciting moment,' he explains. 'They all come down front, beside the audience. You know that Rodgers and Hammerstein gave that song to the State of Oklahoma and it's their State song. They're very serious about it, and when we got to that part in the second act, the audience stood up – as if it were the national anthem – well, it *is* their anthem. It's not very easy to get back into the drama with what remains of the second act.'

† John Kander, the composer, has already offered the 'Cabaret' motif cleverly inverted in the entr'acte and has been presenting snatches of the tune in disguised form throughout the evening, thus preparing our ears for the song.

But not every eleven o'clocker needs to be brilliant or to use the whole cast.* 'Send in The Clowns' in *A Little Night Music* and 'Being Alive' in *Company* and 'What I Did For Love' in *A Chorus Line* fill the bill admirably and each of them is a solo of self-discovery. The heavily dramatic musical play *Lost in the Stars* even went a step further and presented the evening's one amusing song inserted for contrast – 'Big Black Mole' – sung by a young boy. And who can conceive of a more unforgettable duet perhaps a little before the eleven o'clock spot than 'Shall We Dance', from *The King and I*. It distils the tenuous relationship of Anna and the King and never fails to elicit uncontainable applause, the greatest of the evening, bursting out even before the polka is concluded.†

The eleven o'clock number is so often an emotional tour de force that its comic possibilities are often overlooked. Jule Styne whose music gave *Bells are Ringing* its special cachet, had his difficulties with star Judy Holliday when she realised that co-star Sydney Chaplin had an eleven o'clock number and *she* didn't. As Mr Styne tells it:

It had to be written in two days. I talked to Adolph and Betty, [*Adolph Green and Betty Comden were the lyricists-librettists on the show.*] I thought and thought and started eighteen different things. They were all for *singer*-singers, [*as distinguished from actress-singer*] and that wouldn't work. Finally it had to be comedy. I remembered something that George Abbott told me. 'If you're looking for material ... for a comedy number and you're stuck, go back and read the script over to find the biggest laugh in the show. Take that and make a song out of it. It will work in song form too.' All of a sudden it comes to me that her biggest laugh in the show was when they asked her where she worked, and she said she worked at the Bonjour Tristess Brassière Company.

At that point in the play, she made a statement, 'I'm going back where I can be me, and the Bonjour Tristess Brassière Company.' I said, 'Gee, that's funny.' I had these eight bars, and I played them for Comden and Green, and they fell down. I said, 'Don't write it. Let's see if Jerry Robbins [*the director*] likes it. Robbins was in bed. I said to Jerry, 'You've

* Tom Shepard thinks of the eleven o'clock number as gaining momentum. 'Particularly as you're nearing the finish of your show,' he says, 'you don't want to just dribble away to the end. If it's a great number, a star turn, why not?'

† This number has other merits as well, physical and emotional. Who can forget the exquisite peach satin ball gown Irene Sharaff designed for Mrs Anna and the sheer beauty of the couple swirling over the stage to the music. It hits us emotionally as well for it is the first time the King has taken Mrs Anna in his arms, a movement we have been anticipating since their first encounter.

got to put clothes on and listen, because we're having problems with Judy, you're trying to give her different things and she's not taking it. She's interested in her song. "Finish it," she's saying, "give me my number." We threw in all the jokes and it was her biggest number in the show.

PRODUCTION NUMBERS

One of the things that separates a musical from a straight play is the use of production numbers. Three or four times in each act the cast will be assembled for song and possibly dance. Oscar Hammerstein was responsible for making the production number more realistic. In the old operetta days there had been the 'peasants' dance', so unreal, as William Hammerstein comments, 'Well, nobody would believe it, because what the hell are all those peasants doing on stage? They're there because we want to hear the full sound of their voices ... and we can see their lovely costumes ... The girls lift their skirts and the fellows are manly.'

Corny or not, the public dotes on and has come to expect these periodic lavish assemblages and even the most modest musical must make frequent obeisance to being 'grand'. One of the recent grand tableaux is the 'Do You Hear the People Sing?' number of *Les Misérables*. A lot of citizens and students and a lot of flag waving seem to replace, in contemporary musicals, the old-fashioned peasant turn.

Sometimes the number is just shoved in because we haven't had one for a while and shows its stitches as in *The King and I*. Mrs Anna who is teaching the children geography pulls down a map of the world and says, 'For years before I came here Siam was to me that little white spot. Now I have lived here for more than a year. I have met the people of Siam. And I am beginning to understand them.' Then, as Martin Gottfried notes in his book, *Broadway Musicals*, 'with this flimsy clue,* she sings "Getting To Know You".'†

---

* William Hammerstein disagrees: 'I am not simply defending my father. I think that's a perfect introduction and an important [production] number because it firmly establishes her relationship with these children which is going to be threatened in the next few moments by the Crown Prince who says, "I don't believe in snow." And then the King comes in, knowing he has to support his son but he has also to support the 'teechah''. It's a big moment of conflict. By placing it there, having the map pulled down, and showing the children in the class being taught by her you're establishing the relationship and setting the stage for the conflict that's coming up.'

† 'Getting To Know You' was added out of town. It was not even written for *The King*

Hello, Dolly has perhaps the best known production number in all musical literature. Dolly Levi* descending the staircase of the Harmonia Gardens to the acclaim of waiters, guests – and eventually the audience – gives us room for chorus, song and dance. But even in this fine libretto one can find production numbers inserted rather than generic.

For example, in the first act when the impoverished Barnaby (who Dolly thinks is a millionaire) tries to wriggle out of dining at the Harmonia Gardens because he can't dance, Dolly pulls out one of her many professional cards which proclaims 'absolutely no sense of rhythm is one of the primary requirements for learning by the Gallegher-Levi Method'. The number is called 'Dancing', and it turns out to be one of the most charming mini-production numbers in the entire show, though most professionals feel it was inserted primarily to bring movement to the stage.

FINALE

Many pages ago, in discussing the differences between a straight play and a musical, I mentioned that the musical must *finally* leave us with an ennobled feeling no matter how true to life, how bitter, or how tragic its ending may be. The characters must be different from what they were when we first discovered them, they must have grown into something in the almost three hours we have spent with them.

If the musical has resolved its story through the eleven o'clock number or beyond, then the ending should be a bang up musical number – the original Italian meaning of finale, or grand finale. One might emulate Jerry Herman and not be afraid to repeat the closing number for chorus after chorus. Of

and I, but, with another lyric, intended to be sung by Lieutenant Cable in *South Pacific*. The song was deleted in favour of 'Younger Than Springtime', and when a production song was needed for *The King and I*, Rodgers brought out this lilting melody which seems to have an oriental triplet and rhythmic scheme. Hammerstein then wrote what Rodgers calls 'a philosophical theme for the entire story'.

* Michael Stewart, *Hello, Dolly*'s librettist, told me he deplored Barbra Streisand's insistence on wearing a white sequined gown for the movie version. 'I specifically wrote into the script that Dolly comes down the steps of the Harmonia Gardens in a bright *red* gown because I wanted to give a hint that the blood was coursing again through her body and she was putting aside the mousy life of a matchmaker now that she had returned to the place where she had been on her "uppers" as a lady of fashion . . .'

course, the best final numbers are those that seem inevitable. *A Chorus Line* and *Company* have been working all along to their final numbers. 'One', in the former, whose concept and title, like the theme of the play is the selection of a singular star, and 'Being Alive', in the latter, wherein the hero opens his heart at last to let love in. *Ain't Misbehavin'* travels through to a medley of 'Fats' Waller's best known songs to ever increasing tempo and finishes by having the cast vocally imitate the instruments of 'Fats' Waller's combo – a vocal tour de force. *Porgy and Bess* brings us a hopeful Porgy (supported by the entire chorus) deciding to head north in search of his love in the joyful, 'I'm On My Way'.

A few musicals end quietly. Generally they have been miniatures all along, or they are swept along by emotion. *Camelot* reprises the exquisitely moving title song, this time sung by a wiser Arthur, to a boy who represents the continuation of the dream, the next generation: 'Don't let it be forgot/That once there was a spot ... /For one brief, shining moment that was known/As Camelot'. *She Loves Me*, the jewel-box of a musical, set in a Hungarian *parfumerie* ends appropriately with the 'sales-song' that has been woven through the piece, 'Thank you, please call again, madam.' Perhaps the most chilling quiet ending I know is the blackout at the end of *Cabaret* (the show does not use a curtain). The hero leaves 1937 Berlin, Sally Bowles decides to remain. What else would suit the awful fate we know awaits her (and the world) but the opening number reprised by the leering Emcee followed by an insidious, malevolent cymbal hiss.

Sometimes, especially when the eleven o'clock number has not led us to a conclusion of the plot, and we have not seen the characters come to their required understanding, an additional number is needed to complete the transformation. In this case a reprise of what could be the hit number may do the trick. It is an old-fashioned device, but a sure-fire one and was used successfully in *Oklahoma!*, *Hello, Dolly*, *42nd Street*, and recently in *Me and My Girl*. It was even used in much more subtle fashion (only a portion of the song was sung) in *A Little Night Music*. After everybody has settled down with the partner for whom they were intended, the operetta's two protagonists, a wiser Desirée and Fredrik are able to chuckle sagely at their own foibles to a reprise of the show's most rueful ballad, 'Send In the Clowns'.

DESIRÉE: Was that a farce,
FREDRIK: My fault I fear,
DESIRÉE: Me as a merry-go-round,
FREDRIK: Me as King Lear. (*Spoken, with underscoring*) How unlikely life
is, to lose one's son, one's wife and practically one's life within
an hour – and yet feel relieved.

The King and I which ends movingly with the death of the King of Siam and the young prince's edict that henceforth the barbarous ways of his country will be softened gives us a distinctly uplifted feeling that serves to allay our sadness. But it has no actual finale, as William Hammerstein says, 'It's not ha, ha operetta where everybody is on stage and the peasants come back and dance again. Yet a finale has to move you, and here it does move you ... because the King reveals that he has learned really important lessons.'

Unfortunately, this kind of non-finale can cause difficulties in the recorded media where we have not the visual to help enlist our empathy for the characters. Tom Shepard who recorded the show had to 'create' one. Of that experience he states: 'I remember constructing a finale for the record, starting with Anna's reading the letter that the King wrote her. Then I segued into the King reading his own letter because we had to create something that worked for the recording including the creation of new underscoring* based on 'Something Wonderful', Lady Thiang's moving tribute to her husband, the King. From there we go to the 'Coronation' of Prince Chulalong and his speech to his new subjects. Then at the end of the recording, the music swells and overwhelms the sound of the new, young King's voice.'

Liza Eliot in *Lady in the Dark* sings 'My Ship' which is the key to her analysis and transforms her from a career woman to a loving woman. Henry Higgins sings 'I've Grown Accustomed To Her Face' which converts him from a mere pedant to a loving human being.† It's obvious from the above that the evening was worthwhile to them and that their characters have been altered.

---

* See *Underscoring*, page 256.
    † Alan Jay Lerner, master dramatist that he was, concluded the printed edition of *My Fair Lady* with this note: 'I have omitted the sequel (epilogue) because in it Shaw explains how Eliza ends not with Higgins but with Freddy and – Shaw and Heaven forgive me! – I am not certain he is right.

Character growth need not be applicable only to individuals, but can become a new, more modern – perhaps civilised is the right word – way of thinking as in *Fiddler on the Roof*. Here Tevye who has disowned his daughter Chava because she married a Gentile forgives her at last, breaking with an ancient tradition.

Romeo and Juliet ends with little reconciliation after the suicides of the star-crossed lovers, but Arthur Laurents in his libretto for *West Side Story* transforms the ending, leaving Maria-Juliet alive, forcing the gangs to put away their violence and create a spirit of brotherhood as they carry Tony-Romeo's body aloft.* Here is Maria's final speech: (and the voluminous stage directions which can only intensify the drama for the reader, for the actor, and through the actor for the audience.)

MARIA: Stay back.

(*The shawl she has had around her shoulders slips to the ground as she gets up, walks to* CHINO *and holds out her hand. He hands her the gun. She speaks again, in a flat, hard voice*)

How do you fire this gun, Chino? Just by pulling this little trigger?

(*She points it at him suddenly; he draws back. She has all of them in front of her now, as she holds the gun out and her voice gets stronger with anger and savage rage*)

How many bullets are left, Chino? Enough for you? (*Pointing at another*)
And you? (At ACTION)
All of you? WE ALL KILLED HIM, and my brother and Riff. I too. I CAN KILL NOW BECAUSE I HATE NOW.

(*She has been pointing the gun wildly, and they have all been drawing back. Now, again, she holds it straight out at* ACTION)

How many can I kill Chino? How many – and still have one bullet left for me?

(*Both hands on the gun, she pushes it forward at* ACTION. *But*

---

* The ending of *Romeo and Juliet*, however, was, rewritten earlier in 1893 at the request of May, Princess of Teck, who would become Queen Mary, consort to King George V, for use as a festive play to cap her nuptial gala. This was Mary's favourite Shakespearean play, but she disapproved of the deaths of either Romeo or Juliet and insisted the Royal Scribe rewrite the last act to provide a happy ending more suitable for presentation on such a joyous occasion.

she cannot fire, and she breaks into tears, hurls the gun away and sinks to the ground. SCHRANK *walks on, looks around and starts towards* TONY'S *body. Like a madwoman,* MARIA *races to the body and puts her arms around it, all embracing, protecting and she cries out)*

DON'T YOU TOUCH HIM!

(SCHRANK *steps back,* KRUPKE *and* GLADHAND *have appeared in the shadows behind him.* MARIA *now turns and looks at* CHINO, *holds her hand out to him. Slowly he comes and stands by the body.* PEPE *joins* CHINO. *Then* MARIA *leans low over* TONY'S *face. Softly, privately)*

Te Adoro, Anton.

(*She kisses him gently. Music starts as the two Jets and the two Sharks lift up* TONY'S *body and start to carry him out. The others, boys and girls, fall in behind to make a procession, the same procession they made in the dream ballet, as* BABY JOHN *comes forward to pick up* MARIA'S *shawl and put it over her head. She sits quietly, like a woman in mourning as the music builds, the lights start to come up and the procession makes its way across the stage. At last, she gets up and despite the tears on her face, lifts her head proudly, and triumphantly turns to follow the others. The adults –* DOC, SCHRANK, KRUPKE, GLADHAND – *are left bowed, alone, useless.)*

THE CURTAIN FALLS

REWRITING – THE SECOND DRAFT

Once the play is completed, every librettist knows it is time for reevaluation and rewriting. No one should underestimate the value of going over and making changes in a musical. On the wall of my Carnegie Hall studio I kept a bold sign, a quote from Alan and Marilyn Bergman which always reminded me and all the people I ever worked with that 'Songs are not written *they're re-written*'. I guess this is the most difficult part of creating – being able to criticise bluntly one's own work. I find I am able with each draft to come up with a more apt phrase here, a more succinct or dramatic scene there – all of this without changing the dramatic outline. And sometimes I find a whole scene that needs rewriting.

This advice is especially important with a musical, partly

because of the sheer numbers of creators involved, all of whom will be contributing valid ideas to make the project even better than it is at the moment, but mostly because there are inevitably so many last minute changes to make after seeing the musical on its feet, changes so obvious that you wonder how you could have missed them. In a musical it is best to start with as polished a project as one can create. Here are some of the things we look for in the reexamination.

Maintaining the humour

Although a script may be serious, it must not be boring. Musicals, more than serious plays, need to have laughter and joy – but with a handkerchief ever ready. I always think of Charles Chaplin, the master of this manipulation, and a well-known scene from *City Lights*, although a film, the prototype of musical comedy. The tramp buys a carnation from a beautiful blind flower-seller, and stands nearby, gazing at her adoringly. The underscoring is 'La Violetera', a near cloying folksong, and our empathy with both these unfortunates makes the moment *almost* maudlin. Then, while rinsing out her flower cup she tosses the fetid water over her shoulder and unknowingly directly into his face. The tension evaporates in laughter. But it is warm, empathetic laughter without a hint of cruelty.

Every librettist must know when to dissolve moments like that. Even the most tragic scenes must be relieved with humour. The sad situation near the end of *Fiddler on the Roof* is alleviated when Golde tells her daughter in reconciliation that she may write to them. Because they are on opposite sides of the stage she loudly makes the announcement that they will be 'staying with Uncle Abram', hoping to renew the severed lines of communication with her child. Tevye retorts, with mock irritation, 'We will be staying with Uncle Abram! We will be staying with Uncle Abram! The whole world needs to know our business!' in gruff but benevolent fashion. We laugh, because Chava knows (and more importantly, *we* know) he has forgiven her.

Walking the humorous line in a musical is not easy, for the librettist must avoid the tempting scatological and the momentary laugh. The object is to make the people on stage human, telling their jokes as they go about their business. This was no easy feat in the musical *1776* which was about the great debate leading to the signing of the Declaration of Independence. Nobody thought the show had a chance of success, much less have any moments of humour. What the pundits forgot was that debates are invariably good theatre and humour often implies a put-down of the opposing party. *1776* succeeded because it managed to be what some critics have called 'juicy, giving you a good time while it gave you information'. Yet the converse may be true in the contemporary political arena. Current news may get laughs as a political cartoon would but will date quickly. Librettists try to choose a general tendency (the subject of graft, for instance, which is always with us, was handled so brilliantly in 'A Little Tin Box' from *Fiorello*) rather than a specific subject such as Margaret Thatcher's Denis; Reagan's astrology, Bush's wimpiness. To include the headlines would only allow the material to be used effectively in a topical revue, and there the material will have to be updated periodically.

Early in my career, I remember writing a satirical political revue of which I made a demo at what then seemed to me enormous cost. By the time the material reached a possible producer, the situations were hopelessly outdated, the lyrics had to be rewritten, the extravagant demo scrapped and rerecorded.

Bitchy humour ('Welcome to the Theater' from *Applause*; 'Bosom Buddies' from *Mame*) is most acceptable as is unconscious self-description ('A Person Can Develop a Cold' from *Guys and Dolls*; 'He Had Refinement' from *By the Beautiful Sea*). What I've always felt is *not* acceptable is pure dirtiness, mainly the kind that is inserted merely for a cheap laugh.*

When Katharine Hepburn opened the second act of *Coco* with the single word 'Shit!' she embarrassed not only the audience, but herself; likewise when Frank Gorshin impersonating *Jimmy* (Walker) made a swift entrance and exit entirely nude, most of the audience squirmed uncomfortably. Both of the above seemed to be inserted merely to shock and attempt to infuse life into what would appear to be a dead body, and were not called for in the musical.

---

* *Sugar Babies* had some of the raunchiest leeringly smutty humour in recent memory. It did offend some Women's Libbers, but because it was intended as a vaudeville-burlesque, a kind of show where that kind of thing was always acceptable, most audiences declared it inoffensive fun.

In the spring of 1988, the critics welcomed a small musical called *Romance, Romance*, but justly deplored a number in the second act concerning the sexual fantasies of two very old people. That number, unnecessary to the plot, lapsed into the worst taste, and although it got some belly laughs, the show never seemed to recover its momentum after this regression. As for slang! Nothing dates more quickly.

Reprises

Although the question of whether or not to reprise will be more fully addressed in a later section of this book, in the first stage of a musical's development one must remain aware of the comfortable feeling that comes to most audiences on rehearing a song. The playwright may want to expand the script to accommodate just such a possibility.*

Length

In reviewing the libretto, one is wary again of excessive length, as outlined on p. 47 and must take into consideration the time it will take to sing all the songs which are yet to be written, and those that will be added in previews. Dialogue which is sung will usually take four times as long to negotiate as prose and each song may need additional choruses to create balance not previously counted upon. Add in the production numbers, dance and possibly ballet, and we all realise that a show gets longer and longer in rehearsal. So we pare it down to optimum length in its first draft.

---

* Sometimes a librettist must lead up to the reprise and will realise that this very technique can make or break the play. Mark Steyn says, 'I was amused by the way an opera critic criticised *South Pacific* at its recent revival here [in London] . . . yet what is so striking about those reprises is that they're not reprises in the sense of "sing it again". Those songs, so confidently stated at the beginning of the show, like "Some Enchanted Evening". You know "Once you have found her never let her go", were reprised falteringly, uncertainly, because all the confidence of those bold opening love songs has been dissipated. That's what's brilliant about it. They give you a fresh dramatic slant on the material . . . and create an emotional high point for the first act.'

Balance

At this point a professional librettist will look through his script to avoid too many solos or duets or even production numbers following each other, although it is difficult to do at this stage, and will be done again once the score is near completion. Then he might have to shift some scenes for what will become better musical balance. Every professional musical has a judicious balance of slow, fast, solo and group numbers. And it is not too soon to work towards that goal.

Alan Jay Lerner calls this balance one of the 'conventions of the musical theater', and adds that it is the dramatist's job to prepare for this. 'What is exciting,' he continues, 'is to be aware of these conventions and use them for fresh expression. It is not enough that there be a fast song after a slow song. Legitimate dramatic ways must be found so that the character or characters arrive at the emotional moment that demands the right kind of music to balance the score.'

Consistency

Most shows that get critical roasting are faulted because their characters are inconsistent. Even in a generational story characters do not change that much. They can grow wiser and older, but they always develop in a natural, human way. Their dialogue is generic to the character, and every librettist will rewrite his play to avoid any manipulation of character or to delete speeches that are unnatural to them.

For example, Sweeney Todd is a revenge-obsessed villain, but he is believable and every word he utters seems natural to him. Dolly Levi is an ambitious matchmaker with enough energy for ten women yet she is believable. Tevye is beset by more problems than Job but there is nothing phony about him or the ways in which he copes with life. Characters should take up their natural roles, without forcing. And each of the characters should speak in his or her own voice, *never the librettist's*!

Particularisation

If the libretto is to have characters who outshine cliché, they must be particularised in order to be memorable. The melodies and lyrics they will sing will certainly help to clothe them and will hopefully give them a uniqueness that makes them unforgettable to audiences. But the libretto must lift them out of the humdrum by looking at them as multidimensional creatures.

In drama, Blanche Dubois in Tennessee Williams's *A Streetcar Named Desire* and Willy Loman in Arthur Miller's *Death of A Salesman* are as real to most of us as the people we see every day. But they are, respectively, much more than an ageing schizophrenic and a travelling salesman. And so it must be in the world of the musical. Joey in *Pal Joey* is not just a heel, he is a young, good-looking, dancing, ambitious, lying, not-too-well-educated, pretentious, good-in-bed heel. Adelaide from *Guys and Dolls* is more than a blonde who works in the chorus, she is patient, crafty, ageing, psychologically informed, smart, forgiving and streetwise. Similarly, there are many facets to Sweeney Todd, Margo Channing (*Applause*), Nellie Forbush (*South Pacific*), El Gallo (*The Fantasticks*), Tevye (*Fiddler on the Roof*), Rose (*Gypsy*), Mame, and so many of the memorable personalised characters in musicals. Not every person a librettist creates can be memorable, but more than one or two roles that lack particularisation doom a musical to the ho-hum category. Nobody remembers people who fade into the wallpaper.

Timeliness

Of course, a writer for the stage will choose his subject *because* it is timely. For example, in the early 1970s a good musical about a woman who left a comfortable, yet loveless marriage in the 1880s to strike out on her own perhaps in search of love would be daring and timely, and because the idea was almost avant-garde, likely to be produced. Now in the late 1980s, post Women's Lib, it would be old hat.* One would have to find

* The recent musicalisation of *A Doll's House* (1984) as adapted by even so notable a team as Comden and Green closed after a few performances because the juice had run out of its theme.

other reasons for her to leave; perhaps ambition for herself or her children, perhaps self-preservation. But no matter how logical or clever your plotting, I am certain you would have difficulty interesting a producer in the theme. The concept is no longer timely. It has moved on. The favourite theme as we go into the Nineties seems to be abuse: spouse, child, parental or self. Yet no one, knowing how long it takes to write and have a musical produced would take a theme that is in full flower, for it would be a dead stalk by the time the show made it to the stage. We all try to stay with – or better yet – ahead of the relevant and current trends. One doesn't need to be contemporary to be timely, but one *does* need issues that concern us today.

Emotion

A good librettist is not afraid of honest emotion. He wears his heart on his sleeve and may even go overboard into pathos – just to the point of bathos. There is no other art form in today's world that needs so much passion as the musical. Have no fear of going 'over the top' for what is truly 'too much' will be toned down later. And because many lines will be cut when rehearsals begin, the incoming director and actors will need all the emotions there are – honest anger, joy, fear and surprise – to create the stuff musicals are made of.

Clean Copy

Working with a word processor is a great help, and I know many librettists like myself who do so. The processor avoids one of the most boring tasks that librettists and lyricists are faced with. Retyping. And it allows us to see our work while it is still malleable and changeable, while the ideas are flowing and vague. Then when they go into print it makes it so much easier to rewrite a page.

I also know other librettists who swear by their trusty type-writers. Still others who don't type but have someone to do it for them, but no one can proceed any further without at least half a dozen copies of the libretto. Most of these will be distributed to the collaborators, and one or two will be retained by the librettist. We are never dismayed if, even after the first story conference, those are discarded and new ones are called for. That's progress. And scripts change, sometimes daily in pre-production. A musical must go through many drafts while being born.

Every librettist should keep a copy of all his old drafts. As a libretto develops into a fully fledged musical, and other collaborators come into the picture, a script can often go too far afield from the original conception and become a hodge-podge that has the stamp of no one individual's personality. I am convinced that this is where the books of so many musicals go astray. Critics are quick to pick up this and sink a fledgling musical that sounds like a conglomeration rather than a collaboration, so everyone must be vigilant along the way. It is good to look back over the work, or more often and better still, *think back* over the work to see if this final – but albeit first – draft of the musical still retains the glowing idea that inspired everyone in the first place. If not, it may need to be rewritten, scenes restored and speeches retrieved. Then one is always grateful to have the originals to hand.

7 ADDING THE SONGS

Spotting the Scenes to be Musicalised. Taking Dramatic Climaxes from the Libretto. Writing For Character. Working Through Words and Music To a Completed Song. Staging the Song. Work Methods – Working in Order vs Skipping Around; Pulling Tunes and Titles Out of Your Trunk. Songs that Come With a Struggle. Comedy Songs. List Songs. Soliloquy. The Love Song. Reprises. Recordable vs Book Songs. Concerted Numbers. Production Numbers. Key Choices and Transpositions. Consistency in the Score – Creating Unity; Writing a Lead Sheet; Writing a Piano Score. Anticipating the Orchestration. Copyright.

SPOTTING THE SCENES TO BE MUSICALISED

The process referred to as 'spotting' begins once the libretto, that is, the second draft, has been delivered to those who will be responsible for creating the songs, unless the musical will be a through-sung one. Whether it is a team or a single person who will be creating the music and lyrics, this next step is the most crucial one in the life of any musical.

A composer needs to worry less about what has come to be known as 'theatre-opera', where everything or nearly everything is sung, although the obvious difficulty of setting this kind of libretto to music is to ensure that *everything gets equal weight* and nothing stands out. 'Where did you put the news

170

paper?' becomes as vital a question as 'Will you love me for ever?'

Mozart was able to solve this problem by having the unimportant plot information accompanied only by a harpsichord, saving the entrance of the full orchestra for the arias, each of which was devoted to a specific emotion. Audiences then learned to accept the convention. But as opera progressed (so its creators thought) towards increasing believability, this very start-the-music, stop-the-music plagued its originators. Enter operetta and musical comedy and the same sheeplike public was now forced to learn to accept this convention. Although the through-sung musical is presently making inroads, our musical stage is still heavily weighted in the start-stop tradition. And so in these cases dialogue, scenes, ideas must all now be transformed into musical numbers. The script may be plundered and raped in the quest for moments that 'sing' better than they 'speak'. There is nothing wrong with being a 'dialogue thief', as Sheldon Harnick calls himself.* 'I tend to take the best jokes of the book I am working with and put them into the songs so I get the credit and the book-writer doesn't.'

Often these moments are obvious, sometimes a whole scene cries out to be turned into singing and thereby develop the characters. At other times a tender exchange will patently call for a love song, but more often the song-clues are buried in the text. They are generally easy to dig out if you know where to look and approach the libretto with imagination.

The author of *Green Grow the Lilacs*, Lynn Riggs, gave his hero Curley a small and charmingly descriptive speech to Laurey, early in the play. Oscar Hammerstein's perspicacity however, expanded the charm into a memorable song – 'The Surrey with the Fringe on Top'. Here is the speech that inspired it, followed by some of Hammerstein's lyrics:

A bran' new surrey with fringe on the top four inches long – and yeller! *and two white horses a-rarin and faunchin' to go! You'd shore ride like a queen*

---

*Fred Ebb confesses to a similar way of working with the librettist's dialogue. 'You may reshape what may be given to you as a dialogue scene so that it comes out as song. Particularly in *Cabaret*, it seems we did that. Joe Masteroff wrote the whole pineapple exchange. That was a dialogue scene.' [The pineapple song is one of the most charming, lighter, subplot songs in the stage musical. Omitted from the film version because the landlady and her fruiterer consort had been replaced by a younger team, the song chronicles the landlady's overwhelming surprise and joy at receiving an unlikely gift, a fresh pineapple in depression-ridden 1937 Germany.]

settin' up in that *carriage! Feel like you had a gold crown set on your head,
'th diamonds in it big as goose eggs ... And this yere rig has got four fine
side-curtains, case of a rain. And isinglass winders to look out of! And a red
and green lamp set on the dashboard, winkin' like a lightnin' bug! Don't you
wish they was sich a rig, though? Nen you could go to the party and do a
hoe-down till mornin' 'f you was a mind to. Nen drive home, the sun a-
peekin' at you over the ridge, purty and fine.*

*When I take you out tonight with me.
Honey here's the way it's goin' to be:
You will sit behind a team of snow white horses.
In the slickest rig you ever see!*

REFRAIN

*Chicks and ducks and geese better scurry
When I take you out in the surrey,
When I take you out in the surrey with the fringe on top.*

*Watch that fringe and see how it flutters
When I drive them high steppin' strutters,
Nosey-pokes 'il peep thru' their shutters and their eyes will pop!*

*The wheels are yeller, the upholstery's brown,
The dashboard's genuine leather.
With isinglass curtains y'can roll right down,
In case there's a change in the weather.*

*Two bright sidelights winkin' and blinkin'
Ain't no finer rig I'm a-thinkin'
You can keep yer rig if you're thinkin' 'at I'd keer to swap
Fur that shiny, little surrey with the fringe on the top!**

A songwriter like Frank Loesser, always on the lookout for the
moment that sings, must have been touched by the following
dialogue in Sidney Howard's play *They Knew What They
Wanted*. He decided to give his 'hit' ballad in his Broadway
opera, *The Most Happy Fella* to the handsome young drifter
on the farm. Here are the lines that inspired the song 'Joey'.

JOE: I only intended to stay a few days. I'm that way, see? I been here
      goin' on five months now.
AMY: Is that all?

* Hammerstein's lyric (written before the music was created) was set to a country, barnyard-
pecking sound in Richard Rodgers's music for this charmer.

JOE: That's the longest I ever stayed any one place since I was old enough to dress myself.

AMY: You *have* been a rover.

JOE: I been all over – with the Wobblies, you see. Before I come here, that is.

AMY: What did you used to do?

JOE: Cherries an' hops – melons down in the Imperial an' oranges down south an' the railroad an' the oilfields . . . Before I come here. When I come here I just stayed. Maybe I was gettin' tired of bummin'. Now I'm tired of this.*

Turning a dramatic scene into song is more obvious if the locale and time are the same, but it takes more vision to cross international borders and adapt different mores. Perhaps it is hindsight because 'If I Loved You' is a revered classic, but the dialogue Ferenc Molnar created in his mid-European play *Liliom* seems tailor-made for song, yet it took a great imagination to transfer the lovers from mid-Hungary to the New England setting that Rodgers and Hammerstein chose for *Carousel*.

LILIOM: But you wouldn't dare to marry anyone like me, would you?

JULIE: I know that . . . that . . . if I loved any one . . . it wouldn't make any difference to me what he . . . even if I died for it.

LILIOM: But you wouldn't marry a rough guy like me – that is . . . eh . . . if you loved me.

JULIE: Yes I would . . . If I loved you, Mr Liliom.†

Sometimes the setting of a song can make pages and pages of libretto redundant. In the end of this very play *Liliom*, Molnar uses six and a half pages describing Liliom's (Billy's) death. Rodgers's and Hammerstein's moving 'You'll Never Walk Alone', accomplishes far more in twelve eloquent lines.

Librettists who are lyricists as well very often have definite

---

*The exquisite verse of 'Joey' compares the ripening crops to perfumed women. He senses the odour of Oregon cherries, Texas avocados, Arizona sugarbeet and confesses that he must follow the wind to the ripened crops. Thus the songwriter adds another dimension to the dialogue.

†Richard Rodgers, himself an excellent lyricist, was unable to solve the problem of this oblique love song. He felt that this 'dialogue is awkward, hesitant, slightly disconnected – as the two leading characters try to express their feeling. [But then] Oscar caught the mood in a lyric that eloquently expressed the emotions of these two young people.'

ideas about where the songs should come and are often known to lead their composers into the songs.*

Yet it is often hard to know where the ideas come from for setting songs or spotting them into the dialogue of a play. Most lyricists are like squirrels, storing away the nuggets of their experiences and waiting for the moment when they will be appropriate for a show. Sometimes these moments seem to emerge from the subconscious.†

If the songwriting team has superstar status in the realm of Kander and Ebb, or Rice and Webber, they may decide to create moments for characters that don't exist, or even for situations that are not in the play. Speaking of 'If You Could See Her Through My Eyes', from *Cabaret*, lyricist Fred Ebb recalls:

I dreamed it. I had a dream. What happened on this runway was that Joel Grey came out, and there was a gorilla in a tutu. That's the truth. No words, no music, but that was the image. And then I told Hal [Prince, the director] ... and he thought it was kind of baroque ... and then I tried to get a song – I know it is silly – that would fit that image ... Eventually this song came. It was him, [Joel Grey] loving this gorilla. And at the end he said, 'And if you could see her through my eyes, she wouldn't look Jewish at all.' So the song could serve to show how anti-Semitism was creeping in ... We called Hal on the phone, I sang it to

---

*In writing a Broadway opera, *Molette*, Tom Shepard recalls, 'When Sheldon [Harnick] handed me the libretto it was pretty clear what would be recitative and what formal composition. To a large degree he spelled it out. He'd be very explicit in terms of stage directions and if something was an aria, you knew it. You knew it even from the way it looked on the page.'

†When Alan Jay Lerner was writing *Camelot* he needed an oblique love song for King Arthur to reaffirm his love. He says he got the idea several years before from his old friend Erich Maria Remarque who had just married the tempestuous movie star, Paulette Goddard. 'One night when we were having dinner, I said to Erich (not seriously) "How do you get along with this wild woman?" He replied: "Beautifully. There is never an argument." "Never an argument?" I asked incredulously. "Never," he replied. "We will have an appointment one evening, and she charges into the room crying, 'Why aren't you ready? You always keep me waiting. Why do you ...?!' I look at her with astonishment and say, 'Paulette! Who did your hair? It's absolutely ravishing.' She says, 'Really? Do you really like it?' 'Like it?' I reply. 'You're a vision. Let me see the back ... Tonight,' I say 'you look eighteen years old.' And that is the end of her rage." I was as amused as I was admiring and I said to him: "Erich, one day I will have to write a song about that," The song was "How To Handle a Woman" which ends:

The way to handle a woman is to love her,
Simply love her, merely love her
Love her, love her.'

Actually the lyric might have said, the way to handle a woman especially when she is enraged is to flatter her.

him over the phone and he really loved it. He wanted very much to go with it. And in fact, we did go with it.*

The libretto may be further amplified beyond the wishes of even the most famous songwriters who are not always the supreme arbiters; they may have to bow to superstar performers. As already mentioned, Ethel Merman was powerful enough to overrule the legendary Irving Berlin and grab 'There's No Business Like Showbusiness' for herself, even though it had been written into the libretto as a plot-song to inveigle Annie Oakley to join an itinerant troupe of performers in *Annie Get Your Gun*, and Nell Carter, after TV stardom, had enough popularity to wheedle an extra solo in the *Ain't Misbehavin'* revival of 1988, and thus turn what had been an ensemble show into a starring vehicle.

The librettist (assuming that he is not also the lyricist) has the least clout of the creative triumvirate. In most cases he has no choice but to capitulate and adjust his script accordingly, for, although he is the one given the blame if the show is a flop and forgotten everywhere except in the royalties department, if the show is a hit, his voice carries little weight.

The songs that are spotted and inserted into the libretto will rarely be the ones that theatre audiences will hear, but the positions where they occur *will most often be places that will be musicalised*. It is simply that most songwriters, at this point, have not come to an exact distillation of what concepts the show needs until the production is further on.† Sheldon Harnick confesses:

---

*There was indeed much discussion over this song, pros and con of keeping the gorilla and the word Jewish. The final acceptance and the decision *not* to pull any punches are a testament to the visionary power and fearless honesty of all the collaborators in this outstanding musical.

† Stephen Sondheim wrote two 'final' songs trying to resolve *Company* on a positive note: 'Happily Ever After', a scathing indictment of marriage, and 'Marry Me a Little', a tepid endorsement of the same subject. Neither seemed right. Finally, he came to the crystallisation of the concept of the entire musical in a third song, 'Being Alive', which states in essence that marriage may be biting, unpleasant and unsatisfactory, but singleness is impossible. It is one of his most brilliant creations.

Jerry Bock says he and Sheldon Harnick wrote six versions of *Fiddler on the Roof*'s final exodus number, the moving 'Anatevka', and 'something like fourteen songs [for Perchik] until we finally got to "Now I Have Everything"'.

But the record for backbreaking effort is probably held by John Kander and Fred Ebb. In creating their first major Broadway show, *Flora, The Red Menace* for Liza Minnelli, the latter says, 'We worked our asses off – twenty songs for one situation. I had no ego. It was "Which do you like?" That sort of thing.'

I never mastered the knack of getting the right idea the first time around. In fact, what I found out about myself was that each draft acquainted me with another level of a character's personality, so successive drafts made the character more real to me, more three-dimensional, which in turn affected the show as a whole. I always took to heart the truism 'Shows are not written, they are rewritten.'

The first five songs written for *My Fair Lady* were 'The Ascot Gavotte', 'Just You Wait 'enry 'iggins', 'Please Don't Marry Me', (a song for Henry Higgins wherein he announced his resolve to remain a bachelor), 'Lady Liza' (another song for Higgins to calm Eliza's misgivings before she goes to that all-important ball) and 'Say a Prayer For Me Tonight', which would calm her own apprehension. Three of the five were discarded.*

Although the songwriter(s) respect the work of the librettist, they are not, nor should they be, too literal in their examination of the script, for their songs have to help the play's characters achieve three dimensions. It is their imagination *coupled* with that of the librettist that can make an inspired work. One can see below how adaptor-lyricist Alan Jay Lerner took Shaw's rather prosaic speech for Henry Higgins several giant steps further in *My Fair Lady*.

... I suppose the woman wants to live her own life; and the man wants to live his; and each tries to drag the other on to the wrong track. One wants to go north and the other south; and the result is that both have to go east, though they both hate the east wind. So here I am, a confirmed bachelor, and likely to remain so.

---

* 'Say A Prayer For Me Tonight' was used in Lerner and Loewe's next musical – this time written for the screen – *Gigi*. Benny Green in *A Hymn to Him* reflects that there are 'striking parallels between the two plays, and especially between the two heroines, both of whom begin as ugly ducklings, both of whom are taken in hand by a sophisticated man, and both of whom fall in love with their mentor'. At the time *Gigi* was first seen, several critics complained that the songs sounded like the remnants left over from *My Fair Lady*. There was some truth in the observation, but it had nothing to do with any failure on the part of Lerner and Loewe to change gears from Shaw to Colette. It was simply that the basic situation of each play was identical.

The partners had a difference of opinion over the merits of 'Say A Prayer For Me'. Lerner disliked the song, saying of its disappearance from the score 'I was not sad to see it go, I never liked it. Fritz did. I told him I thought it sounded like a cello solo. He said it *did* sound like a cello solo, but a very nice cello solo. It would never have found its way into *Gigi* except Fritz, that dirty dog, played it one night for Arthur Freed and Vincente Minelli when I was not around, and the following morning I was outvoted three to one.'

Lerner later retracted, saying that the sequence in the picture in which Leslie Caron sings the song to her cat, 'was one of the most touching moments in the film'.

In 'I'm An Ordinary Man', some of which is quoted below, Lerner and Loewe amplified Shaw's diatribe about the impossibility of a woman in a man's life. The song also provides a comic interlude in the first act that is lacking in Shaw's speech, and with its musical shifts from slow speech-singing to rapid annoyance, the orchestration and tempi help to punctuate Higgins's frustration with Eliza. In fleshing out Higgins's character it allows us to laugh at the selfishness which permits him to comprehend no point of view other than his own. It also exposes his erudition and snobbishness. But despite his self-proclaimed 'ordinariness' and his generalising about women, we find him quite naïve. This naïvety plus his vitriol produces, in his case, charm.

SONG: **I'M AN ORDINARY MAN**

I'm an ordinary man;
Who desires nothing more
Than just the ordinary chance
To live exactly as he likes
And do precisely what he wants.
An average man am I
Of no eccentric whim;
Who likes to live his life
Free of strife,
Doing whatever he thinks is best for
him.

But let a woman in your life
And your serenity is through
She'll redecorate your home
From the cellar to the dome
Then get on to the enthralling
Fun of overhauling
You.

Oh, let a woman in your life
And you are up against the wall!
Make a plan and you will find
She has something else in mind;
And so rather than do either
You do something else that neither
Likes at all.

TAKING DRAMATIC CLIMAXES FROM THE LIBRETTO

Every dramatist builds towards climaxes, turning points with which he hopes to keep audiences on the edge of their seats; in musical theatre this can be even more exciting because tense moments can get an added emotional kick from song. Sadness, humour, malevolence, unmitigated joy – in fact, all the strong emotions are wonderfully amplified by music.

Often it is in soliloquy (*see* page 199) that this crucial change is communicated to the audience. In *Carousel*, Billy Bigelow decides to pull off a robbery and although his noble motive is to get money for his unborn child, the result will lead to his death. The whole plot and the whole second act depend on this. Rodgers and Hammerstein made it valid and more moving than words alone could be in their famous eight minute 'Soliloquy'. Another turning point is to be found in the delicious (no pun intended) 'Ice Cream' number from *She Loves Me*. Preceding it, the heroine, Amalia, who called in to her job pretending to be sick, has just been brought ice cream when she was visited by Georg, the head of the shop where she works. These two have a running feud throughout the play, and each has been corresponding with a 'dear friend' whom they have come to love through their letters. They don't suspect it is each other until Georg sees Amalia waiting at their appointed rendezvous. Of course he is unable to talk to her about it. Shortly before the 'Ice Cream' number he invents a fat, bald, older gentleman for the 'dear friend', and leaves Amalia who will write to him. Here is Sheldon Harnick's brilliant lyric for this turning point:

Dear Friend ...
   I am so sorry about last night
   It was a nightmare in every way
   But together you and I
   Will laugh at last night some day.
(Meditating)
   Ice Cream
   He bought me ice cream ...
   Vanilla ice cream
   Imagine that!
   Ice cream,
   And for the first time
   We were together
   Without a spat.
   Friendly ...
   He was so friendly,
   That isn't like him.
   I'm simply stunned.
   Will wonders never cease?

Will wonders never cease?
It's been a most peculiar day.
Will wonders never cease
Will wonders never cease
Where was I? Oh ...
(Rereading)
I am so sorry about last night, it was a nightmare in every way, but together you and I will laugh at last night some day ... I sat there waiting in that café
   And never guessing that you were fat
(She crosses this out)
   That you were near.
   You were outside looking bald ...
Oh my ...
(She takes a new piece of paper)

Dear Friend ...
  I am so sorry about last night ...
(Meditating)
  Last night I was so nasty
  Well, he deserved it ...
  But even so ...
  That Georg
  Is not like this Georg,
  This is a new Georg
  That I don't know
Somehow it all reminds me
  Of Dr Jekyll and Mr Hyde,
  For right before my eyes
  A man that I despise
  Has turned into a man I like!

It's almost like a dream,
And strange as it may seem
He came to offer me vanilla
Ice cream!

Another brilliant turning point is the first act curtain of *Sweeney Todd*. The moment finds the revengeful barber needing to dispose of the body of a competitor whose throat he has just slashed. Mrs Lovett, enamoured of Todd for a long time, asks him, 'What are we going to do with him?' and Todd answers disinterestedly, 'Later on, when it's dark, we'll take him to some secret place and bury him.'

'Well of course we could do that, I don't suppose there's any relatives going to come poking around looking for him. But ...' Mrs Lovett declares, and then a chord from the orchestra indicates a light-bulb has just been turned on inside her brain, and she adds 'You know me. Sometimes ideas pop into me head and I keep thinking ...' (She begins to sing, and although the music enters almost innocuously, this is the kind of moment that is best served in song – the musical pauses can be built into the dialogue, and the number can become more and more animated.) 'Seems a downright shame' ...

TODD: Shame?
MRS LOVETT: *Seems an awful waste ...*
  Such a nice plump frame
  Wot's-his-name
  Has ...
  Had ...
  Has ...
  Nor it can't be traced.
  Business needs a lift ...

> *Think of it as thrift,*
> *As a gift . . .*
> *If you get my drift . . .*
> *No?*
> *Seems an awful waste.*
> *I mean,*
> *With the price of meat what it is,*
> *When you get it,*
> *If you get it . . .*

TODD: (Becoming aware) Ah!

MRS LOVETT: Good, you got it.

> *Take for instance,*
> *Mrs Mooney and her pie shop*
> *Business never better, using only pussycats and toast.*
> *And a pussy's good for maybe six or seven at the most.*
> *And I'm sure they can't compare as far as taste . . .*

As the gruesome humour continues, they both imagine meat pies made from humans in various professions, (piccolo player pie is piping hot; politician is so oily it's served with a doily, etc.) ending the act with a full-blown waltz called 'A Little Priest'. From that number to the end of the play Sweeney embarks on his bloody search for fresh victims. All this leads to the melodramatic finale and to Todd's and Mrs Lovett's eventual downfall.

But the turning point is not always so obvious. Sometimes it may even be achieved by a happy accident. Harvey Schmidt, composer of *The Fantasticks* remembers that when they had cast Jerry Orbach as El Gallo (his first role), 'we took what had been a rape speech in the Barnard [Colombia University] production (because he was so marvellous we wanted to give him more to do musically) and turned it into "The Rape Song".'*

Generally, after living with the plot for a while, the turning points will emerge and make themselves clear. They will invariably be the most songful, and often the most moving moments of the entire score.

---

* When it was mentioned that it would seem a natural moment for musicalisation, that the first act would be constructed around the explosive turning point of 'The Rape Song', Tom Jones, the show's lyricist admitted, 'If we had been more knowledgeable about things, we probably would have done it in that way for those reasons. We were knowledgeable about some things, but not much about the structure of musicals.' [The song is not as sexual as its title would suggest, the 'rape' that is planned is to steal the young girl away from her father, more like an elopement.]

WRITING FOR CHARACTER

'Larry Hart, brilliant as he was, was not a dramatic lyric writer, nor was there any reason for him to be,' says Alan Jay Lerner. 'A musical in the twenties and thirties had no dramatic or emotional validity and the wit was the lyric writer's, never the character's. Oscar Hammerstein, on the other hand, was very much a dramatic lyric writer and as even the most elementary primer on theater will tell you, with *Oklahoma!* he and Dick Rodgers radically changed the course of the musical theater. The musical comedy became the musical play.'

Things have progressed more and more in that direction, so that today's musical almost does not need specific extractable songs. But what every musical *does* need is character identification through its lyrics or a kind of musical signature for its protagonists. Without these essentials it is sure to become unbelievable and sink under a critical barrage.*

When Alan Jay Lerner was writing *Camelot* and approached King Arthur's first number, both he and Fritz Loewe knew that they had to show him frightened and shy at meeting his bride. The number 'I Wonder What the King is Doing Tonight' is full of amusing terror in the lyric, 'that appalling clamouring/ that sounds like a blacksmith hammering/ is merely the banging of his royal knees', and replete with short gasped melodic phrases 'He's numb!/ He shakes!/ He quails!/ He quakes!'

Guinevere's entrance almost immediately after needed to reveal the bloodthirsty, romantic yearning of an adolescent girl longing for knights in armour to woo her with feats of heroism. Her song was 'Where Are the Simple Joys of Maidenhood?' and in it she asks her patron saint, 'Shan't I be young before I'm old?' Here again the melody, using long spinning phrases, almost like a madrigal, adds a subtext of subtle elegance to lines like 'Shall a feud not begin for me?/ Shall kith not kill their kin for me?' We know we are in medieval times, but are well aware that we are in the theatre and in the hands of a lyricist with a strong sense of humour.

---

* Andrew Lloyd Webber's 1989 London success *Aspects of Love* is a notable example of the plot taking over the whole musical. Although sung from beginning to end in quasi-operatic style, the music never enthralls us, but the libretto which adheres closely to the excellent book from which it was adapted intrigues us with its twists and turns.

To present Lancelot, the team rightly felt the melody should have a strong, French feeling, which it does and with the pompous lyric, 'C'est Moi', is an almost comical exaggeration of his overblown dedication to righteousness, chivalry and chastity. The lyric often places the adjective after the noun for humorous literal translation. ('A French Prometheus unbound/ To serve at the Table Round'.)

Thus, each of these characters is given quite a different emphasis, even though each gets a slightly humorous song, the melodic and lyric tone are particular to the individuals, and yet, (and this hardest of all to do) each has the *flavour* of fifteenth-century Camelot without being a museum piece. Lerner, while setting one foot in contemporary Broadway, keeps one foot in Arthurian antiquity.

WORKING THROUGH WORDS AND MUSIC TO A COMPLETED SONG

Every team or every solo songwriter* will choose similar methods for spotting, creating climaxes and developing character through the songs they write. They will probably have healthy arguments about the merit of some of their work, but their working methods may vary. Richard Rodgers told me that he and Oscar Hammerstein often wrote several songs for a situation in their plays and then much later selected the one that appealed most.†

When writing *Fiddler on the Roof*, lyricist Sheldon Harnick says, 'we would both read the source, [the libretto] then Jerry [Bock, the composer] would go off to his studio to work on musical ideas which he would then put on to tape . . . to get the momentum going, it was much simpler to have music first. Then I didn't have to search for the form. Lorenz Hart also liked to have Richard Rodgers write the music first and then he would present the composer with the completed lyric.

---

*Thomas Shepard believes 'a fine music and words man like Jerry Herman could look at a script and know where the songs should come.' He is certain that pages of dialogue could be removed because they would sing better than they would play. Of Mr Herman, he adds, 'he's underrated because he's so skilful, neat, elegant – very much like Irving Berlin.'

† Mary Rodgers, an eminent composer herself, says her father told *her*, he never wrote more than was called for in the libretto, except when they were on the road, making changes. Perhaps he was idly boasting to a younger theatre man.

(Sometimes he would deliver several startlingly different lyrics to the same tune, which not only proves Hart's virtuosity but betrays that Rodgers's music then did not have so definite a profile as to suggest an inevitable lyric.) Later, when Rodgers worked with Hammerstein, and the words became an indispensable part of the play, the lyric was written first. But in most of their scores there are one or two songs in which the music was written first.

The tradition of having the music written first which is still the most prevalent among established songwriting teams began many years ago when operettas were imported from France and Austria into Britain and America. These scores mostly by Offenbach, Lehar and Strauss were so well known that lyricists had merely to translate and adapt the melodies to the English language. Conversely (and except for Gilbert and Sullivan), whenever British or American librettists wrote their own lyrics and expected the Continental composers to set them, they were horrified at the result. Composers who had emigrated to Britain and the United States were unaccustomed to the English language and created abortive and laughable accents on their lyrics.*

There was an additional reason for ensuring that the music precede the lyrics: ragtime, followed in the 1920s by jazz. Most versifiers in the early part of the century preferred to let the composer have his head and lead the way into these unfamiliar rhythms. And as dancing became more and more of a craze indulged in by people of all ages, the songs had to be danceable. The lyricist felt it was safer to trail along after the composer. Oscar Hammerstein calls this habit of writing the music first with the words after, 'an illogical one, but not entirely without compensating virtues. Writing this way,' he continues, 'I have frequently fallen into the debt of my composers for words and ideas that might never have occurred to me had they not been suggested by music. If one has a feeling for music – and anyone who wants to write lyrics had better have this feeling – the repeated playing of a melody may create a mood or start a train

---

*One of the most amusing misaccentuations I know of occurs in *The Rise and Fall of Mahagonny*, an opera whose libretto was supposedly set somewhere in the United States. It was written by Bertolt Brecht with music by Kurt Weill. The hero's aptly chosen Irish-American name, Jimmy Mahoney, invariably comes out as Jeemie *Ma*honey in Kurt Weill's musical accentuation, immediately destroying the author's statement that Jimmy is a red-blooded Yankee.

of thought that results in an unusual lyric. Words written in this way are likely to conform to the spirit of the music. It is difficult to fit words into the rigid framework of a composer's meter, but this very confinement might also force an author into the concise eloquence which is the very essence of poetry ... In our collaboration, Mr Rodgers and I have no definite policy except one of complete flexibility. We write songs in whatever way seems best for the subject with which we are dealing, and the purposes of the song in the story which we are telling.'

In non-collaborative work, the songwriter generally gets the concept and title, perhaps a feel of the rhythm, works a few bars of music, and then – and this is important – moves directly to the end of the song. This is the way Jerry Herman and Stephen Sondheim, the theatre's two most eminent composer-lyricists, operate. Herman says, 'I construct my songs like a jigsaw puzzle. For example, I'll get a title idea and musicalise the opening phrase, and then skip to the end. Knowing I am going to end the song "I Won't Send Roses", with the phrase and "roses suit you so", I musicalised that then I went back and filled in the middle, like doing an enormous jigsaw puzzle – that's my way.'

Sondheim's method is remarkably similar. 'When you're wearing two hats writing to your own music, you're the other person [the lyricist]. You don't want to hamstring yourself as a composer. That's the easy part of working with yourself, you can make the adjustments as you go along. Once the lyric starts to take shape, I don't want to get too far ahead of the music, and vice versa. Then it's a matter of developing both simultaneously. I generally do it section by section, and I generally make a kind of long line and know what the key relationships are going to be in the various sections of the song and how the general long line is going to go – down or up, or cover the third or fifth or whatever that is. But it is just a matter of shaping a little bit at a time, like doing a jigsaw puzzle. It gradually closes in until it's all there ... I think it's useful to write the last line first – not necessarily the last line, but the thought at the end.'*

---

* Frank Loesser, who wrote pop songs before he wrote for the theatre had his own way. He used to put all the book material into the verse, so 'you would have a verse that goes something like "Thanks for electing me governor, you'll all be paid back. I'll fulfill my promises to you, you really voted for the right man." Then the *chorus* goes, "How'm I Doin?/ Hey, Twee-twee-twee, twa-twa," etc.'

STAGING THE SONG

How deep need the songwriter delve into his imagined staging of song? I've always believed that if the creator pictures, and better yet, hears the song *being sung* on stage, a more theatrical work will emerge. Of course when a composer is his own lyricist it is easier to imagine the whole number being performed on stage, and most composer-lyricists working in the theatre have a built-in theatrical sense. In practice, and always, once the show gets on its feet, lyricist-librettists generally talk to the stage director about staging while the composer talks to the musical director. As Tom Shepard puts it, 'Obviously you cross-pollinate all the time, but basically I am far more worried about the music being performed wonderfully and cleanly, while Sheldon [Harnick] is far more concerned with the dramatic values.'

But any concept of staging that inspires the songwriter may simply be a suggestion for it certainly does not mean that the director or choreographer will be forced to use that vision. They may modify it or 'improve it'. Because of its flexibility, Mitch Douglas calls the mental images that come to a composer or lyricist, 'turning oneself theatrically on. Whatever mental image works for you as a writer is fine. Some people work verbally. Wouldn't it be funny if I wrote a song where I rhymed all the words with "port"; someone else may say, "this scene is in a dressing room and the dressing room is going to have a bunch of fans on the walls, what if I let each fan have a different meaning?"' But Mr Douglas cautions all of us to let the people in charge of staging actually *do* the staging, just use the scene for inspiration.

Stephen Sondheim feels differently. 'We should stage each number within an inch of its life, in our own heads when we write.' And Jerry Herman agrees. He will often visualise specific staging. Of the opening number in *La Cage Aux Folles*, 'I Put a Little More Mascara On,' he says:

> I got this idea of the audience seeing the transformation from a middle-aged man in a tatty bathrobe into a glamorous creature named Zaza ... By using all the MGM tricks I lived through ... I *see* the number. I *saw* Albin physically change into Zaza. I saw the makeup table and the color of the bathrobe. I described the scene in detail to Theoni Aldredge [the costume designer] and Arthur Laurents [the director]. I said 'I see steps

coming out at this moment in the lyric, and at the end I see Albin descending a step at a time.' Everything I visualized was on the stage. I was fortunate enough this time to be working with a team that respected and did *exactly* what I visualized. It's thrilling for me to see my dream actually on the stage, not just in music and lyrics, but the whole picture I had in my head.

Sondheim not only sees colour and design, but often imagines a whole dramatic playlet which he describes amusingly: 'We should be able to tell the director and the choreographer, "All right, now when he starts to sing the song he's sitting down in a chair. Now around the second quatrain he gets up and crosses to the fireplace and throws her note in the fireplace, then he sings the third quatrain directly to the audience, then he goes back and shoots himself and sings the fourth quatrain." '*

Songwriters have been known to fall into the trap of murdering their musical's chance of production by imagining a staging so costly, requiring such a lavish set or needing so gigantic a production that producers will back away. We generally start by staging the intimate numbers as we write them and progressing from there to the more lavish. But always keeping in mind the musical's scope and budget.†

WORK METHODS

Every team or solo songwriter has developed a method of creation that ensures its best product. As noted on page 182, whether words or music come first, what is important is that there is a meeting of ideas. In order to accomplish this, Sheldon Harnick, who collaborated with Jerry Bock on *Fiddler on the Roof*, evolved a method:

---

*The importance of the creators imagining a number's staging is brought home in Sheldon Harnick's statement that 'Jerry Bock and I once wrote a number for *Fiorello*. They couldn't find a way to stage it. So it was dropped.'

† Stephen Sondheim's staging of 'The Worst Pies in London' from *Sweeney Todd* is a good example of how to build the total dramatic scene effectively into the song. Here it is again conceived as part of the creation *by* the songwriter, and it will be part of the number for ever, for the staging is written into *the very notes of the song*. There are rhythms, drumbeats and rests in the song where the singer must slap the dough, flour the board, form the pies, scrunch a bug found in the dough under her foot, and the like. Heavy staging like this may sometimes be resented by an insecure director aiming to stamp 'his personality' on a production or a star not wishing to use a predecessor's interpretation, but truly imaginative staging by composer and lyricist will give the number a life that no director or star could possibly breathe into it.

We would both read the source material, [the libretto, together.] Then, Jerry [Bock, the composer] would go off to his studio to work on musical ideas which he then put on tape. The tape might have anything from a dozen to two dozen musical ideas worked out. I must say that on the tape Jerry would say, 'Well, I see this number for the butcher' or 'I think this number is for somebody else.' My reaction was almost always, 'Wrong. That's not the butcher.' The most exciting numbers were almost always the ones where I would hear his voice saying 'I don't know what this is.' For some reason, those were always the best.

Bock and Harnick finally came to agreement and produced songs where music and lyrics seem to have a seamless unity. Stephen Sondheim believes in an even closer collaboration and gives this advice:

When music and lyrics are done by different people, the best way for the lyricist to collaborate with the composer is in the same room whenever possible. Very close collaboration is the best. First you must talk very clearly about what the number is to accomplish emotionally, in terms of the plot, in terms of the character. I mean *overtalk* it so you are sure you are both writing the same song. Then there's more chance that you'll be able to work together, to give each other enough kind of supple space to invent and not be restricted.

Working in Order vs Skipping Around

As a kid, I remember eating my favourite food, the meat off my plate, first and then plodding through the vegetables. There is no reason why this same principle should not be applied to writing songs, for actually, if the libretto has been well organised, one can always come back and work on the sections of the plot that do not immediately inspire you. In fact, working on a section that attracts you enormously can often create an inspired work.* There are, however, two cautions, the first being the opening, as found in Jerry Bock's following words:

---

* If one is lucky, inspired, and the number is essential to the plot, those songs written in non-chronological order may always remain as part of your score. Sheldon Harnick calls those moments the 'obligatory moments, moments which would have to remain no matter what changes were made in the book along the way ... One such moment I thought had to stay comes late in the first act [of *Fiddler on the Roof*], Tevye has given his oldest daughter permission to marry the tailor, even though he's already made a match for her with the butcher, and to persuade his wife, he invents a dream. I thought, "that's a moment that's always going to stay ... that dream which was written in September of 1961 ... [the show didn't premiere until three years later] was never changed."'

> Some people work in order. Sheldon [Harnick] and I are skippers ...
> except for the opening number ... It is very important for it is the key
> that opens the door to your show. So you have to be wise and tell your
> audience what's going to happen. Tell them what the evening is about.

The other caution to butterflying comes in the bio-musical.
Most of us find the events in the life are the stimuli so we work
on them in order. And as for the vegetables, once you begin
work on a number that doesn't particularly inspire you, by
thinking about it deeply, the inspiration often comes unasked
for.

Pulling Tunes and Titles Out of Your Trunk

The Gershwins were justly proud of the magnificent music
and lyrics they had created in 'The Man I Love', and every
time it was bounced out of a show they inserted it in another
until it became a hit; the Kern-Wodehouse 'Bill' went through
several incarnations (once even suffering the indignity of being
sung to a dollar 'bill') before settling down as a moving if tear-
drenched song for Helen Morgan in *Show Boat*. But it is rare
in today's theatre, which is so dependent on tone, texture,
character and mood, that a song which was written for one
musical will be appropriate for another – even if the stories'
settings and time frames are similar. The contemporary
musical theatre no longer accepts 'hit songs' that can be sung
by any character* or transferred from show to show and still
make sense.†

In discussing his own work, Sheldon Harnick who wrote
lyrics for two musicals having scenes in a Jewish ghetto (*Fiddler
on the Roof* and *The Rothschilds*) says, 'Songs we write and
don't use do not end up being trunk songs that can be used
elsewhere. They seem to be locked into the shows for which
they were written,' as he recalls:

---

* See notes on 'There's No Business like Show Business' (page 175) and 'Say a Prayer For
Me Tonight' (page 176).

† Luther Henderson feels that 'it is only acceptable to pull songs out of your trunk when
you remember you have the license to rework them like taffy to fit this show. If you feel you
must take the song in toto you are not only restricting yourself, the song will somehow sound
like it doesn't belong in this particular show.'

One of the songs that we had written for *Fiddler* was a number early in the show called 'The Richest Man in Town'. It was a very pretty song in which Motel the tailor tells Tzeitel that he has nothing – but, because she loves him, he is the richest man in town. Well, for one reason or another, it was not used in *Fiddler*. [Obviously it would conflict with another 'rich man' song: the showstopper 'If I Were a Rich Man'.] When we did *The Rothschilds* I thought that it was an even more appropriate song for Meyer Rothschild. We didn't tell our director and producer that this was something that had come from *Fiddler* when we played it for them. When we were finished, they said, 'That's a very pretty song, but you know something, the *texture* doesn't seem right for this show.'

But not every songwriter can be so cavalier. Cy Coleman who wrote what he thought was 'a great show', [an untitled bio-musical about Eleanor Roosevelt] felt he was faced with a terrible dilemma. As he states, 'Everybody disliked the book, but the book writer didn't want anybody coming in and changing anything. So the show could never be produced. Yet the show contained one of our best scores? [The lyrics were written by Dorothy Fields.] The score didn't completely die, however, he adds. 'I raided it. We used "It's Not Where You Start", and "Scream", went into *Seesaw*. In *Barnum*, the music to "Out There", is the Teddy Roosevelt song. There's a lot more. I hated doing it, but I just figured it was good, and I wanted to do something with it.'

SONGS THAT COME WITH A STRUGGLE

There is a word in the English language that has done more to stifle creativity than any other. That word is 'inspiration', a lame excuse for dilettantes but a most annoying one for professional creators as it implies that ideas, words and music are gifts from heaven. Oscar Hammerstein always maintained that his writing was very hard work, and that no professional sat around waiting to be inspired. Like him, they went to work every day. 'Some days,' he wrote in his book, *Lyrics*, 'the work comes easier than other days, but you keep going because the chances of getting good ideas are more likely while you are trying to get them than when you are doing nothing at all.'

Hammerstein, like all lyricists and composers, struggled with lyrics, and described the process as a long wrestling match in which the lyric gets to be the enemy. While working on *The King and I* he had an especially difficult bout with the only love song in the show. It was made more difficult because Anna and the King are never, nor could the conventions of the time allow them to be, in love in the usual sense. His first draft was a song called 'Tom', to express Anna's love for her dead husband. After a month he abandoned that idea in favour of a version called 'Home'. That was finally discarded and a third called 'I Have Been in Love', was written. At last, and in his words, 'you get a death grip on it,' and he wrote 'Hello, Young Lovers', one of his most successful love songs in 'a final burst of perspiration' in forty-eight hours.

Lyric writing and music composition are hard work indeed, and I do not believe you should put a song that refuses to come easily aside while you wait for inspiration. Everyone knows that the Youmans-Caesar classic 'Tea For Two' was written in twenty minutes, but do they know about the songs that take twenty days?

Tom Jones, lyricist of *The Fantasticks*, has said he is not afraid of hard work. 'You love [a song] if it comes out perfect the first time, but I am very suspicious of depending upon a thing coming out the first time. I feel better about the ability to go back and work again and work again without losing the shape of the piece.' Even Jerry Herman often mistrusts a song that comes too easily: 'I wrote "Before the Parade Passes By" [from *Hello, Dolly*] in about twenty minutes in a hotel room in Detroit under the most awful conditions, with everyone screaming at me because the first act finale wasn't working. I love that song. I love what it says and the way it says it, the simplicity and it really just poured out ... I must add, though, I had worked on the musical and the mixmaster had been going for about a year. I had been thinking about those people and what they would say and how they would sing for a year of my life, so I don't honestly know whether I wrote "Before the Parade Passes By" in twenty minutes, or a year and twenty minutes.'

COMEDY SONGS

One of the most essential ingredients of a musical must be comedy; in fact such a large segment of the public expects hilarity during their evening watching a 'musical comedy', that the generic term refuses to be replaced with just plain 'musical'. But as the musical has marched into the modern era, what constituted comedy before has changed greatly.

In the adolescent days of the musical, comedians were brought in to do their 'schticks', frequently being given a few lines that constituted the subplot. They often stopped the show and held up the libretto while they discussed the political situation of the day (Will Rogers) or did a famous sneezing routine (Herman Bing). Shows were three, sometimes four hours in length, and once the comic performer had his audience going, he liked to keep them going. Performers were hired specifically for the purpose of distracting the audience, and since most of the show's main plot was inconsequential, to say nothing of the subplot, it was more important for audiences to leave the theatre having had a good time than for the drama to be tightly constructed or even believable.

And the humour itself was often what we find offensive today. Blacks, Jews, Irish, Orientals, homosexuals and other minorities were frequently the brunt of jokes in song and libretto. Humour, and not only burlesque humour often included dropping one's pants or stepping into some mal-odorous substance. Women, especially blondes, were generally portrayed as dumb sex objects who were always at the service of their 'hubby' or family, and secretaries, well, in mostly every show they had ludicrously large breasts, nasal voices and wiggling fannies.

But somewhere around the time of *Oklahoma!*, all that changed. Lyricists and librettists realised their audiences needed to understand and empathise with the people on stage in order to find a song amusing.* Joseph Stein puts it succinctly:

---

*William Hammerstein has a clear-cut vision of the kind of humour his father brought to the character of Ado Annie in *Oklahoma!*. 'Ado Annie, in Lynn Riggs play is a kind of moronic dim-wit and she became the butt of jokes. My father took her and made her a real buddy of Laurey's, and I thought that was a marvelous use of character and comedy. I was rehearsing a girl in the part who had never seen a performance of *Oklahoma!* and on the first day of rehearsals she began singing "I'm just a Girl Who Can't Say 'No'" in a wanton way, like a girl who just wanted to climb into bed with everybody. I had to convince her that the humour derived from Ado Annie's innocence; it had to be the comedy of charm. Just as in the finale,

'Larry Hart wrote funny lyrics, but not the kind used today which become part of the story.' Richard Kislan in his excellent book, *The Musical*, puts it more alliteratively, in those days 'comedy was cosmetic . . . now it is comedy in context.'

Fred Ebb's lyrics in *Cabaret* are often moving and trenchant. At the end of the first act, however, the script calls for a light-hearted moment during the engagement party of the Jew, Herr Schultz and his German landlady, Fraülein Schneider. This will occur prior to a malevolent scene and hymn that intimates the Nazi horror to come. Mr Ebb's song for Herr Schultz is amusing, honest and much admired by his peers. It is doubly effective because it seems exactly like the kind of song Herr Schultz would sing after a glass or two of sweet wine at his own engagement party.

> SCHULTZ: Now – the only word you have to know in order to understand this
> song is the Yiddish word 'meeskite'. 'Meeskite' means ugly, funny-
> looking. 'Meeskite' means . . . (*HE sings*)
>
> *Meeskite, meeskite,*
> *Once upon a time there was a meeskite, meeskite,*
> *Looking in the mirror he would say, 'What an awful shock,*
> *I got a face that would stop a clock.'*
>
> *Meeskite, meeskite,*
> *Such a pity on him, he's a meeskite, meeskite,*
> *God up in his heaven left him out on a shaky limb,*
> *He put a meeskite on him.*
>
> (*Spoken*) But listen, he grew up. Even meeskites grow up. (*HE sings again*)
>
> *And soon in the Chader, (that means Hebrew school)*
> *He sat beside this little girl,*
> *And when he asked her name, she replied,*
> *'I'm Pearl.'*
>
> *He ran to the Zayda (that means grandfather)*
> *And said in that screechy voice of his,*
> *'You told me I was the homeliest!*
> *Well, Gramps, you're wrong, Pearl is!*
> *Meeskite, meeskite,*
> *No one ever saw a bigger meeskite, meeskite*

---

when she comes out of the barn with Will Parker and she's got some hay stuck to the back of her dress; it's charming, you know she's discovered something she didn't know before.'

Top left: Composer Richard Rodgers and lyricist Lorenz Hart collaborated on forty-seven shows between 1926 and 1943 until Hart's alcoholism forced Rodgers to seek a more stable partner in Oscar Hammerstein. Hart, who measured 4′11″, was called the 'diminutive giant' by Alan Jay Lerner and insisted that all photographs of him showed him standing next to Rodgers seated at the piano. Top right: *On Your Toes*, which incorporated a full Balanchine classical ballet starring Vera Zorina and Jack Whiting, flopped in 1937 London which was only interested in escapist shows. Above: Revived in 1985, starring Tim Flavin and Natalia Makarovia, it was more successful.

The three biggest money-making shows of all time, all of which were brought to the stage by producer Cameron Mackintosh.
Above: *Les Misérables* the first collaboration of Schönberg-Boubil. Left: *Cats*, a British triumph that was soon to be staged in forty countries worldwide. A hit because of Gillian Lynne's slinky choreography, John Napier's junkheap scenery, Trevor Nunn's imaginative direction and Andrew Lloyd Webber's melodic setting of T.S. Eliot's verses.

Right: *The Phantom of the Opera*, (Michael Crawford) passionately cajoling Christine (Sarah Brightman) to come through the mirror with him. The work had its finger on the beauty-and-the-beast syndrome of the times.

Above: Cameron Mackintosh, who started producing shows at the age of twenty, and except for the flop with Cole Porter's *Anything Goes,* has had a long string of hits. Below: Hal Prince, the producer-director of most of Stephen Sondheim's shows, at a rehearsal of *The Phantom of the Opera* which he directed. Composer Lloyd Webber is to his right while choreographer Gillian Lynne looks on.

Above: Stephen Sondheim listening contemplatively to a play-back. Below: The opening 'Beautiful Girls' number which introduced the entire cast of *Follies* in its 1989 London revival. The rewritten libretto worked even less well than the original, but the score still shone like a diamond.

Left: Michael Ball and Ann Crumb in *Aspects of Love.* Below: Trevor Nunn at rehearsal.

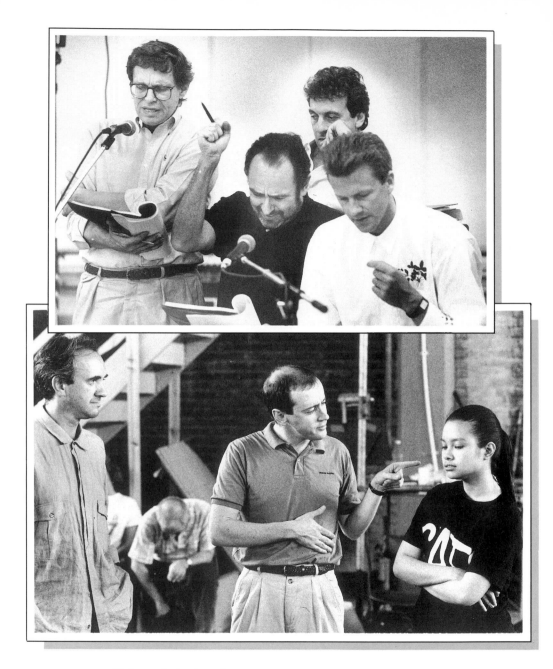

Rehearsals for *Miss Saigon*.

Top: Richard Maltby Jr., standing, who with Alain Boubil, right, wrote the lyrics. Between them, conducting is Claude-Michel Schönberg who wrote the music. Standing is David Caddick, the music supervisor. Above: Nicholas Hytner directing Kim (Lea Salonga), the tragic heroine, and The Engineer (Jonathan Pryce) her protector-pimp in *Miss Saigon*.

Left: The chorus of whores sing and dance the bombastic opening number 'The Heat is On in Saigon'.

Right: The exquisite love scene: 'The Last Night of the World' sung by Kim (Lea Salonga) and Chris (Simon Bowman).

Left: Cole Porter, who was left-handed, wrote words and music at the piano always using a pencil to avoid ink smudges.

Above right: A scene from the London production of Porter's *Anything Goes* (1936), whose landmark hits were 'Your're the Top', 'I Get a Kick Out of You', 'Blow, Gabriel, Blow' and 'All Through the Night', as well as the bouncy title song. Below: Elaine Page in the 1988 London revival, which added 'It's De-Lovely', 'Friendship' and 'Easy to Love'.

Everywhere a flaw and maybe that is the reason why
I'm going to love her till I die.
'Meeskite, meeskite,
Oh, is it a pleasure, she's a meeskite, meeskite,
She's the one I'll treasure for I thought there could never be
A bigger meeskite than me.'

So they were married.
And in a year she turned and smiled,
'I'm afraid I am going to have ... a child.'

Nine months she carried
Worrying how that child would look,
And all the cousins were worried too,
But what a turn fate took!

Gorgeous, gorgeous,
They produced a baby that was gorgeous, gorgeous,
Crowding round the cradle all the relatives aahed and oohed,
'He ought to pose for a baby food.
Gorgeous, gorgeous,
Would I tell a lie? He's simply gorgeous, gorgeous
Who'd have ever thought that we would see such a flawless gem
Out of two meeskites like them?'

Moral, moral
Yes indeed, the story has a moral, moral
Though you're not a beauty it is nevertheless quite true,
There may be beautiful things in you.

Meeskite, meeskite,
Listen to the fable of the meeskite, meeskite,
Anyone responsible for loveliness, large or small,
Is not a meeskite at all.

Mr Ebb confessed at a Dramatists' Guild discussion that he was asked by Hal Prince, the director, if the song exposing Herr Schultz's Jewishness 'could possibly be funny ... So I called my mother ... My mother told me that exact story. It was about two very unattractive people that she had known and they had this fabulous-looking child.'

'I think we are all a little bit like that. People who write tend to remember things. You store them away, and then you never know when you are going to use them or when they are going to just jump to the front of your head for some reason. But that's how that happened. It wasn't a story I really invented, it's a story I heard.'

Original or not, the humour fills out the character in the play, and that in turn enriches the whole musical.

Joe Stein amplifies the point when he tells us that the comedy songs and humour come from the situation. 'Jokes don't mean anything in the theater. They don't work. Relationships and characters are what count. If you have the right relationships and characters as a springboard, you'll find the humor. And much of the humor comes as a surprise – it's not carefully planned, as a joke would be.' Terence McNally, librettist of *The Rink*, feels pretty much the same way. 'If you're just being funny with words,' he says, 'you'll never get the kind of laugh that comes from an audience caring about your people.' And Jules Feiffer adds that the situation is more important than the basic song lyric, for 'very few songs make you hysterical with laughter when taken out of the context of the show.*

But it is more than the situation and placement that makes us laugh. For different audiences laugh in different spots, particularly at previews which are often attended by specialist groups. What is hilarious to the East Enders may be greeted with stony silence by Sloane Rangers. Those employed in the theatre who usually attended a Sunday night Actor's Benefit laugh at a script's subtleties while the ticketholders at a union benefit sit on their hands for the same material.

Russell Baker, one of America's foremost humorists, suggests laughter is sometimes invoked by peer pressure. 'Somebody has to say, "Funniest damn evening I've spent in the theater in years", and then these people will buy tickets and go, and they'll laugh. And laughter begets laughter. A small audience in a big house sits apart from one another, and it's deadly. It's as though people were insulated from each other. Put that same audience into a small house where they're packed together, and when one guy laughs it's infectious – everybody laughs.'

He adds that the essence of comedy lies in watching the unexpected. 'What's funny usually results from disappointed

---

*My personal favourite, in *Candide*, is Cunegonede's surprised song after encountering Candide, 'You Were Dead, You Know' only strikes a sense of humour when you realise the two protagonists are a pure contraption of Voltaire's imagination. Leonard Bernstein's purposely heavy-handed music adds to the amusing quality. And the number is mercifully brief. But taken out of the musical it is not funny at all, but rather senseless, almost boring.

expectations. An old woman walking down the street slips on a banana peel and falls – that's not funny. A man in a top hat slips and falls – that's funny because people in top hats aren't supposed to be *able* to fall. There's a sudden upsetting of your expectations.' Our expectations often derive from the context of the show. For example *Oklahoma!* is a homespun, wholesome, family show where every girl is virginal and every man honourable, so when Ado Annie sings 'I'm Just a Girl Who Can't Say No', it is funny not only because the lines are witty and naïve, but because it is truly a surprise. Put Ado Annie amid all the lithe prostitutes in say, *House of Flowers*, and her song would fall flat.

Additionally it is *the placement* of a humorous moment that is important. Dale Wasserman inserted 'A Little Gossip' into the ending of *Man of la Mancha*, between the scenes of Don Quixote's dying and his death and as Richard Kislan says, 'It eases the mounting gloom of the former moment as it sets up the audience for the incisive drama of the latter.' Audiences seem to enjoy the contrast of happy, sad, happy, sad which was the stock-in-trade of the old-time revue. Ballad, comedy skit, ballad, comedy skit. Somehow with their emotions thus exposed through laughter followed by tears, they seem to have a thoroughly cathartic experience.*

LIST SONGS

The list song has been a useful tool of musical theatre ever since earliest operatic times. One of the 'hits' of Mozart's day was to be found in *Don Giovanni* at the spot where Da Ponte's libretto calls for the Don's servant to list all the countries in which his master has seduced women. The song is truly comic and the audience's laughter increases as the catalogue lengthens. In truth, the list song has not changed much in the

---

*The converse is true as well. Arthur Laurents remembers: 'Because it came after the "Mr Goldstone" number with its comedy juggling and dancing, one of the sensitive songs in *Gypsy* wasn't getting a hand and Jerry [Robbins] just cut it. Jule [Styne] asked Jerry to put "Little Lamb" back in and Jerry said no. He said "It doesn't work. It's out." I remember sitting in the theatre and Jule [Styne] coming onstage – very nattily dressed as he always is – and he came down to the footlights and he said "Mr Robbins, I have spoken to the Dramatists' Guild in New York, [which has written into composers' contracts with directors that no song can be cut without the composer's permission] and I want to tell you I am withdrawing my entire score as of tonight, unless "Little Lamb" is put back. It *was* put back.'

last three hundred years. It is simply a series of parallel lines adding to the same concept.

In the then contemporary musicals of the Thirties and Forties the indisputable master of the list song was Cole Porter with Noël Coward running a close second. Porter's glib humour carried him from the well-known hits like 'I Get A Kick Out of You', in which he itemised all the things that bored him to 'Let's Do It' which mentions all the classifications of animals that can fall in love. (Heavy sexual innuendoes implied that the 'it' was much more than heavy kissing.) 'Cherry Pies Ought to be You' presents us with glittering quadruple rhymes concerning all the loving objects in his repertoire as Mercury sings to his beloved Chloë of things like Don Juan, Rita Kahn, Cupid with nothing on and Leda without her swan. Reprising the same number for a quarrelling Niki and Juno, Porter lists only hateful things, like withered grass, lethal gas, sour old applesass, Balaam's ass. Because he rhymed so glibly and with such an irreverent admixture across the centuries,* every one of his shows was expected to have a list song. And he never seems to have disappointed. A special favourite of mine is an unjustly obscure gem called 'The Physician' sung by a *Nymph Errant*. It lists all the parts of her body the physician wants to make love to and succeeds more than most list songs for it adds another dimension – unrequited love. I quote a few lines below, but the entire song which is quite lengthy is worth investigation because it accomplishes what all good theatre music should: it is consistent with the character who is singing, it remains constantly inventive and never reaches the point of diminishing returns.

> *He said my maxillaries were marvels,*
> *And found my sternum stunning to see,*
> *He did a double hurdle*
> *When I shook my pelvic girdle,*
> *BUT HE NEVER SAID HE LOVED ME.*

Nöel Coward, who could be as glib as Porter often shot his darts deeper into society. Because he was so clever with words, he seems to have had a special penchant for the list song. Gems

---

* 'You're the Top', from one of his greatest successes *Anything Goes* (1934) lists such anachronistic rhymes as Mahatma Gandhi–Napoleon brandy; Bendel bonnet–Shakespeare sonnet; O'Neill drama–Whistler's mama; Tower of Babel–the Whitney stable; a dress from Saks's–next year's taxes, etc.

like 'Don't Put Your Daughter on the Stage, Mrs Worthington' excoriate both pushy mother and untalented daughter; 'Why Do the Wrong People Travel?' attacks the nouveau riche. More than most artists, who generally put their heads in the sand when it came to warfare or socio-economic issues, Coward's barbs could devastate with list songs like 'Don't Let's Be Beastly to the Germans' and 'The Stately Homes of England'. Serious or droll, he was the master of the list song. The last chorus of 'That is the End of the News', hilarious throughout, is printed below. Notice the A^1, A^2, Bridge and A^3 form.*

> *Heigh Ho, what a catastrophe,*
> *Grandfather's brain is beginning to atrophy.*
> *Last Sunday night after eating an apple,*
> *He made a rude noise in the Methodist Chapel.*
>
> *Good egg, dear little Doris*
> *Has just been expelled for assaulting Miss Morris.*
> *Both of her sisters*
> *Are covered in blisters*
> *From standing about in the queues.*
>
> *We've been done in*
> *By that mortgage foreclosure*
> *And Father went out on a blind.*
> *He got run in*
> *For indecent exposure*
> *And ever so heavily fined.*
>
> *Heigh Ho, Hi diddle diddle,*
> *Aunt Isabel's shingles have met in the middle,*
> *She's buried in Devon*
> *So God's in his heaven,*
> *And THAT IS THE END OF THE NEWS.*

Because our contemporary musical theatre has come to expect a libretto to advance the action at all costs, the basic list song, usually included to bring a moment of lightness into a play, has fallen somewhat out of favour. It is, after all, the lyricist's solo ballgame (for the plot has halted and the composer has, hopefully, written his simplest tune to keep out of the way of the lyrics). The best of today's list songs do more. The list is

* For an explanation of this form see p. 55.

generally combined with some character elucidation rather than a straightforward list.

Take for example Stephen Sondheim's 'Liaisons', rich old Madam Arnfeldt's recollective song in the second act of *A Little Night Music*. Before nodding off, the aged ex-courtesan browses through a listing of remembered lovers. She catalogues their gifts to her (which puts the official stamp of 'list song' upon it), but she also deplores today's world 'where the princes are lawyers', and where what was formerly a gown and train has become merely a frock. Thus, the now respectable dowager lets us in on her philosophy as well – and a lot of Sondheim's own – and the entire musical gains by having one of its characters, albeit minor, more fully fleshed out.*

Composers and lyricists generally have a sixth sense about when to insert a list song into a score. It works best in a spot where the libretto gives us much similarly classified information. In his notes on 'Company' Stephen Sondheim writes: 'I started a list of what's company. Then I started to expand the lines. "Love is what you need is company. What I've got as friends is company. Good friends, weird friends, married friends, days go, years go, full of company ... Phones ring, bells buzz, door clicks, company, call back, get a bite." '

Then the whole notion of short staccato phrases occurred to him. And he states that by the time he had listed his general thoughts, he had the smell of the rhythm of the vocal line.

The list song can be either a series of short rhyming lines as in 'Gee, Officer Krupke' or 'The Lady is a Tramp', or it may be a series of (usually 8-bar) sections as in 'To Keep My Love Alive' written by Rodgers and Hart for the revival of *A Connecticut Yankee*, in which each *section* outlines a different murder. The first chorus – there are three wonderful ones – is quoted below. Since the lyrics are so generally amusing and shocking, Richard Rodgers chose to write the melody in simple A^1, A^2, Bridge and A^3 form. The rhythm, somewhat like a gavotte, helps make the murderess's demeanour even more demure and this adds to the humour of the premise.

> *I married many men, a ton of them*
> *And yet I was untrue to none of them*
> *Because I bumped off ev'ry one of them*
> TO KEEP MY LOVE ALIVE.

*Most theatre buffs and ageing chanteuses alike would give Stephen Sondheim the credit for having written the best list song of the past two decades, 'I'm Still Here', from *Follies*.

Sir Paul was frail, he looked a wreck to me
At night he was a horse's neck to me
So I performed an appendectomy,
TO KEEP MY LOVE ALIVE.

Sir Charles had insomnia
He couldn't sleep in bed,
I solved that problem easily,
I just removed his head.

I caught Sir George with his protectoress
The rector's wife – I mean the rectoress,
His heart stood still – angina pectoris.
TO KEEP MY LOVE ALIVE.

Some theatrical list songs worth investigating are 'Gee, Officer Krupke' (*West Side Story*); 'I'm Still Here' (*Follies*); 'He Had Refinement' (*A Tree Grows in Brooklyn*); 'Friendship' (*Du Barry Was a Lady*); 'Monotonous' (*New Faces of 1952*); 'The Little Things You Do Together' (*Company*); 'The Lady is a Tramp' (*Babes in Arms*).

SOLILOQUY

One of the advantages a musical has over a dramatic play is that in the latter we only come to understand a character either from overhearing others discuss the subject or by coming to know what a person is feeling through their dialogue. That is not necessary in the musical theatre. People can tell us about themselves.

Although we haven't accepted a spoken soliloquy since Shakespeare's day, we readily believe, and even treasure, overhearing a soon-to-be-father talking to himself for eight minutes about his hopes and fears for his unborn child in Rodgers and Hammerstein's *Carousel*. Whenever we think of a musical soliloquy this particular one comes to mind, perhaps because it was entitled 'Soliloquy'. In this number, a true soliloquy in drama textbook terms, the performer-character resolves a crisis. But Mitch Douglas takes a different view of what soliloquies must accomplish. He believes 'they don't necessarily have to resolve it, but the motivation has to be there for them to launch into song. "I've Grown Accustomed To Her Face" in *My Fair Lady* is certainly a soliloquy, but Higgins doesn't resolve his dilemma. He comes up with a statement "My God! She's gone." And she's become a part of his life and he doesn't know how he's going to live without her. Then he imagines a whole picture of her future: she's going to marry Freddy; she's going to be bored; he's going to walk out and she's going to become a piece of garbage. He comes to the same conclusion he started out with, only now, he comes to accept it. So it's not the character *resolving* the situation, it's the character *exploring* the situation.'

In Langston Hughes's and Kurt Weill's *Street Scene*, Anna Maurrant spends almost as much time exploring her life and musing about why things never worked out for her and why she needed an extra-marital love affair to take away the 'greyness' from her existence. Her soliloquy is called 'Somehow I Never Could Believe', and it fills a void that would take pages and pages of dialogue. She tells us how she expected joy and laughter, and thought she was getting that from her husband, and then her dreams got drowned in the greasy soapsuds in the kitchen. Now, even though her children don't seem to need her, she has not given up hope. That is a large piece of a life to display, and the musical number gives us background and empathy with the character whose murder late in the second act will provide the stunning climax to the play.

Song serves another purpose as well, for, although we take it for granted as one of the axioms of all musical theatre, music *combined* with lyrics can set the mood. For if the words are basically a distillation of thought, the music expresses the protagonist's most intimate disposition, letting the audience enter into the singer's 'mood'.

The soliloquy is often (as so many theatre songs are) a list song. [*See* Page 195.] This form is so prevalent because it keeps the person who is speaking from meandering, as the list song must zero in on a particular mood. In 'The Colours of My Life', from *Barnum*, Michael Stewart's sensitive lyric lists the autumnal colours Mrs Barnum prefers, and contrasts her 'browns and greys' with her flamboyant husband's 'reds and golds'. Thus, the song-soliloquy creates unity at the same time as giving the audience a clue into her retiring, mousy character.*

---

* Thomas Shepard (as well as many other knowledgeable theatre people) feels that soliloquy

In *La Cage Aux Folles*, Jerry Herman gives us a wonderful character song, which is not to be confused with a soliloquy. In the number – the opening of the show – Zaza, the leading character, a female impersonator, is sitting before his make-up mirror getting ready for his act. Depressed with the examination of his ageing face, he tells in amusing choruses how he puts 'A Little More Mascara On'. The number is one of those 'can't fails', being full of amusing quips and including a transformation in full view of the audience, at the end of which Zaza is in full drag.

Sometimes a soliloquy can show us a new side of a character even as it is pivotal to the plot, for after all, the soliloquiser is alone, with only the audience listening in. Anna's soliloquy in *The King and I* displays quite a bit more spirit than we have seen before from this lady. She talks about the barbarism of the king and the audience think she will leave Siam – but then (and it's the music that does it here) she remembers 'the children, those little faces looking up at me', and we know she cannot be parted from them. As in Billy's soliloquy in *Carousel* we have a raison d'être. Most of the time the singer comes to a *definite realisation at the end*.

Sometimes, if a character is transformed in the second act – like Rose in *Gypsy* – that transformation can develop into a powerful soliloquy. Coming so far into the second act, this particular soliloquy gives lyricist Stephen Sondheim a chance to reintroduce snatches of Jule Styne's previously heard songs, creating unity in the best operatic sense but still maintaining a show biz quality.

The moment in the final scene is devoted to Rose, alone, after a blow-up with her now successful daughter, stripper Gypsy Rose Lee. When Gypsy asks her momma 'What'd you do it for?' Rose at last levels with the audience:

ROSE: *You wanna know what I did it for?!* Because I was born too soon and started too late, that's why! *With what I have in me I could have been better than ANY OF YOU! What I got in me – what I been holding down inside of me – if I ever let it out there wouldn't be signs big enough! There wouldn't be lights bright enough! (Shouting right out to everyone now) HERE*

---

implies transformation, and calls this kind of solo, where a character talks about intimate thoughts, a 'credo'. I suppose that under that criterion, Hamlet's speech that starts 'To be or not to be', would be a credo as well.

*SHE IS, BOYS, HERE SHE IS WORLD! HERE'S ROSE! (She sings)**

The solo which moves through snatches of 'Some People' has references to the 'Mr Goldstone' number. Rose here ruefully examines her stage-mother career, which provided her merely with 'scrapbooks full of pictures with me in the background', and finally ends the number as a true soliloquy with Rose coming to the realisation that 'this time "Everything's Coming Up Roses"'. The beauty part is the change in the final line from "for you and for me" to 'this time – for me! for me! FOR ME!" '†

Other soliloquies, character exposés, solo turns or 'credos' worth exploring are 'I Won't Send Roses', from *Mack and Mabel*, 'The Twin Soliloquies' from *South Pacific* and Fannie Brice's determined soliloquy in *Funny Girl*, 'Don't Rain on My Parade'.

THE LOVE SONG

If the musical theatre differs from the dramatic play or comedy, it is because of its heavy reliance on emotionalism. Two lovers in a scene will often start slowly and the librettist will work out the dialogue so that it builds to an expression of their feelings for each other. As said many times before, when the emotion becomes too strong to be spoken, it is sung. Those who work with music will tell you that one can say things with rhyme or in song that would sound maudlin in dialogue.

---

*As mentioned in another context, when the emotion gets too big to be handled in mere words, the addition of music can take the musical an impassioned giant step further.

† Stephen Sondheim remembers: 'That was originally going to be a ballet with Rose seeing her past as sort of nightmare figures ... The ballet was not cut until rehearsal. "Rose's Turn" was written during rehearsal because it became apparent that the whole ballet idea was simply not in keeping with the rest of the show. It was much too pretentious and entirely wrong ... In terms of performance, to have her come out and sing thirty-two bars, even twice would simply not have done what was intended. So the idea was to carry out the nightmare quality that Jerry [Robbins] had wanted, only do it entirely through music and lyrics.

'Well, how do you do that? You do that with a kind of interrupted consciousness technique. The original idea of the ballet was that it was going to be a visual reprise of her life. When we decided to do it not as a ballet, but as a song, we held on to the reprise idea by making the number a nightmare vision of the various songs we've already heard in the show. So "Rose's Turn" is essentially a series of variations on songs you've heard before. There are some melodic variations with dissonant accompaniments and some lyrical variations and they play off all that you've heard and seen all evening, which gives the number a kaleidoscopic feel.'

It is difficult to convey to the reader the total effect of how much music glorifies and amplifies a lyric, but I have chosen show songs that are all recorded and I would invite you to listen to any recordings you're not familiar with.

The Love Love Song

Even love songs have had their evolution. The earliest musical comedy ones, however, had lyrics that were matter-of-fact, perhaps obvious is a better word. They always used the words 'love', 'kiss' or 'heart' in their titles, and told little about those who were singing them. Librettists wanted their audiences to be moved by the spirit of loving rather than by the situation in the play which was usually replete with cardboard characters anyway. That does not mean that they did not hit their emotional centre, merely that they relied more on soaring, rangy melodies, reaching for high notes (which is in itself an emotional high) and the delicious combination of male and female voices frequently singing in harmony.

Kern and Hammerstein's 'You Are Love' which capped an emotional scene in *Show Boat* starts simply with the voices in very low register . . .

> *You are love,*
> *Here in my arms*
> *Where you belong,*
> *And here you will stay.*
> *I'll not let you away,*
> *I want day after day with you.*

But by the time it has reached the end of its lyric which is the unremarkable 'Where you go with me, heaven will always be', Kern's music has led us through a range of two and a half octaves, we have had an evaded cadence and a repeat of the last couplet with the voices joined, the soprano has held a high B flat and the tenor an equally intense high G. Although the characters might be substituted for any other pair of lovers, the audience are riding on the power of 'romance' and find themselves emotionally involved.

'You Are Love' is not unlike Cole Porter's 'So In Love'. This stirring ballad may or may not have been written with tongue in cheek, for Porter was writing of the vicissitudes of a theatrical marriage where sincerity is not uppermost in anyone's mind. Nevertheless, the song, with its dark, minor opening leading to an impassioned outpouring, remains one of the musical theatre's most important love songs. It begins ...

> *Strange, dear, but true, dear,*
> *When I'm close to you, dear,*
> *The stars fill the sky ...*
> *So in love with you, am I.*

The form of this romantic song is A^1, A^2, Bridge, A^3 [*see* page 55] with the pitch rising to a higher note in each succeeding A section, and the rhythm is a relentless beguine. This will certainly increase the tension as the song heads for its climax. The relatively long closing section [not italic] serves somewhat like a postcoital cigarette.

> *So taunt me, and hurt me,*
> *Deceive me, desert me,*
> *I'm yours till I die!*
> *So in love,* so in love
> So in love with you, my love
> *Am I.*

Most of the above feelings, of course, exist in operettaland, but even in the late Eighties musicals such as *Les Misérables* with a song title like 'A Heart Full of Love', and *The Phantom of the Opera*, seem to revel in that domain.

Some other songs that wear their hearts on their sleeves and discuss nothing but the emotion of love are: 'I Love You' (I know at least four with that title), 'I Loves You, Porgy', 'I'm in Love Again' and 'I'm in Love With a Wonderful Guy'.

The Quasi-Love Song

Sometimes a lover will try to deny his or her love, but this denial will only serve to affirm it to the audience. Typical is 'This Can't Be Love'. The negative side is taken as well in 'People Will Say We're In Love' wherein a lover is admonished for being too demonstrative. Then there are songs like 'If This Isn't Love', 'I've never Been in Love Before' and 'I Don't Know How To Love Him' which hint at insecurity. The hit song in Andrew Lloyd Webber's 1989 opus, *Aspects of Love*, is called 'Love Changes Everything' and talks in romantic terms about how 'love', personified, can throw a monkey wrench into the best-laid plans.

Other characters will flirt with the periphery of love, which is romance as in 'It's Almost Like Being in Love'. They all use the word 'love' in their titles but they don't come at it straight on. I call this a 'Quasi-love song'.

The Reflective Love Song

One of the important selling points of musical theatre is nostalgia. Our most popular hits have been musicals that are set in a period other than our own. And coupled with this our sentimental theatre often resorts to older characters reflecting on their own past or simply reminiscing. *La Cage aux Folles* has its 'Song on the Sand', *She Loves Me*, its 'Days Gone By' and *The King and I* allows its heroine to recall her own love affair while observing the emotions of the principals in the subplot when she sings:

> *Hello, young lovers*
> *Whoever you are,*
> *I hope your troubles are few.*
> *All of my mem'ries go with you tonight*
> *I've been in love like you ...*

The Oblique Love Song

In today's musical theatre, we can no longer stop the head-long action of the play to dwell on the past or spout a thesis on love as an emotion. Our love songs have to illuminate character while they carry the plot further in a fresh* way. For want of a better term, I've called this 'oblique', since it almost doesn't

---

*Charles Strouse who wrote the music for *Bye Bye Birdie*, *Annie* and *Applause* among many other musicals feels that this freshness should create a feeling of surprise. 'It's that ... which would seize my imagination. If you know that he loves her, it's obvious that he's going to sing "I love you". But it's the moment *before*, when he's tying his shoe and feels the crick in his back that interests me, because the audience wouldn't expect a song about it ... Lee [Adams, his longtime collaborator] sees that the best line for a song title would be "Oh, My Back", and not "Oh, I Love You". The audience would be bored with the "I Love You" song.'

feel like a love song until we examine it with hindsight. Perhaps it is easiest to understand the contemporary love song by examining a few of them.

In Rogers and Hammerstein's *Carousel*, Julie and Billy have a strong emotional and physical magnetism that will grow in intensity until the end of the play, but each is basically timid. When Julie conveys her uncertainty about the handsome carnival barker she has met to her friend Carrie, the response is 'You're a Queer One, Julie Jordan'. Later when Billy appears, and the two are alone we come to understand that the blustering barker is fundamentally timid. Our perception is clear, *not* from the dialogue but from the song whose title is 'If I Loved You'. (Rodgers sets this all-important word 'If' on a stressful downbeat and waits two beats on the word so we come to understand that this is a very big 'if'. The word is a clue to these two bashful people who can never come totally out of their shells because they fear rejection so desperately. Thus, we have a love song that elucidates the personalities of the two main characters in the story at the same time that it charms us.

Even more roundabout is the song Jerry Herman gives Mack Sennett to sing to Mabel Normand in his underrated musical *Mack and Mabel*. Brash and reckless Mack tells his girl 'I Won't Send Roses' and goes on to list his myriad faults – he talks mostly about how unsentimental he is. However at the song's end he tells her intimately and tenderly, 'and roses suit you so'. The audience comes to realise through that final line that Mack is really much softer than he pretends to be (this is known as subtext) and creates a tremendous empathy for the singer and the song.

Mabel, for her part, is not dissuaded by Mack's lack of gallantry for she answers gently ending her own chorus with 'So who needs roses, that didn't come from him?' Again, the down-to-earth quality of the singers shines through while we are struck with the originality of the approach.

Of all the oblique love songs my particular favourite occurs at the end of *She Loves Me*, (*see* page 178) a delicious confection where Amalia sings 'Ice Cream' which seems to have nothing, and everything to do with her lover Georg. Finally she discovers by analysing why he brought her the ice cream, that she loves him.

Today's love song avoids the word 'love' in its title, but it need not be unromantic. It can be sassy and bright as 'Bewitched, Bothered and Bewildered' or 'Cherry Pies Ought To Be You', or more often, medium slow as 'Right As the Rain', 'My Heart Stood Still', 'On the Street Where You Live' or 'Some Enchanted Evening'. It may even be terribly intense as 'Body and Soul' or 'Being Alive'.

REPRISES

Since audiences love them, second acts generally contain at least one or two reprises. The discreet use of reprise can make us feel, as Lehman Engel says in his book *Words With Music* 'like we are seeing an old friend once more'. Most composers like to include reprises, while most lyricists do not.*

But, according to the most avant garde composers (read Stephen Sondheim and his school), the technique is rapidly becoming obsolete. They will tell you that only the old-fashioned musicals continue to be built around the 32-bar song which might easily be reprised: they now have themes in the operatic tradition, what might be called a *leitmotif*, and portions of these melodies come in and out through the evening. *Aspects of Love* uses its hit song, 'Love Changes Everything' in more of a pop way, trying to fix the tune in the audience's head, and sometimes in a way that is totally irrelevant to the play. While this kind of usage may make for a whistleable series of songs, none of it helps to create a stronger and more memorable work. In this case it is because the tune is reprised with so little care as to what the situation on stage is at the moment. Different lyrics are literally thrown on top of the tune, and the melody assaults us again and again. In any case, when we speak of reprise technically, we mean the *same* music and words, only the circumstances are different.†

Second acts seem to call for reprises, but there are other cases where a reprise is acceptable – even desirable. The 'Take That Look Off Your Face' and the 'Letter Home' in the *Song*

---

*Stephen Sondheim recalls his collaboration with Richard Rodgers (*Do I Hear a Waltz?*) 'Rodgers wanted a reprise of "Take the Moment". I asked why. He said "I want to hear the tune again." For me, that isn't enough.' [Ed. Note – The reprise *was* included in the final production.]

†William Hammerstein puts it succinctly: 'A reprise should be a reminder, and a thought that you've heard that song in the first act ... It should bring back a whole slew of emotions to remind you that this is how we started out, and this is where we've come.'

section of Don Black's and Andrew Lloyd Webber's *Song and Dance* are part of the fabric and construction of the show. In those cases, because the plot is exposed through the letters a British girl in the US sends home to her mum, the reprise needs essentially new lyrics.

The other kind – those that use the same lyrics, but in totally new contexts – appeal to me emotionally, while list songs with new or opposite lyrics as Cole Porter's 'Cherry Pies Ought To Be You', from *Out of This World*, are rarely emotional, but always amusing. In this case it was using the tune for a hateful rather than loving effect. Another example, in *Gypsy*, the 'Let me Entertain You' song is used as a childish vehicle throughout the show, generally in 3/4 or waltz clog tempo. At the moment where Gypsy makes her debut as a stripper, she sings the number in a totally different context, and in an insinuating, sexual manner. Now the orchestra adds a backbeat (strong accent on the second and fourth beats of the bar, typical of striptease music), and the lyrics which contain phrases like 'do a few tricks', 'make you feel good' changes the meaning of the very same words from naïvety to raunchiness.*

Although most of his earlier shows (*Anyone Can Whistle*, *Gypsy*, *Do I Hear a Waltz?*, *A Funny Thing Happened on the Way to the Forum*, *Follies*) sprinkled reprises liberally, Stephen Sondheim has often stated his disapproval of the technique. Here are some of his comments from an interview.

> I find the notion that the same lyric can apply in the first act and the second act *very* suspect. In writing a play, if a character is undergoing the same emotion late in the evening that he went through before, you can reprise a line, can't you? Or, in a musical, reprise a song? Well, most of the time it doesn't happen. Most of the time the character has moved beyond, particularly if you are telling a story of any weight or density. *Company* was a show where we could have used reprises, because it is about a fellow who stays exactly the same; but I didn't want him to be the essential singing character, so I decided not to. In the case of *Forum*, we did a reprise for comic intent. That is to say you heard the song again,† but in an entirely different context, and in fact with a different lyric.

Romance, Romance which is two small musicals, one set in Paris in the 1890s and the other in East Hampton nearly a hundred years later and uses the same song – first presented in pure operetta style and later, reprised with rock rhythm and feeling. Somehow this seems to work.

† The song was 'Beautiful' and originally sung by the love interest as was appropriate and charming; reprised later by the male servant in drag it becomes hilarious.

Maybe there are instances where it *does* happen, but even if you are using the same musical material it seems to me something has progressed, and unless the book throws new light on the subject, the lyric can't be the same. Satisfying as it is for an audience to hear a tune that they've heard before, I think it is more satisfying that they follow and be excited by and intrigued by the story and the characters. It's nice to be able to combine the two if you can find an instance. I have found places where the music could be reprised, but I've never found one where the lyric could be reprised.

I'm not downgrading reprises, I'm saying it's very difficult to find a way that is honest for the evening and therefore doesn't break the audience's concentration and doesn't remind them that they are in a Broadway theatre listening to a reprise of a song that still maintains the mood and yet is a reprise. I just think it's very hard.

But Mitch Douglas, who is an avant garde lyricist as well, questions Mr Sondheim when he says: 'The fact that Sondheim doesn't use reprises doesn't mean they can't be used effectively. Actually Sondheim reprises his themes, he'll set up a motive and repeat it. Perhaps it's an old-fashioned idea, but look at the way "Happy To Make Your Acquaintance" from *The Most Happy Fella* pulls the whole scene together.'*

Perhaps the most theatrical, and even pathetic use of reprise (expressing the feelings most theatre people have about reprises in general) is to be found in the Sondheim–Fueth *Merrily We Roll Along*. The scene is a posh Manhattan party given by the gushing wife of a rich producer to celebrate a new musical written by a young creative team. Dressed to the nines, this woman shushes the assemblage, announcing they are in for a treat – the hit song from their up and coming musical. And indeed, a treat it is, one of Sondheim's most felicitous ballads, 'Good Thing Going', (some of which has been quoted on page 64). But then the hostess, applauding vociferously, asks the guests rhetorically, 'Wasn't that wonderful? Wouldn't you like to hear it again?' and reluctantly the performers must oblige. They get halfway through when someone (in counterpoint) asks for a drink, and other voices join in, resuming the party and obliterating the song. The performers are left struggling

---

*By way of explanation: In this song Rosabella, Tony's new wife, has, with difficulty, finally taught him, an Italian immigrant, the proper phrase for introductions – 'Happy to make your acquaintance', and in a charming reprise when Rosabella introduces Tony to see her close friend, Clio, he at last gets to use the phrase. Of course, out of nervousness he garbles it, which only makes him more endearing.

to completion, and a bit wiser when they learn, to paraphrase Alan Jay Lerner, 'that the sequel is never equal'. Almost everyone involved in the creative musical theatre has been trapped in this humiliating position. We often forget Sondheim's rueful illustration when they are clapping their hands off and we are hungry for applause. Remembering it would spare us an experience we could live very well without.

RECORDABLE SONGS vs BOOK SONGS

In the Fifties, popular music which consisted mainly of Rock, Country, Heavy Metal and R and B began diverting from show music as we know it today. Prior to that most of the pop hits were derived from musicals, and audiences would go to the shows knowing the songs they heard would be the ones they'd be humming over the next few months.*

In the early days of the musical, and later, when the revue ruled supreme, producers used what they called 'interpolations' as a guarantee of success. Someone would be sent over from a publishing house in Tin Pan Alley to play an assortment of songs for a spot in the show and the producer would pick the one that looked most like a hit. One of the biggest hits Irving Berlin ever wrote, 'Blue Skies', was interpolated (over their vociferous objections) into the musical, *Betsy*. Even though the team of Rodgers and Hart, who had written a complete score, was well known, the producer insisted on some extra insurance of success by asking reigning 'hitmaster', Irving Berlin, to write an obvious winner. So the tradition of musicals aiming for hits was spawned, and it flourished for several decades. But gone are the days when every theatregoer knew all the songs already and would often burst into spontaneous applause as the theatre orchestra struck up a

---

*Perhaps a *rapprochement* is taking place. 1989's big hits are 'Love Changes Everything', from *Aspects of Love* and 'Losing My Mind', from *Follies*, and have risen to the top of the pop charts. In both these cases the treatment was heavy with drum machines; in the latter Liza Minnelli approached the recording from hard rock anger rather than self pity. Although this is the reverse, it is not unlike the phenomenon that went on in the Forties when simpering pop vocalists took hard-hitting show tunes like 'Bewitched' and by sentimentalising them were able to impel them to the top of the hit parade.

familiar ballad in the overture.* Recently, apart from *Jesus Christ, Superstar*'s 'I Don't Know How To Love Him', *Evita*'s 'Don't Cry For Me, Argentina', *Cats*' 'Memory', and *Les Misérables*' 'On My Own', there have been few megahits emerging from the theatre.† It is truly unfortunate that this divorce occurred, because it means not only a loss of revenue for composer and lyricist, but a loss of the feeling of anticipation for modern audiences attending a show on Broadway or in the West End.

Perhaps it sounds altruistic, but Sheldon Harnick's remembrance of a conversation he had with Marvin Hamlisch best analyses what a theatre song must accomplish:

> He [Marvin Hamlisch] had never done a show, and he was working with the very gifted lyric writer and composer, Ed Kleban [on *A Chorus Line*]. They articulated the fact that they had a choice; they could have tried to write songs which might have had a chance in the commercial record market; or they could let Michael Bennett steer them in the very specific directions towards songs which would probably be limited to their use in the show. They made the wise decision that they couldn't be in better hands than Michael's. They listened to him and they wrote numbers which served the show exclusively. They made the decision right at the top not to worry about what songs might be recorded but instead to ask themselves what is the situation? What would these characters say? What's going to be effective on the stage? How can we serve the *show*? Only the last song, 'What I Did For Love', was an attempt to go for that hit. The show itself is an extraordinary knitting-together of all theater elements. I can't help feeling that Hamlisch and Kleban made absolutely the right decision.

I have to agree. Not only does *A Chorus Line* hold the record as the longest-running musical, but its original cast album has sold millions. It continues to move audiences because it is honest with its material. Except for the brilliant flash in the pan of a musical like *Hair*, the era where many hits emerged

---

*Stephen Sondheim remembers 'going to *Hello, Dolly* when the title song was already a hit. The feeling the audience had was of welcoming an old friend. That doesn't happen any more. Today, some of the biggest hit shows don't have any hit songs.' And Jule Styne recalls his feelings of box-office insurance as long as he knew there were several recordable hits in his latest show. He said at a recent interview: 'At the time of *Gypsy* or *Bells Are Ringing* we could walk into a record company and say "Here it is: So-and-so will record this number and so-and-so will do that one." And you had eight singles before the show opened!'

† Each of these was written, recorded and arranged in a commercial manner *and plugged on radio* months before the show opened. The song title was often advertised along with the show title and would help the producers to build up a large box-office advance.

from a musical has long since vanished. Add together all the brilliant shows Stephen Sondheim has written and then realise he has had only one song, the moving 'Send In The Clowns'* that has attained hit status and become a standard.

Certainly the day of the musical as the major source for material that is in the top forty (or even the top 100) is gone, never to return unless – once again – the songs take precedence over plot and book. But isn't it true, as Mark Steyn says, that many composers and lyricists rule *themselves* out from having widely successful scores by filling them with proper names, references to streets and plot which make them too specific? He continues:

> Without wishing to sound pompous, I think it was Goethe (who never wrote any pop songs), who said 'the poet should seize the specific, and if there's anything lasting about him, he'll articulate the universal.' When Sheldon Harnick was a kid in Chicago he heard the Irving Berlin lyric on the radio, 'They Say It's Wonderful'. He thought it was a great song. What a pretty ballad. Then he went to New York and saw the show and realised that the lines, 'I can't recall who said it, I know I never read it' had a different meaning in the context of the show. Of course Annie Oakley had never 'read it'. The plot makes a big point of the fact that she was illiterate! And that is what a musical songwriter should do. Make the song specific for the character, but not *so* specific that it can't be understood by all those people who buy the records or hear it in night-clubs or on the radio.

With Rodgers and Hart's *Babes in Arms*, a fairly successful show of the Thirties, saddled with a tired plot concerning a group of kids who pay the mortgage by putting on a show, the public couldn't have cared less for the story. What they came to hear was the score, for *Babes in Arms* contained at least five memorable standards including 'My Funny Valentine', 'The Lady is a Tramp', 'Where Or When', 'I Wish I Were In Love Again', 'Johnny One-Note' and the title song.†

---

* This is said notwithstanding Liza Minnelli's 1989 hit recording of 'Losing My Mind', for this crossover rock treatment is aimed at the pop market and approaches the song from the point of view of anger rather than the 'torch' manner in which it was originally presented in the theatre.

† Critic Mark Steyn would like to roll back the clock too. Speaking of the newest musicals he says, 'We hear all these recitatives and extended musical scenes and strange dissonances and we're impressed by it. But at the same time, you go around the corner and you see *Anything Goes*, and you get to the title song, hearing it go into its 6th or 7th chorus and you get an exhilaration that you don't get from these new kinds of scores.' [Ed. Note: Besides the magnificent title song Cole Porter's *Anything Goes* boasted five other standards: 'I Get a Kick

For the health of the musical theatre – for we are now deep in a cinematic age where a musical runs or folds depending on the believability* of its book – it seems fortunate that we have progressed beyond that naïve time. The only possibility of creating a show score that would climb on to the pop charts could be in a revue, and since that form has fallen into disuse in the last three decades, that seems hardly likely.† But cast albums of standards like *Show Boat, South Pacific, Carousel* and *My Fair Lady* and recent megahits like *Jesus Christ Superstar, Les Misérables, The Phantom of the Opera, Me and My Girl* and many other long-run shows have sold well into the millions of copies. Thus, even though they don't compare with the instant popularity, nor do they make the money that songs on the charts may, albums can have a very long run. As long as the show has. Still, the monetary rewards are nowhere near what the superstar pop composers earn. The most any composer-lyricist can hope for is to have an occasional hit song emerging from a score – seeking more than that, it seems, will almost certainly imply a commercialism that will doom the show to failure.

CONCERTED NUMBERS

The basic reasons for using counterpoint in musicals were touched upon in Chapter 3 (Composer's Training). Certainly counterpoint, along with small ensembles, is something that composers (and lyricists to a lesser degree) need to be able to add to every musical worth its salt today. As the composer-lyricists plan to add songs to a naked libretto, they keep one eye on the balance between solos and duetted and group numbers. (Contrapuntal or concerted numbers should not be confused with production numbers which are discussed later.)

The counterpointed backstage gossip in *The Phantom of The*

Out of You', 'Blow, Gabriel, Blow', 'You're the Top', 'Be Like the Bluebird', and 'All Through the Night'.]

   *Even in fantasy like *Cats*, or *The Phantom of the Opera*, the book must somehow be logical and interesting enough to be believable.

   †Stephen Schwartz had two enormous rock hits that were recorded by the Jackson Five – 'Day By Day' from *Godspell* and 'Corner of the Sky' from *Pippin*. Yet he says, 'I really don't think in terms of the pop market. "Corner of the Sky" was the philosophy of Pippin – the hero's attempt to find a place for himself in the universe. In the case of *Godspell*, I was writing so fast, I was lucky to get the music done.'

Opera seems a natural theatrical harangue; the 'Ohio' duet in *Wonderful Town*, the 'Politics and Poker' quintet in *Fiorello* and the 'Soon', 'Now', 'Later' triple counterpointed melody and lyrics that introduce the principals early in *A Little Night Music* are unique to those musicals. Counterpoint is an essential, and without voices and musical lines tumbling one on top of the other, there would be no lyric stage.

A splendid example, called 'Cocktail Counterpoint' may be found in Jerry Herman's score for *La Cage Aux Folles*. It occurs in the pre-dinner scene where Georges is trying to hide his homosexuality from M and Mme Dindon, his prospective and bigoted in-laws. Jacob, the flamboyant 'maid' is passing round cocktail titbits to the usual cocktail chatter. Georges declares he knows nothing of the notorious nightclub next door and pretends to have enlisted in the macho Foreign Legion. Even a read-through of the lyric shows that this number does all that it should. It allows us simultaneously to enter the minds of the swashbuckling pretender, the easily shocked Mme Dindon and her 'petit-functionaire' husband and the opinionated 'maid'. These sentiments could only be expressed in a song, and it is to Jerry Herman's credit that everybody sings in true, natural rhyme while the tempo and musical setting is animated enough to create the exact feeling the songwriter was aiming for. Pandemonium.

GEORGES:	MME DINDON:	DINDON:	JACOB:
I joined the	Oh what lovely	That is	It's appalling
Foreign Legion	Dishes	Even	To confess
With a saber	They're so	Worse	Our new
In my hand	Delicate	Than I feared	In-laws
And crawled	And frail	The son is	Are a mess.
Across the desert	Mine have	Strange	
With my belly	Naked children	The father	She's a
In the sand	I believe	Is weird.	Prude
With	They're on-	To meet	He's a
Men who loved	Ly male.	The wife	Prig
Their camels	Oops, I think	I'm actually	She's a
And their	They're playing	Afraid	Pill,
Brandy and	Some exotic lit-	I prefer	He's a
I swear	Tle game	That	Pig.
Nobody dished	Oops	You	
Nobody swished	I think	Remain	So zis
When I was a	That	An	Zis
Foreign	Leapfrog	Old	Zis
Legionnaire. . .	Is its name . . .	Maid! . . .	for your papa!

As our musical theatre grows more and more to resemble operatic form, increasing its through-sung* segments, Stephen Sondheim, faced with the second act opening of *Sweeney Todd*, chose to write the ultimate concerted number. Hal Prince, who directed the musical, says, 'he envisioned tables set across the stage in an arc, surrounding Mrs Lovett's pie shop. The customers (our chorus of twenty) were to devour meat pies, swilling them down with beer and beating the tables for "more hot pies". Meanwhile, Sweeney, above in the barber shop, was awaiting delivery of his new lethal barber's chair. Mrs Lovett, torn between the demands of her customers and Sweeney's heightened euphoria becomes crazed. For all of this, Steve created twenty separate dramas, each uniquely consistent with one of the chorus members' eating and drinking.'

Prince, who was at a loss as to how to stage this nearly impossible scene, finally came up with the idea of seating the choristers at one long table thereby focusing the audience's attention on three elements: Mrs Lovett, Sweeney, and the hungry mob. With so much counterpoint going on, Prince admits, 'you couldn't understand the brilliant lyrics, but you got the point.'

Semi-production numbers demanding this kind of counterpoint are relatively rare. Musicals generally stick to two or three emotions that can be exposed simultaneously.

In all counterpointed numbers, composer and lyricist must work especially closely together. It almost goes without saying that if the lyrics are to be heard, each part should first be sung as a solo and then the new one must enter.† Musically, especially when there are only two parts, the lines are most commonly contrasted with one moving at slow pace (perhaps by whole and half notes), while the other could be angular and rapid (using quarter and eighth notes).

---

*Through-sung scores like *Aspects of Love*, *Sweeney Todd*, and *Miss Saigon* are frequently mislabelled 'through-composed'. Technically, through-composing implies a line that never turns back on itself to repeat. (An exemplary through-composed melody is the well-known first theme of Rachmaninoff's Second Piano Concerto; its long line spins through sixty-seven long measures without repeating.) Only elements or recurrent motifs give through-composed music its unity.

† A clever musical director will soft-pedal the already heard lyric and spotlight the entering one.

PRODUCTION NUMBERS

The general public loves to see large numbers of choristers, singers and dancers dressed in gorgeous costumes, moving in an expensive, artfully lit setting with everybody gyrating and singing at ultimate amplified sound. This is called a production number, and few musicals can survive without three or four of them sprinkled throughout the evening, for they are one of the major differences between the legitimate theatre and the musical theatre. When used thoughtfully as in *Oklahoma!*, *Oliver*, *The King and I*, *Evita* or *Fiddler on the Roof* (and many others) they can give a musical tremendous vitality and zing. For in these cases we are not even aware that the libretto has been manipulated by the clever librettist to allow the songwriters to have a judicious balance of solos, group numbers, counterpointed and production numbers. But some musicals like *42nd Street*, *Ziegfeld*, *Sophisticated Ladies* or *Chess*, seem to me to rely too heavily on lavish splash and then become merely a collection of production numbers.

Some obvious production numbers that grow beautifully out of the plot are the ballroom scene in *My Fair Lady*, the clambake in *Carousel*, the scene on the grand staircase in *The Phantom of the Opera*, the Lambeth Walk in *Me and My Girl* and the wedding scene in *Fiddler on the Roof*.*

By now the production number has become so beloved of the general public that even musicals with modest-sized casts like *Baby*, *Company* or *A Little Night Music* are expected to contain production numbers involving the entire company but obviously on a smaller scale.†

In order to compensate for this reduced scale and achieve the heart-thumping, show-stopping effect audiences go to musicals for, a production number must be cleverly manipulated.

One can repeat with chorus after chorus, lifting keys, adding more voices and more amplification, which was done in the

---

*A memorable production number was a hilariously maladroit dance called the 'Spanish Panic' in *Once Upon a Mattress*. Here the choreographer, aided by Mary Rodgers's beautifully awkward music, sets this fairy-tale court into suitable pandemonium to end Act I.

† A most intimate musical, *Romance, Romance* opened in New York in 1988. With only four in the cast, most of the dialogue and singing was given to the two featured principals. A quasi-production number effect was achieved from time to time by having all four come on stage in voluminous costumes. The producer cleverly booked the show into the Helen Hayes Theater which has a tiny stage. Four actors dressed in flowing attire, singing and dancing in such tight quarters cluttered the stage and gave an amazingly lavish effect.

finale 'One' number in *A Chorus Line*. Yet there is a better way, which is to write two numbers which are woven together. This was done in the 'Side By Side By Side' number in *Company*.

Given the need to insert relaxation, smiles and a bit of benevolence into this archly acerbic musical, Stephen Sondheim chose to open Act II with a typical ABAC Broadway show tune (albeit with his ever present wry twist). This gives the protagonist Bobby his first non-ballad song, and in it he tells us how comfortable and safe life is for him 'side by side by side' as an onlooker to marriage. Then the mood and the point of view changes to the five couples whose marital adventures make up most of the plot of this concept musical and they ask 'What Would We Do Without You?' After this alternate side of the relationship is explored we are brought back to the first 'Side By Side By Side' number, fully amplified, broadened, hat-and-caned, and because it is familiar now, irresistible.

Production numbers are often the last to be conceived and written, because they are difficult for artists to create since they must use accessible tunes and will end up as a product of the choreographer's or director's art. But uninspiring or not, they must be completed and choreographed before the show goes into previews, for costumes and sets will take time to be created and executed. Among the first questions to involve the producers are, of course, how many production numbers will the show have, and how lavish they will be? For obviously the cost of putting the show together, the running costs, the size of the backstage crew will all depend on the production numbers.

KEY CHOICES AND TRANSPOSITION

Everyone who has ever sung a song knows the uncomfortable feeling of finding oneself in a key that is too high or too low. Either diction is lost or pitches strain (especially with men) into a falsetto that audiences find humorous. What is worse for the songwriters performing that song at a backers' audition is the fact that whoever is in the audience – it might be a producer or a group of producers – stops listening to the meaning and import of the song and begins to look embarrassed and turn away from the singer. To avoid this, when the project is fairly well developed, demos can be presented with professional singers experienced at getting the words and music across. But early auditions are most often given by composer and lyricist. I always suggest to songwriters creating a musical that once they have completed a song, they transpose it to a comfortable key for presentation, and that they learn how to perform every song in their score in a range that suits their voices.

As far as the creation of the song goes composers often have their own favourite keys. Noël Coward preferred to work in E^b. He used to say he could 'manage' in B^b or A^b but was hopelessly 'lost in a sea of sharps'. Randy Newman likes E and A, perhaps because they sound so natural on the guitar. Irving Berlin is reputed to have written in the key of G^b because he says he played on the black notes, and I like to work melodies in straightforward keys like G or F but sometimes I prefer what I call the warmth of a bunch of black notes and work in D^b.

But whatever key composers write in, they always remember to rewrite the song in a suitable key for the character who will sing it and (it may or may not be the same one) they themselves use.

Stephen Sondheim wrote the roles of the two protagonists in *Sunday in the Park With George* for soprano (Dot) and baritone (Seurat) because it seemed to him that 'Dot should have a kind of brightness to her voice.' 'Seurat,' Sondheim stated, 'is very repressed and withdrawn – a very contemplative and compact kind of personality. A baritone.' They ended up with Mandy Patinkin who is a cantorial tenor and Bernadette Peters whose voice, Sondheim adds, 'is lower than anyone. It works perfectly.'

The necessity for open-mindedness and flexibility in writing a musical is illustrated further in the casting of *West Side Story*. The part of Tony was written for a tenor, 'but every tenor', Sondheim says, 'who could hit a high note was terrible! So we cast Larry Kert who, when we first cast him could only hit a G and later an A.' For the part of Maria, Leonard Bernstein also wrote a high A^b for the top of their duet, which would indicate a lyric soprano. Carol Lawrence who was chosen to play Maria has a chest voice which can comfortably negotiate a D at the utmost. Beyond that chest voices must go into 'legit' or head tones – which will create a thinner sound. Bernstein wanted those high notes to remain in the score, always hoping someone would come along who could sing them. He was adamant, as Sondheim says, and 'made her sing it [the high A♭] every night. And every night the voice thinned out – and the show suffered at that moment because when you wanted a strong sound, Carol couldn't hit it. That's the danger of writing for individual ranges and insisting the singers *match* the ranges.'

It is important to be aware of the capabilities and limits of the human voice when writing and the range of the singer must be considered. A soprano's lyrics will be lost if the composer sends her below middle E, or above high G,* but in rehearsals music directors, rehearsal pianists and the composers themselves will often suggest new key changes that suit their 'stars'.†

CONSISTENCY IN THE SCORE

If the characters in a musical must be woven into a whole cloth, so indeed must the musical score. The time has long passed when several composers and lyricists working on a single project could create a unified evening. Interpolation can mean death. Every artist of any stature speaks in his own highly recognisable voice – or should! Shows where numerous creators' names are listed in the right-hand column opposite the songs are generally suspect. If they open at all, they are usually flops. Canny audiences guess that the score may have been in trouble out of town, perhaps the principal composer or lyricist had run dry and couldn't be galvanised into further invention, so 'fresh blood' was called in to give a shot in the arm to what looked like an anaemic failure. What producers and directors

---

*There are, of course, exceptions. Two outstanding ones are Barbara Cook and Christine Andreas. Ms Cook's magnificent coloratura was the inspiration for the role of Cunegonde in Leonard Bernstein's *Candide*. In the 'Glitter and Be Gay' number he took her up to a stratospheric E♭ *above* high C! And yet her eloquent diction made every word understandable. Ms Andreas seems to have taken over Ms Cook's roles these days.

†Depending on the spirit of the work, some composers like Sondheim and Bernstein may vary their flexibility of range. In *Sweeney Todd* and *West Side Story* the chosen cast was obliged to fit into the score; that means only singers who could encompass the notes were considered, for these scores were more like operatic works, whereas in *Follies* or *Wonderful Town*, pure musical comedies, keys were frequently changed to suit the artists who had been pre-chosen. (Non-singers Alexis Smith in the former and Rosalind Russell in the latter.) Changing keys allowed the music director to place the musical line so as to get the optimum sound out of their non-trained voices.

don't realise is that they probably stand a better chance of success with the score sounding all of one voice rather than an admixture of styles.*

It is a deplorable and common fact that when shows are revived, sometimes after a decade, sometimes after a generation, hits from that songwriter's other shows are often added. This was done in *Irene, No, No Nanette, Singin' in the Rain*, the still reigning hit, *Anything Goes* and several others. In every case they didn't help much, and only served to antagonise the purists who were familiar with the original matter.

Creating Unity

Depending on the work itself, that is to say if the style is a serious one, we expect the score to be not only homogenous, but to have the same melodic and lyrical themes recurring throughout. With so many of today's successes using the operatic technique of non-stop singing, it was only a question of time before themes that represent specific characters would be introduced. *The Phantom of the Opera* uses a spooky chromatically descending passage every time the author wants to suggest that the Phantom is nearby. But the operatic *leitmotif* need not be used heavy-handedly.† Notice how Jerome Kern used the melody of 'Ol' Man River' *upside down* for his 'Cotton Blossom' opening of *Show Boat*.

Cot - ton   blos-som   Old   man   ri - ver

*Richard Rodgers's enormous talent was understandably waning late in his life when he wrote his final shows, *Two By Two* which had lyrics by Martin Charnin and a few others, and *I Remember Mama*. The latter show involved a group of songwriters in addition to Rodgers. Both shows were disasters which were certainly not improved by the diversity of styles in which their composer-lyricists worked.

†Although Stephen Sondheim's *Follies* is basically a light-hearted score, it deals with some important and rather depressing issues. Its 'cracked face' logo and musical motif (the song was removed before the Broadway opening), still intrudes itself in a healthy and troubling way from the overture to the final curtain. It is to be observed that when the show was recently restaged in London, the 'cracked face' logo was replaced with one showing a marquee sign with a crooked letter, thus suggesting a disused theatre rather than ageing Follies girls, and lightening the public's first visual impression of the musical. However, the intense, beautiful and sometimes depressing motif remained.

The Lead Sheet

The musical shorthand known as the lead sheet is an expedient means to creating an approximation of a composer's ideas. It was a valuable tool for those who only knew rudimentary chords or who needed a professional to write down the melodies as they sang them to an arranger. But if a composer wanted more than the root of a chord in the bass, or if he wished a chord constructed in any manner but ascending thirds, the interpretation became so complicated to write in lead sheet form that it became *easier* to fall back on notation. Because of this, the best composers, Rodgers, Arlen, Gershwin, Lane, Strouse and many others always wrote their own piano scores and only relied on a lead sheet for sketching. Since today's composers know they can only approximate the sound they want, their shorthand method is often to commit their music to tape* so that they won't forget what they have just created, and then go directly to the piano score. The lead sheet then is back where it started, the refuge of the untutored. Here is how Stephen Sondheim feels about it:

I've never used lead sheets, and neither has any self-respecting composer with any training. Give me a melodic line and I'll harmonize it one way, you may harmonize it another way. It's an entirely different song, even though it's got the same melodic line. Music is made up of a number of elements, and it is the putting together of all those elements that gives the song its flavor, character, quality, weight, texture, everything else. Lead sheets have nothing to do with anything as far as I'm concerned. If you leave it up to the orchestrator to fill in the textural detail in the orchestra, it becomes essentially an arranger's score. That's what the word 'arranger' really means: somebody who takes a lead sheet and chords and makes an arrangement of a tune. Now for my money, that's the composer's job, otherwise he's not composing. A lot of people aren't trained to do that and need arrangers, but not any of the composers whose work I respect.

---

*Thomas Shepard, who is best known for recording original cast musicals, does not record his own creative work at the outset. 'I usually forget' he says, 'I *do* have a tremendous fear that what I've just played will escape me, so rather than making a tape, I try to make some barely legible sketch right away. If I had a studio with a permanently set-up tape machine and a writing desk, I think I would, but more often than not, I just have the music in front of me and my hands.'

In the theatre, audiences will hear the song sung with an orchestrated background, but in order that the reader may see the progression of a song from conception to realisation, I have printed below a few bars of an original show tune in (1) lead sheet form, (2) piano vocal score, (3) combo arrangement, for use in a small theatre or workshop, and (4) full orchestration suitable for the West End or Broadway stage.

1   The lead sheet

He thinks I'm beau-ti-ful ⸻ He told me so

2   The piano score

3   Combo arrangement for use in a small theatre or workshop

4 Full orchestration

ANTICIPATING THE ORCHESTRATION

Although the piano score will not be fully orchestrated until the show has been optioned, directed and rehearsed, the composer and orchestrator will want to have frequent meetings to discuss the final sound of the show. After this, many orchestrators, aware of the last minute rush to add underscoring, introductions, finales and the like to a finished score, always against a deadline, will make notes *on the piano copy* of some of their ideas for orchestration.

If the show is to go directly to a workshop or fringe production it may be presented only with piano backing, but there are some theatres like London's King Head, New Jersey's Papermill Playhouse or Chicago's Dramatist Workshop whose budgets for development include enough money for a small orchestration and even paid rehearsal salary for the band. These will eventually be expanded to full orchestrations when the show gets on its feet.

Jonathan Tunick says: 'Before you actually begin to work on a show, you must absorb the music and decide on what the general style of the score is. In the case of *Company*, it was a very contemporary, urban sound influenced by pop music ... *Follies* was a glorification of every pit band that ever played.'

COPYRIGHT

With a completed book, lyrics and music, the show has now become an entity, and although it will go through many changes between the present and the time it opens for public viewing, and may end up looking quite different from its original state,* it should always be copyrighted again. Two dozen scripts and as many copies of the score are generally printed up. The business of getting the show on its feet is about to begin.

---

* *Legs Diamond*, Peter Allen's musical about a gangster that opened and closed in early 1989 went through five years of drastic changes – right up to opening night. Characters came and went and the focus of the show changed from Legs' murdering and mayhem to a sympathetic anti-hero who takes up a life of crime out of frustration for failing in a life of show business. Dramatic scenes and songs had to be cut and shuffled, and a major co-starring role (Christine Andreas as Legs's wife) was cut in rehearsal at great expense.

8 PUTTING IT TOGETHER

Getting an Agent: Making a Demo: The Score. Singers and Instrumentalists. Back-Up and Overdubbing.

GETTING AN AGENT

By the time a musical is completed, rewritten and rewritten again, every professional team will have talked to other show biz personalities and will have chosen a producer and director. A star director, one who has had successes before, may have worked with a member of the writing team and even be able to encourage a producer to join the venture. A director may be chosen because the collaborators have worked together successfully and comfortably before, as the Hal Prince–Stephen Sondheim team, or if it is a new relationship (like the choice of Arthur Laurents for Jerry Herman's *La Cage Aux Folles*), because he has a certain affinity for the material.

What works for professionals is not always available to amateurs, and in order to arrive at even this stage, the untested collaborators will have to work very hard to *get* a director and later on a producer. They will have to make a demo and get it to workshops who develop properties. In order to accomplish this I advise everyone to get a theatrical agent. Get a good one. Here are some no-nonsense comments from one of the best, Mitch Douglas at ICM:

225

If you know anyone in the business who has an agent and they're successful, ask who their agent is and ask for a personal introduction. If you live in a small town and assuming you don't know anyone in show business, I would write to the organizations who would know agents and try to get an agent list. There are a number of ways to do it. I would write The Authors' Guild, The Dramatists' Guild, ASCAP, and BMI [BASCA in the UK] asking for a list of people who handle agents. Then there is Samuel French, Dramatists' Play Service, or Tams Whitaker at Theater International. One might write and ask who are the people who sell musicals. And then write a very good query letter. The effective way is to write 'Dear Mr Thus and So' or 'Ms Thus and So, I have written a musical about ———. I have a complete script. I have a demo tape. May I send it to you for review?' Say something that is intriguing about your work. If you have no credentials, you just don't have them. If you do, you might add, this play is being considered by and has gotten to the top reading levels of several regional theaters which leads me to believe it's produceable and commercially viable. If it's won awards, say so. List any works you have had published. NOT, I have written songs for my high school play, or my relatives like it, that's no qualification. If you can get a recommendation from someone in the business that's the best. Also get a list of regional theaters and write enough about your show so that they might audition it. Don't say that it's the best thing since Stephen Sondheim, or nobody writes like you either. Don't send anything to any agent without asking – otherwise they return it to you. They don't accept delivery.*

On pages 301–4 in the appendix of this book, you will find a complete list of theatrical agents in the US and Britain.

MAKING A DEMO

A demo can be anything from a home recording with the composer and/or lyricist singing, to a full orchestral score with soloists and chorus. Most of the time, the most complicated demos are a pointless extravagance because the show will be changed. As Jerry Herman says: 'If a producer can't tell whether a score has value by listening to a good pianist and a good singer (I don't say it has to be done by the composer)

---

* But even the most talented newcomers may have trouble getting representation. When asked about getting an agent for his first show, Jerry Herman said: 'If you can find one, [it's the best avenue to pursue]. I couldn't. Before I put work on the stage, I had to go knock on doors.'

then he has no business being a producer of musicals. To spend a fortune on those orchestrations is ludicrous, because they won't be what will ultimately be done. [My advice to amateurs is to] present your work with all the love and care you possibly can, and hope that your producer doesn't have a tin ear.'*

I believe the 'good pianist and good singer' mentioned above should be recorded in a professional studio. This will facilitate your agent going through the workshop route.† Some studios in New York and London that specialise in demos are listed in the appendix of this book, but the classified section of every telephone directory carries a list of recording studios.

The Score

Time (especially in a recording studio), is money – often a great deal of money – for a professional studio with a capable engineer and good equipment (in early 1991) costs about £100 or $200 per hour. An hour's work for a good demo singer adds a good £50 or $100 per hour as well. All of which means that studio time is not to be wasted. Since the singers and instrumentalist(s) have only the notes on the page between them and the microphone, the score should be clean and legible before one goes into the studio. Takes and retakes should only occur because of unclear diction or because the artists are unfamiliar with the material. These are unavoidable. But with or without a producer, no one wants to pay for time spent deciphering the notes. Nothing is more amateurish and discouraging to other collaborators, especially if they consider the future possible liability of working against deadlines with a composer/lyricist whose score is illegible.

---

*You might also hope the producer has had a good night's rest before auditioning your show. One of my most painful experiences was playing and singing a musical for a well-known producer, (nameless here) while watching out of the corner of my eye as he was nodding off.

†Sometimes, if a show has a major star committed and eager to do the role, a demo is unnecessary. Luther Henderson says: 'I don't think we'll be doing a demo for *Mr Jellylord*. The reason is Gregory Hines. This is a special instance, for we have in tow an extraordinary artist and an extraordinary person in the movies and everything. So for whom are we demoing or demonstrating? I can't imagine having any difficulty getting money to do a show starring Gregory Hines on Broadway about a legendary jazz figure who called himself Mr Jellylord. Anyway, I believe they already have the money ... maybe the Schuberts. One of the reasons it wasn't presented before, I'm told, is that the book didn't make sense.'

The Singers and the Instrumentalists

Demo singers have to be fabulous sight-readers. With the composer and lyricist over their shoulders checking every note and syllable they utter, they need nerves of steel. They also need to be able to match a phrase they have just sung so that the engineer can patch it into the tape. They even have to be able to change the timbre of their voices to create a particular kind of sound requested (young, old, tired, fresh, sexy, and yesterday's). Sopranos have to be able to sing alto and tenors need a range big enough to encompass baritone and bass lines. It has been frequently pointed out that demo singers never go on to become singers on stage. Most of them will tell you that it is because they don't want to leave home, which is generally required of a show in progress. Don't believe them. I am sure it is because they have developed their considerable art to its fullest capacity. Everyone I have ever worked with takes special pains to make every syllable of every lyric super-comprehensible. Usually they have to do it with very little rehearsal. But they never have (nor should they have) that special star quality or individuality that stage performers need. They are the work horses, not the sleek race horses the public will see. One male and one female, are generally able to handle all the songs of a musical.

Even where a musical is already cast most professionals find it preferable to hire demo singers rather than let theatrical personalities do the recording. This ensures that the score will be clear, tempi are unvarying and songs are not theatricalized.

Although some composers like to make their demos with a trio for backing, (piano, bass, drums), that kind of demo has recently been considered overkill. Piano and vocalist is enough, and the pianist may be the composer. But often I have found that composers are not good enough pianists to cope with the material. And if they can negotiate all the notes, sometimes they may be too emotional for demo recording, which really doesn't want to create theatre on tape. It is often hard for the theatrically emotional personality to keep the tempo steady. That's why most professionals rely on that all-important person, the rehearsal pianist. Besides, the composer and lyricist belong in the studio control room, critical of every sound as it is being recorded on to the tape.

Back-up and Overdubbing

Remembering that the word 'demo' is short for demonstration, a demonstration that will bring the necessary agents, directors, producers and eventually backers into the project, professionals limit its scope. Back-up, the kind that was used in Stephen Sondheim's 'You Could Drive a Person Crazy' from *Company* is not only unnecessary, but is to be avoided. It only serves to cloud the lyric. Overdubbing, creating a massive sound using a few singers, is generally an expensive waste of time.*

---

*For one of my early musicals, where I needed a production number, I remember creating a full chorus using four principals by overdubbing each part several times. When the number was finally finished, it sounded like an army of a thousand, but the words were incomprehensible, the singers exhausted and the producer furious because the cost was astronomical. Worst of all, the number was cut from the final demo.

9
AUDITIONING

Auditioning in General. Working with a Star. Writing a Show for a Star. Showcasing. Auditioning for Backers.

AUDITIONING IN GENERAL

Howard Dietz, lyricist and skitwriter for the revue *Flying Colors*, was especially distressed when he had to audition the endless vaudeville acts that would be interspersed between sketches and songs in that show. He commented: 'One day I was sitting with Helen Broderick at an audition watching a man whose act was to do a violent and comic prizefight with himself. He actually made his nose bleed. Incredulous, I asked if he made his nose bleed at every performance. "Oh no," replied Helen, "only at auditions."'

And now the moment comes for the artists to bloody their own noses. For whether it be a search for a star, a workshop, a director, a producer, or simply to spread the word that it exists, the material has to be presented for review. Even if a musical has been written with a particular star in mind, that star will have to audition and having auditioned at the musical's inception may be called upon by the producer to audition again

230

when the show gets on its feet.* Katharine Hepburn had to audition for *Coco*; it was touch and go with Rex Harrison before he was hired for *My Fair Lady*.

WORKING WITH A STAR

In the first half of this century a majority of all musicals were written with particular stars in mind. Revues would often be built about popular performers, only to close when that personality tired of appearing in them. The serious book musical had not yet arrived and overtime costs for backstage help, crucial to a producer's budget today, was negligible. This allowed a performer like Al Jolson, who did not feel alive unless he was electrifying an audience with his showmanship, to stop the slight plot of *Sinbad* and sing a half hour's worth of his hits. Bert Lahr too found his own life in clowning and taking his audience away from *their* lives. They had what is known as star power, the vital electrifying element that flows from performer to audience. Revues and musicals were tailored around them. Eddie Cantor, Fanny Brice, Sophie Tucker, Ed Wynn, The Astaires, Ethel Merman† and a hundred others all had this indispensable gift, and their appearance alone guaranteed a run for the show.

Most of today's songwriters follow the Richard Rodgers tradition of being more fussy about the performance of their material than the comfort of their stars. Jerry Herman, an exceptional composer who follows only the lasting traditions of show business, says: 'I revised several *Dolly* numbers for Carol Channing because I wanted her to be comfortable. I believe in the comfort of a star above anything else. I would throw out the best song in the score if it did not sound comfortable in the star's mouth.'

---

*Gloria Lane who starred in Broadway opera auditioned and was given her first featured role while pregnant on the condition that she reaudition after the baby arrived. Gian Carlo Menotti, the director, wanted to be sure childbirth had not changed the quality of her strong mezzo-soprano voice. Mr Menotti later proclaimed that motherhood had, if anything, improved Ms Lane's vocal timbre, and awarded her the key role of the secretary in *The Consul*, thereby launching her into a long operatic career.

† Critic Martin Gottfried sums up some reasons for Miss Merman's unforgettability when he says: 'She was the essence of the musical theater ... so innocently obsessed with gripping the audience that she felt no embarrassment as she strode downstage, planted both feet squarely beneath her, reared back, and blasted the back wall of the balcony.'

Throughout the Thirties and beyond, movie personalities like Mae West, Lucille Ball, Jack Benny, Robert Preston, Janis Paige and the like were often imported to help an ailing show. But as the musical developed into a larger and more expensive entity, with companies mushrooming all over the world, any particular star's indispensability necessarily declined.*

Although composers and lyricists often keep a visual image of a star and hold on to the sound of a particular voice in their heads for inspiration, it is not always possible for them to see their dream performer on stage, but Jerry Herman, who, as was mentioned in an earlier chapter, believes in staging a song in his mind while composing it, is often imagining the star who will sing it even then. He says:

> I suggested Angela Lansbury for *Mame*, and the producers thought I was just demented. Their feeling was, 'This is a brilliant actress, there's no better actress in the world, but she's not a musical comedy performer.' But I had seen her in a Stephen Sondheim show, *Anyone Can Whistle*, and I remembered this lady belting out a song, very, very well. So I said, 'She's a musical comedy performer and all I want you to do is to get her a ticket to New York. I'll do the rest.' They were so pleased with the score I had just written that they gave me the three hundred dollars to bring her in. [After the audition] she had the contract in about two hours.†

Of course, a musical is more than stars. The bulk of the company will be the featured players and 'gypsies'. The dance captain, in these days of choreographic directors, usually has a group of reliable professionals he or she has worked with in previous shows to call upon for the current project.‡ But featured players may be more difficult to find especially if parts are demanding. One is often forced to settle for less than ideal performers. Sheldon Harnick recalls a 'real problem with

---

*Andrew Lloyd Webber wrote the role of Christine in *The Phantom of the Opera* for his wife, Sarah Brightman. After singing the role successfully for a year and a half in London, the New York production was announced with Ms Brightman. But American Actors' Equity declared only Michael Crawford in the Phantom's role was indispensable and Christine's role might just as well be sung by a US citizen with no harm to the production. When Mr Webber threatened to withdraw his score, Equity came round and allowed Ms Brightman to play the role in New York as long as she liked.

†That year Angela Lansbury won the Tony award as Best Actress in a Musical.

‡Leonard Bernstein remembers casting *On the Town* and aiming for realism, 'so when we were casting the chorus, instead of the most beautiful people we could find, we picked people who could realistically be identified as music and piano teachers along the Carnegie Hall corridors, people who could really sing and dance well.'

casting *Fiddler on the Roof*. We wanted people who would look as though they could conceivably be linked with this community at that time, [a central Polish ghetto in 1915.] ... Jerry Robbins [the director] and Joe Stein [the librettist] were looking for people who could act ... In auditioning Tevye's three daughters, Joanna Merlin was the best actress for the role ... and by the time we got into rehearsal, we had only one daughter who could really sing – that was Julia Migenes,* as the second daughter. The third daughter, Tanya Everett, was a dancer essentially, and as I say, Joanna was an actress ... The song we had originally written to open the show was called, "We've Never Missed a Sabbath Yet", and it was too difficult for them. Jerry [Bock, the composer,] took part of the melody of that song and converted it into "Matchmaker, Matchmaker" ... We knew the problems we had to face with these three girls, so it was written to be something they could handle.'

As Jerry Bock adds, since 'Matchmaker' was one of the hits of the show, 'it is a case in point of writing a song *after* you've cast the show, and having it work out better.'

The public's adoration of stars may be considered a kind of insurance, but sometimes, if the star and the role do not gibe, their presence can act as a kind of 'de-surance'. John Kander and Fred Ebb who had written a large part of Liza Minnelli's material, wrote the main role, the mother who has been left to manage an unsuccessful business in *The Rink*, to star another good friend, Chita Rivera, whose acting, singing and dancing talents have graced Broadway since the days of *Bye Bye Birdie*. The secondary part, an overweight sort of vagrant daughter who returns home after walking around all night with a knapsack, was written for no specific actress. But their friend Liza Minnelli, who was having emotional problems, *asked* to be in it. Lyricist Fred Ebb reports:

We are very close, and she came to me and said, 'Can I be in it?' She wanted to work. I called John [Kander], I called Jules Fisher, who was producing, and Terence McNally, who wrote the book, and I said, 'We can have Liza in the show, but my vote is against it ... And Liza was saying, "Don't change a thing. I'll sing the score exactly as it is written." She hadn't even heard it. "I'll take second billing to Chita" ... She was

---

*Julia Migenes has since become internationally renowned as a reigning star of the Metropolitan Opera, the Royal Opera at Covent Garden and the Vienna Opera.

wonderful, everything you could ask for in an actress. But the people who managed her considered this is a terrible move for her. They were obstructive in every possible way. They changed their mind about the billing, and there was a large negotiation about it. One name was a little elevated, the other a little down. It became a mess, all of which Liza seemed to have no part of. These people were horrified that Chita had more songs and the audience-pleasing numbers ... The show was tough and I think the casting of her was a fatal mistake ... So we closed. So what is the moral of that story? I mean, how do you say no to a friend that you love as much as that and who has done as much for us as she had?'

If it is hard to get a star out of a show where she doesn't fit, it is harder to get one *in* where her presence is needed, especially for a minor part. Once the principals had been chosen for *My Fair Lady*, Alan Jay Lerner, the librettist-lyricist worried about casting the small but key role of Professor Henry Higgins's mother who has a brief appearance in the second act. Both Alan Jay Lerner and Moss Hart, who directed, had set their caps at the great British actress, Cathleen Nesbitt, but, as Alan Jay Lerner reports in his memoir, *The Street Where I Live*, he felt she would never accept the role.

'It's too small a role for Cathleen Nesbitt,' I said to Moss. 'I know it is,' said he, 'but I'm going to try.' He personally called her and invited her to come to the office to discuss it. The manner in which he did left me weak with awe. He said to her: 'Cathleen, the role of Mrs Higgins was never a great role and it is even smaller in the musical version. Furthermore, I want you to know it will not get any bigger and might even become smaller on the road. But we want you very much. Cecil [Beaton] has designed some ravishing clothes, you will look beautiful, and you will receive your usual salary.' He leaned forward. 'Also, Cathleen, I beg you consider this. For years now you have been appearing in very large roles in very bad plays, to which all of your friends have come out of loyalty and suffered through the evening. I believe they will have a very good time at this play and I think you owe it to them to give them a nice evening in the theatre.' Cathleen was completely bewitched – as who wouldn't be – and the following day she called Herman [Levin, the producer,] to say she would accept the part.

WRITING A SHOW FOR A STAR

Sometimes, as with Liza Minnelli's appearance in *The Act*, written by close friends John Kander and Fred Ebb,* the fortunes of a musical, a product of a like-thinking creative group will be permitted to rest on the fragile shoulders of a generally mercurial personality. But producers have a large investment to protect and so, over the succeeding decades there developed a search for a *particular kind of star*, as when Alan Lerner and Fritz Loewe conceived *My Fair Lady* with the 'educated' British voice of Rex Harrison in mind. (They were canny enough to know they would have to pit his spoken-singing against a true soaring soprano of an Eliza.) Harrison, magnificent as he was in the role of the English professor, Henry Higgins, has been followed successfully by any number of stentorian voiced British actors.

Today, even the most popular star cannot keep a panned musical from sinking, as when Peter Allen went down along with *'Legs' Diamond*, but the lack of a star can submerge one that is barely afloat. Television superstar Nell Carter's ill-considered withdrawal from the *Ain't Misbehavin'* revival caused the barely profitable production to founder.

Besides wanting to terminate contracts when they please, a star may make other more drastic demands when it comes to the final agreements. Astronomical salary, a piece of the creative royalties, name above the title, not performing at matinées, are a few of the common terms they may exact.

But even more heartbreaking than a super-entertainer's ruinous terms may be their mercurial change of heart. Arthur Laurents, the librettist of *West Side Story* and *Gypsy* among other hits, spent a year and half of his life writing a show for his good friend Lena Horne. At the last moment, Horne told him she did not want to appear on stage any more.

Ethel Merman's well-known refusal to allow young Stephen

---

*Kander and Ebb seem to be the designated court songwriters for Liza Minnelli as Haydn was for Prince Esterhazy. They wrote *Flora, the Red Menace* in 1965 especially for their friend. Next, after creating some special nightclub material for her, they wrote *Cabaret* with her voice in mind. (Hal Prince, who directed the show turned her down for the stage role, saying Sally Bowles was supposed to be British. The movie's solution, to make Sally a transplanted American never occurred to anyone connected with the stage play.) She got the part in the movie, (and won the Academy Award). Then in 1978 they wrote *The Act*, and in 1982 allowed her to appear in *The Rink*.

Sondheim to write the music and to confine him to writing lyrics for *Gypsy* is nothing compared with the demands of Lauren Bacall when *Woman of the Year* (1980) was going through its creative process.

Before the project was begun, producers David Landay and Lawrence Kasha had obtained an agreement from the star to appear in the show for what is considered a very long run, a year and a half, if she approved of the librettist, lyricist and composer. Librettist Peter Stone speaking for co-collaborators John Kander and Fred Ebb* says, 'I dare say we'll never do it again, but we tailored a show to a star, thereby increasing the hostage situation.' Mr Stone continues:

The book was for her, the score specifically was written for her singing range which is not wide. Finally, when we would go into rehearsal and out of town if she didn't like something, there was no way we could really express ourselves beyond saying, 'How *would* you like it?' We had no basis for suddenly saying, 'no' ... It was a strange, difficult time till we opened in New York ... We found a certain amount of comedy in the agony of it. In large measure, the material and the star were compatible, so the show worked, and it ran. We all won our Tony awards, and she won hers, and everybody should have been happy, but we weren't.... Now, she had a right to go on vacation for two weeks, so we went about looking for someone who could keep the curtain up during those two weeks, and somebody hit upon the idea of Raquel Welch. She came in and did the show for two weeks and was a sensation. This added to our problems immeasurably because, for us, Raquel was O.K. in the part, it wasn't anything near what we had intended, but we were intrigued with her success. And I must say, she looked spectacular on the stage. Second, there was the matter not, of *how* she was doing it, but *that* she was doing it at all, which really intrigued the critics. So she got marvelous reviews. Bacall was infuriated. God forbid that anybody should have said a kind word to her about Raquel. When [her contract expired] Bacall left the show, Raquel agreed to come back, and she could have played it for a long time. But she left precipitously without giving us any advance warning, and we again were hostage to the star aspect of the show. We made a desperate attempt to recast it and even had to close for a few weeks to get a new star in. It didn't work. We cancelled the show. It couldn't come back after that.

---

*Kander and Ebb were an ideal team for such a project because they had the experience of tailoring their material in *The Act* to friend Liza Minnelli's unique talents.

Although *Woman of the Year* was a successful show garnering its share of Tony awards, and may have suffered from 'star syndrome', its production difficulties can nowhere be compared to the vicissitudes of outrageous ego suffered by the revered classic *The King and I* in which the 'I' was suggested by the great British star, Gertrude Lawrence, and the hostages this time were the team of Rodgers and Hammerstein. Here, from Richard Rodgers's autobiography, *Musical Stages*, are some comments on star and property:

> Early in 1950 we received a call from Fanny Holtzmann, Gertrude Lawrence's lawyer, asking if we would be interested in writing and producing a musical adaptation of *Anna and the King of Siam*. It had been both a popular novel and a successful moving picture, and Gertrude was convinced that it would make an appealing and colorful vehicle for her.
>
> At first our feelings were decidedly mixed ... we had never before written a musical specifically with one actor or actress in mind, and we were concerned that such an arrangement might not give us the freedom to write what we wanted the way we wanted. What also bothered us was that while we both admired Gertrude tremendously, we felt that her vocal range was minimal and that she had never been able to overcome an unfortunate tendency to sing flat.

Both Rodgers and Hammerstein were enchanted with the idea for the play, but would have preferred not to have been locked into a contract with a particular star. Of course, this was impossible. In his book, Mr Rodgers then goes on to discuss an antagonism Ms Lawrence displayed to him from the first day of rehearsal because, not believing in the reliability of her voice, he decided to have *all* the female songs introduced to the assembled cast by the silver-throated ingenue, Doretta Morrow. Then he continues with:

> It was unthinkable to replace Gertrude, so I did the only thing possible: I hired an excellent vocal coach to work with her on the songs ... Still he couldn't cure her of singing flat ... Taking no chances, though, I was careful to write songs for her that were of relatively limited range – 'I Whistle a Happy Tune', 'Hello, Young Lovers' or 'Shall We Dance' – while saving the more demanding arias and duets – 'We Kiss In a Shadow' or 'Something Wonderful' – for those singers whose voices could handle them. Even after the show opened on Broadway and was attracting huge crowds, audiences were noticeably uncomfortable during her singing and showed it with muffled but audible sounds.

When Gertrude Lawrence died of cancer, after appearing for well over a year as an unforgettable Anna in *The King and I*, a great star dropped out of the firmament of our musical theatre. Constance Carpenter, Patricia Morrison, Valerie Hobson and Deborah Kerr assumed the role after her, but they really never filled it. As Richard Rodgers himself admits, 'each brought something special to the role, and each was certainly more vocally secure than Gertrude Lawrence. Just the same, whenever I think of Anna I think of Gertie.'

SHOWCASING

With or without a star, every musical will need backing, and will need to be seen by members of the show business family. One of the favourite ways these days is to set up a showcase. Using people who may be cast in the roles or performers who may be currently appearing on local stages, the showcase is the musical in microcosm.

A studio is rented, the author reads a synopsis of the plot which is interspersed with some of the songs from the show. The whole process must take less than an hour. It is best scheduled (in New York) at lunch hour and the studio should be in midtown.* All the material should be rehearsed as carefully as if it were a production, with nothing amateurish about it, otherwise these sophisticated auditors who have given up their midday break might just walk out. The 'star' of the project ought to be performing to give the showcase importance; the pianist again, usually not the composer, must know the score well and the singers should have memorised their songs. The audience will have been invited several weeks earlier and a production assistant will have checked a few days in advance to be sure all the bigwigs will attend. Amateur creative teams simply have flyers printed which describe their show, and have them sent indiscriminately to agents, producers and directors. This is certainly an unprofessional way to get a hearing. Here is what Mitch Douglas thinks of it: 'I cannot tell you how astounded I am by the number of flyers I get saying, "there

*Off-Broadway, off-off-Broadway and fringe theatre projects where all concerned have not been able to give up their 'day-jobs' frequently hold showcases after working hours. (6 or 6.30 p.m. seems to be the rule in New York. In London it's slightly later.)

will be a reading or a showcase of my musical" . . . and that flyer says absolutely not one thing about the property. It may say Camille – A Musical. Well, Camille – the rock and roll girl?, Camille, the girl who died of tuberculosis or Camille, the drag queen? Which Camille? Tell me something to intrigue me. Give me a hint. I'm not going to see something I know nothing about! Or I'll get something [in the mail] that is so bloody cryptic, I still don't know what it's about.'

After the showcase the agent or production assistant will call the people who have attended to find out how deep their interest in the project goes.

AUDITIONING FOR BACKERS

Jerry Herman says that before he had an opportunity to do a full-length score, producer Kermit Bloomgarden auditioned the songs he had written for revues *Parade* and *Nightcap*. 'I am really impressed,' Mr Bloomgarden said, 'but can you picture me hiring you to write the score for a million dollar musical?' Mr Herman goes on to say, 'I couldn't get anybody to pay serious attention to me for years.'

Formerly, the only way to get somebody to pay 'serious attention', was to invite them into a living room for a backers' audition. Generally, it was assumed that by the time this was done, the show had a director and producer,* but often they may not have been chosen yet.

David LeVine, executive director of the Dramatists' Guild says that the living-room audition is not dead. It goes on in Guild headquarters which has a room with all the advantages of being set up as an elegant living room, having a wonderful grand piano and a midtown location above Sardi's the well-known theatrical restaurant. 'Our members use the office for

*William Hammerstein, whose father, coming from a successful theatrical family, never had to worry too much about raising backing, states that 'the best auditions I've ever sat in on were done by composers and authors – and if the director had been set by this time – the director explained the plot. Those are the people who feel the material the best. They may perform it badly because they're not performers, yet, again, you're making "rules" for a show. The "rules" you make when you sit people in a living room and that guy gets to the piano are: These people are not performers. They're not going to give you what you would eventually see. They're going to explain the story, and they're going to sing some of the songs for you – but they're not singers. And so the audience accepts that and are frequently charmed by these terrible voices. What captures them is the enthusiasm.'

backers' auditions. We must have one or two of those a week during the winter. I think fewer productions than was the case years ago are backed by individuals, most of them now have corporate investors or have investment from film companies.'

There are other ways to handle the auditioning process, especially if the show is being prepared under special auspices like a foundation. The Shepard-Harnick collaboration on *Molette* was done for the O'Neill Foundation. Since the composer, Shepard, didn't want to divide his attention between playing the piano and presenting the score, he 'made a pretty good tape of the piano part and then sang over it. It worked for the O'Neill people and the publisher, Theodore Presser, who will release the score.' After two weeks of workshop in Connecticut, where the production changed almost nightly, the work with essentially the same cast was transferred to an audition theatre stage in Manhattan.

Because of the large investment needed for productions, workshops or foundations which sponsor play readings are typical of the route most musicals follow to Broadway today. One doesn't get 'a producer', but 'several producers', a new one with each of the groups the show goes through.* As one theatrical lawyer stated, 'You do the show small, and then large.'

---

*Creators must be careful not to go through too many workshops because each will want a piece of the eventual profits and with too much of the pie (perhaps in the sky) given away, bottom-line, business-minded producers might not want to option the remains.

10 WORK-
SHOPPING

Getting to a Workshop. Further Development.

In recent seasons the sink or swim risks in bringing a new musical to the Broadway or West End stage have multiplied. Things are not so bad in Britain, because there are so many daily papers. Additionally, most European audiences go to see their favourite stars in spite of what critics may say, and costs of production are half what they are on Broadway. But New York has only one meaningful paper, *The New York Times*, and its powerful critic (Frank Rich) can make or break a theatre work. Whereas a straight play with a small cast can be put on for half a million dollars, a first class musical, the kind Manhattan audiences are accustomed to, will generally cost ten times that amount. The 'tired businessman' has been brought up on the lavish extravaganza, and although younger audiences embrace a 'small' musical like *Little Shop of Horrors*, or are amused by the zaniness of *Nunsense*, only a fool of a producer would attempt to sell even an off-Broadway success to one of the innumerable theatre parties who often buy out a theatre evening *before* the show opens.

But worse than that is the fact that American audiences are only interested in super-success. The same has happened in Britain which seems to have developed a taste for the old style sweeping event.* New, untried, perhaps daring musicals

---

* Mark Steyn says: 'This kind used to exist. I don't think it's anything new ... what you see with these shows of Andrew Lloyd Webber are the sort of shows that both London and New York had a century ago. The very extravagant use of technology and a highly musical

241

catering to a special audience, all do the workshop routine, while the big, lavish more commercial musicals usually have a single producer who most often leads the show to its final destination.

But even if it is a new idea, and not a large size musical, costs are still in the million dollar range. And risking so much money on an untried work is an unwise gamble. That is why producers have endeavoured to hedge their bets and pull out of a show that is not working in its 'workshop run'. They can send the creative team back to the drawing board for repolishing, then have yet another reading. This is called the development process, and lately opinion has been sharply divided as to its value.

Stephen Schwartz says 'the workshop doesn't make sense any more because they cost $500,000 and you're so limited in terms of rules that you don't have room to move freely, try things out. It's not like when we did our *Godspell* workshop, when everybody met when they felt like it and said, "What'll we do today?" It was a much more creative process then. Now it's just like rehearsal without the scenery; that's all it is, just doing the show without the scenery!'

Taking the other side, producer Michael Davis says, 'Without a development process, it's like deciding to have a baby after a one-night stand.' But even he allows that since the workshop run can be so expensive, many projects are abandoned.

GETTING TO A WORKSHOP

Amateur and professional may work differently, but before any work is optioned it must have a demo which will be approved by the directors of the theatre. This can be sent in by an agent, or in many cases it arrives over the transom or through the letter box. After a few weeks, assuming the creators have the commitment contract in hand, they will meet for their first

---

score, but with nothing else to recommend them. I think Andrew is the sort of Reginald de Koven [the most famous composer of historical operetta from 1890 to 1910, *Robin Hood, Student King, The Jersey Lily*, etc.] . . . looking back on this period fifty years hence we will wonder why did people go to *Phantom of The Opera*, what was their interest in *Cats?*'

conferences with the director and musical director of the theatre.

Frank O'Donnell who had his first work produced recently in workshop recalls:

> At our first meeting with the directors we were told there was much they liked about our show, but there were revisions they felt the book needed. Since these changes were very broad, it took me a few months to get them done. The revised book in hand ... a workshop was indicated.
>
> Seeing and hearing living, breathing actors speaking my lines and singing our songs was a revelation. One thing that became immediately obvious was that the lines I had considered sure-fire gags almost invariably sounded flat and contrived, whereas the ones that fell naturally from the characters' lips resulted in genuine humor.

Most professionals have been through several workshop experiences. My own most recent experience has included going through a workshop at the Paper Mill Playhouse in Millbrook, New Jersey with a show called *One More Song* for which I wrote music and lyrics. The Paper Mill Playhouse is the state theatre of New Jersey and like many counterparts in the US (although charging admission) its development projects are funded by the State, and the good news is that unlike Broadway, *they don't want to make money*!

Their programme which is like Milwaukee, Denver and many others all over America is a three-part one. In part one, they workshop five shows every season. Of the five shows selected they like to have one, preferably two, dealing with a black or minority theme. (The show that was workshopped before ours and preceded us on to the Paper Mill Playhouse stage concerned a black dancer in slavery days who falls in love with a white woman.)

Workshopping in an Equity theatre like the Paper Mill seems to have developed into a science. It is not done on the cheap – in fact to produce this show for two performances cost much more than one would imagine. They set one of their directors on the project – in our case the talented Philip McKinley – and we went through the intense job of casting twenty-one principals and chorus, (The total swelled to thirty-one once the assistants, stage managers, assistant musical and stage directors, etc.) were added. They hired a choreographer, commissioned orchestrations (from Luther Henderson), brought Leonard Oxley back from Alaska (where he was still touring as the pianist for *Ain't Misbehavin'*) and hired a five-piece orchestra.

We rehearsed for three weeks at the Minskoff studios on Broadway where they rent a large studio and several smaller studios for individual rehearsals by the year. The whole score had to be copied by approved Local 802 union copyists, which cost an amazing $10,000.

At the end of three weeks, cast and orchestra and all the assistants were bussed to the theatre in Milburn, New Jersey for all-day rehearsals, dinner and performances. During the rehearsal period, the cast was trained to hold the script in at least one hand at all times. Were they to set it down, it would not be what is known as a reading and would come under the costs of performance, under an Equity ruling. In a 'reading' the cast can be paid at a lower rate.

The first phase, or reading, was done with no costumes and a minimum of props on the Paper Mill's enormous stage (which had been set up for the current production, *Naughty Marietta*). The reading, given on Monday and Tuesday nights, when the theatre is normally dark anyway, is free and open to the public. Everyone is provided with a form and asked questions about what they liked and disliked about the workshop, with the zinger at the end being – 'Would you like to see a full-scale production of this work?' In our case, the overwhelming answer was happily yes, which becomes the theatre's cue to get State of New Jersey financing for the second stage. Playwright, Robert Anderson, who is a friend of mine, and has gone through several workshops on both sides of the footlights, feels the 'criticism on individual questionnaires has no meaning, but the general consensus taken as a whole, can give you an indication of popular feeling. Then you are free to take to heart what the public has said or to throw it in the trash basket.' Many other theatre pros feel that workshopping, while it does iron out the flaws, finally ends up flattening the show. And no one can deny that regional workshops have regional audiences. As Michael Bennett has said, 'what they find amusing in Iowa will fall on its face on Broadway.'

FURTHER DEVELOPMENT

The second phase is a six week workshop in Paper Mill's small auditorium which seats seventy-five and is adjacent to the big stage. Actors are paid Equity salaries and scripts no longer need to be held in hand. The production uses modest sets and costumes and just a minimum of choreography. Every night other professionals are invited and the libretto and songs are gradually hammered into what they call 'proper theatrical form'.

This is followed by 'the third phase', which includes a full-scale production on the main stage – not in front of any other production's scenery. Full productions, even in a regional theatre in the 1990s are budgeted at $1.5 million and Paper Mill, like all the other regionals, hopes the production will then go on to Broadway. Since they are a non-profit group, they are not too concerned about receiving a piece of the proposed profits, but they are very anxious for prestige and insist that every future production carry a byline in its programme, such as 'Originally presented at Paper Mill Playhouse.'

In the United States, many workshops exist in New York and throughout the rest of the country. (A complete list of theatres looking for material to develop in workshop is found in the appendix of this book.) Workshop is one of the few ways open to untried, unknown musicals as well as the famous. Peter Stone and Howard Ashman, both librettists, (*Kean, 1776, Woman of the Year, Sugar* for the former and *Little Shop of Horrors, Smile* for the latter,) complain of being on so many lists to see workshops. Mr Stone conjectures that the reason is because in the mercurial theatre somebody may be fired and they will be needed.

Most of the later Sondheim musicals have gone through workshops to good effect. *Into The Woods* was polished that way, but many canny theatre people, Peter Stone among them believe 'workshopping is almost of no value'. He, like most others who have no faith in the vision of the group, does believe in an older theatre device: out of town.

Fred Ebb is another who doesn't like it. 'I'd rather travel with a show – go out of town and get reviews,' he says. 'I can't see that it helps a writer very much, because the audience you're inviting [in the later stages of workshop] are friends. You're going to fill fifty, sixty seats with cast members' friends, your friends. And I think they're apt to be quite tolerant.'

11 REHEARSALS AND PREVIEWS

Arranging. Orchestration. The Overture. Underscoring. Exit Music. The sound engineer. Previews: Cuts and Additions. Play Doctors. Preview Audiences. Freezing the Show.

Prior to a Broadway or London opening, if a show has not been through workshop performances, there are generally six to eight weeks of intensive rehearsal before previews.

Even though the cast will be exhausted every night from working at feverish pitch, for the first few weeks this is generally everybody's happiest time. Although much remains to be done, and everybody is working at a frenzied pace, the opening night is far enough away to look rosy. To theatre people, always the optimists, the project looks infallible, everyone assures everyone else that all the tiny flaws are correctable, jealousies and cliques among cast members haven't yet surfaced, and best of all, everybody is being paid a full salary! The opening night end of the rainbow looks like a certain pot of gold.

During this time the remaining music will be written; sets built; costumes emerge from sketches on a costumier's drawing board to cloth and sequins; lighting designed; the score orchestrated; overture, ballet music and amplification decided upon. All these things will be done simultaneously, approved by the producer and his myriad assistants, but generally suggested by the all-powerful director.* Schedules vary, but most directors will timetable a six day week, 10 a.m. to 6 p.m. with a ten minute break in every hour period, as insisted upon by American and British Equity. The stage manager and assistant director who will be chosen at this point will be in charge of attendance, absences and calls. The studio will be selected and reserved. It should be central, and have a large rehearsal room and several smaller ones. Upon the floor of its main room, a diagram of the size of the stage of the first preview house will be taped.

The cast will begin to work in earnest following the changing schedule which is written at each day's close of rehearsal on the studio call-board. Individuals will be selected to splinter from the full cast and work in groups, or individually, with the composer and then with the rehearsal pianist to hammer out the songs. Jockeying these intensive 'private' drills into the fabric of full-cast rehearsal is like putting together a human jigsaw puzzle, and for this reason experienced stage managers are much in demand.

Now comes the time for routining, which is converting the song into a performance. It will be decided who will sing the song, which of the chorus singers will take solo lines, how many choruses will be done and at what tempo and volume.† Keys will be shifted around trying to find the optimum range of each singer's voice. Routining also means deciding whether there will be back-up to a solo voice and sometimes decisions are made about underscoring.‡

Producer, director and cast will be working hard for these six weeks, constantly aware of that terrible deadline – the necessity of announcing the show on a certain date, to guarantee there will be a suitable theatre available and to build up the ticket sale, which is known as the 'advance'.

---

* In directing *West Side Story*, it was Jerome Robbins' unique concept to keep the Jets and Sharks apart as groups in rehearsals, even to eating their meals as separate gangs. Stephen Sondheim recalls at first he 'thought it was pretentious, but of course, it was perfect, because without any animosity or hostility, there was a sense of each gang having its own individuality, so that you had two giant personalities onstage.'

† Tempi decided upon by the director will be an important clue to the orchestrator, who may put more notes into a slower-moving orchestration; volume will be his clue as to how many instruments he will decide to use behind the voice.

‡ A good director will try to have the songs rehearsed and routined so the orchestrator and his considerable staff of copyists will not be obliged to go on the road with the show. Taking this extra contingent along to work around the clock in New Haven or Leicester can cost the producer thousands extra in overtime.

Postponements are suspect in the theatre, smacking of deep trouble. Nobody wants to buy tickets for a musical that needs more time to patch itself together. Theatre aficionados, Americans definitely, and more frequently these days the British, only want to attend hits and can smell a flop from its first announcement. Who can blame them for staying away from these turkeys, especially today with the inflated price of theatre tickets?

Just as making *The New York Times* best seller list seems to assure a book's continuing success, so can passing the hundredth performance of a musical practically ensure a long run. But it is a rare producer of a musical that receives so-so notices who has put by enough of his advance (known as 'overcall') to keep the show running beyond its first few weeks.*

ARRANGING

Arranging has to do with the adaptation of the composer's music, his lyrics and melody to the demands and necessities of the libretto. Demand for the arranger came in when the untrained melodist could not get people to listen to his tunes for an entire evening. Before the days of harmonic sophistication, this untrained melodist was never equipped to do more than write a harmonised melody and had to get a trained musician to do it for him. For example, if the play calls for a singer coming from a village abroad and singing a hypothetical song called 'I'm Going to Like it Here', assuming this artist got a job in a New York nightclub, she would not be able to sing the song in the same fashion as she did abroad. She would have to use the equivalent American accompaniment, arranged perhaps with back-up or with a rock beat, reharmonised and reset.

---

* Discussing Cameron Mackintosh, producer of *Les Misérables, Phantom of the Opera* and *Miss Saigon* among other hits, Mark Steyn indicated his admiration for this unique kind of producer. 'It doesn't matter to him whether the show he intended to open in September gets delayed to November or December. What's important is that *when* the show opens it is the show that he intended to open in the first place. There's none of these things as in the case of '*Legs Diamond*' where something starts, and within a couple of days the word around town is that the show's in terrible trouble, and they're frantically rewriting. They don't know where to go and they're sacking everyone, hiring new librettists, kicking off the choreographer. They get more and more demented and stand around in this little circle with no idea of what needs to be done.'

When asked if arranging was not perhaps the composer's job, Luther Henderson said:

> Arrangers didn't come into play until it was necessary to produce a finished show in something less than four months. Opera composers could take a year or two to do their work. Musicals don't have that luxury. The composers are very busy in the last months writing new songs to replace the ones that don't seem to be pleasing the tryout audiences, so somebody's got to help out. But it's more than just taking some of the burden off the composer's shoulders. Take a composer like Jule Styne, for instance. I guess he could arrange, but I don't think he chose to. Composing is a very closed operation, and you must use your materials with more economy than you would as an arranger. Once you have this kernel the composer has composed, as the other things emanate from it, it will never lose its identity. To have both turns of mind, the one that can create the raw material and the other that can refine it and send it into fanciful areas is rare.
>
> With *Mr Jellylord*, that music done back in the '20s, '30s and '40s is nice. Jazzy and light. But it was done in a nightclub and is not engaging enough to interest people sitting on the other side of the proscenium. We have to do something special with the songs; maybe different lyrics, add another chorus in a different key, add a dance. And all good arrangers keep in the back of their minds how they would like the arrangement to sound when orchestrated.

ORCHESTRATION

In the professional contemporary theatre, the composer or songwriting team usually get together with the orchestrator at about the same time as the overall director is having his first conferences with the scenic designer. The latter will not talk about whether the set should be big or small, but rather about their feelings of what the show should be visually. Both of these conferences will set the scope of the show, and, as Stephen Sondheim says, the score will be discussed without a note of music.* 'I remember saying in the case of *A Little Night Music*, that it should feel like perfume,' Sondheim goes on to explain. 'I have no hesitation in using generalized images, because my

---

* Sid Ramin, co-orchestrator with Leonard Bernstein and Irwin Kostal of *West Side Story*, points out that the orchestrator is often influential in the important decisions as to the style of the score and the kind of orchestra chosen. In *West Side Story* and *Gypsy* we didn't have any violas ... in *Forum* we used no violins at all, only violas and cellos in the string section.

orchestrator doesn't want to be told, "I want six cellos and four violins," that's what *he* will decide. And he knows more about it than I.'

Stephen Sondheim's initial discussion with orchestrator Jonathan Tunick re *Sweeney Todd, the Demon Barber of Fleet Street*, was slightly more specific: 'First of all,' I said, 'we have to have an orchestra that can scare people. I wanted him to use an electronic instrument and an organ ... because for me the loud crashing organ sound is as scary as anything and also has a wonderful Gothic feeling ... and electronic sounds can unsettle you too. I kept saying, "I want it to be unsettling, and I want it to be scary and above all I want it to be very romantic, because it is a very romantic show."'

We all know that orchestration is a special art, and those of us who have heard *Sweeney Todd* know that Mr Tunick came up with a romantic *and* scary contribution to the show. Although he modestly pooh-poohs his work we are aware that good orchestration is much more than what Jonathan Tunick calls 'making devilled eggs'*, for in most shows the orchestrator is called upon to write introductions, endings, segues and underscoring. But what makes the orchestrator's contribution even more special in the musical is that the sounds emanating from the pit invariably become an integral part of the show. The specific art of instrumentation must take care of all the details and the orchestrator must be able to achieve these details without overshadowing the voices onstage.

Although listed in the programme, orchestrators' names are generally overlooked by the general public. They shouldn't be, because they are the public's only link with the music. Every note the audience hears will have been filtered through the orchestrator's pen. Composers are aware of this and many have formed collaborative teams as close as the fraternal-like composer-lyricist alliances. Richard Rodgers's music was always orchestrated by his alter ego, Robert Russell Bennett. Jonathan Tunick has performed the same service for nine Sondheim shows. Bill Brohn who worked electronic instruments, gamelin and wind chimes into an Eastern-Western sounding orchestration gives insight into the special qualities

---

* Mr Tunick explains: 'Orchestration is a way of enhancing a song – using the devilled egg metaphor – by taking it, mashing it up, adding some ingredients, mixing it, and putting it back together again.'

needed to orchestrate Claude-Michel Schönberg's massive score for *Miss Saigon*.

> Our first meeting was in Cameron Mackintosh's New York office, and it took the better part of an hour for an intercommunication to be set up. This is a different composer than one would regularly encounter – very much a unique voice – so my questions to him were very different. After getting acquainted with the script and the demo, on which he himself played the piano and sang all the voices, (incidentally, this is the best insight an orchestrator can have into a composer's desire,) it was necessary for me to start picking his brains. I wanted to know what it was he heard as far as their translation into orchestral terms when he played and sang. The orchestrator takes what is probably an accompaniment on the piano and converts that into instrumentation. It was really necessary for me to hear him express in concrete terms, passages at the piano where he distinctly heard brass chords, percussion, exotic Asian instruments which he knew from trips to the Orient. Of course, some of those sounds had to be incorporated into the score. And so that was where the working began, and it was a long process, not just a couple of hours.

Mr Brohn was requested to orchestrate six numbers from the score as a sort of demo to see if he would be the man for the job. As he says, 'the result was a sort of 50–50, some of the pieces turned out rather dreadful and far off the mark, far from what Claude-Michel and Alain Boubil had in mind for the show. On the other hand there were a couple that seemed to hit the mark closer, if not right on the nose, and interestingly enough, I think the one that got me the job was the very first notes of the score. The overture, the one I tried to find a sound for was an East meets West thing, and in what I did, Claude-Michel felt there was a distillation of all the sound that this entire piece would need. There followed a whole series of meetings in New York and London. After that we got down to the notes of each number, and "what are you going to do here?" and "what sound will we have there?"' Orchestrators rarely thank their producers who are always complaining about the cost of orchestrating and reorchestrating. Mr Brohn is an exception. He says: 'More helpful than anything I've ever worked on in getting to the essence of this score, was the allowance by Cameron of time – which orchestrators rarely have – and the means to put together an orchestra to do some readings.'

Mr Brohn feels himself an important part of a creative team, and as with all other collaborators the orchestrator must put his ego aside for that old chestnut – the good of the show. Similar to what happens in motion pictures, where background music should be unobtrusive, the audience must *not* be aware of the orchestration. If we are, it is generally too overpowering. The orchestrator must not star but is responsible in large part for the show's success.

But that is considerable and like a signature, the instrumentator's stamp is for ever branded on the musical. One could not conceive of *Gypsy* without Sid Ramin and Robert Ginzler's brassy burlesque sound, *She Loves Me* minus Don Walker's mittel European shlaag, or *Sweeney Todd* lacking Jonathan Tunick's screamingly eerie instrumentation.*

But no matter how innovative an idea the orchestrator has, he is still somewhat limited in its execution by an old and preposterous clause in the Musicians' Union contract. He cannot bring in a sweeping semi-symphony for a musical about Alt Wien or a six-piece combo for one about a nightclub without either angering his producer or the union of musicians. Each of the Broadway theatres has a specified minimum number of musicians that *must* be hired. Twenty-six in the St James and Imperial, twenty in the Alvin and so on.† Even if they don't play, if they simply sit and read the newspaper in the musicians' lounge, they must be paid. Of course, more than the minimum number of players may be hired, but with the costs of musicals constantly escalating, producers are as reluctant to do that as they are to pay for musicians who sit through the evening without ever playing a note.‡

---

* Stephen Sondheim points out that orchestrator Tunick is very aware of subtext. 'In *Follies* there is a song called "In Buddy's Eyes", in which the character says that everything's wonderful at home and that she's so happily married. Nothing in the lyric nor the music tells you that maybe it isn't true, but there is something in the orchestration ... Jonathan has orchestrated it so that every phrase which refers to her husband is all dry, all woodwinds. Whenever she refers to herself it's all strings again.'

† When Luther Henderson orchestrated *Ain't Misbehavin'* he wanted a true jazz band of Fats Waller's time. This numbered considerably fewer than were called for by the Local 802 contract with Broadway's Longacre Theatre. The idle musicians could always be found during performance time smoking cigars and involved in a hot game of poker in the bowels of the theatre.

‡ Thomas Shepard's production of *Follies* in Concert (1985) sounded magnificent in the Philharmonic Hall, Lincoln Center. And with good reason. The virtuoso orchestra backing an all-star cast was none other than the hundred and ten-piece *New York Philharmonic*.

THE OVERTURE

Ever since the classical period in the opera house or the concert hall, a proper overture was written in strict sonata form.* But from the time of the Savoy operettas of Gilbert and Sullivan, audiences have seemed to delight in a selection of songs from the show they are about to hear. It is, of course, a way of plugging the songs at the same time as putting the audience into comfortable, and especially if they have heard the music, familiar surroundings.

But an overture must not merely be a soporific, and should not be something that audiences talk through. It is the first indelible impression given of the show, and as in the classical period, it should give the essence of the show in microcosm. John Kander did just that in his overture to *Zorba*. As he says, '... in the original 1968 version, Hal Prince's version, which I dearly loved, we had the sounds of the Greek instruments behind the curtain, [the sound of the drums] and the sounds of the crowd. When the curtains parted, there was this very smoky place, and little by little, the music came out of that ... you were in a Greek nightclub, and one by one people came forward to the microphone. It was electrifying. It set the tone.'†

The overture is a composer's chance to show himself and is the only opportunity at that performance when the audience can concentrate on the music without distraction of words or scenery. And as such composers want it to be heard and cherished. Jule Styne, raconteur par excellence, tells my favourite show biz story about the first Broadway performance of his now classic overture to *Gypsy*.

I wanted to do something in the overture that would let the audience know it was about burlesque, among many other things. So I wrote this with Sid Ramin and Robert Ginzler, the orchestrators. We worked it out

---

* Sonata Allegro form is used for the first movement of symphonies and concertos as well. In essence this satisfying form consists of three parts. (1) The exposition – the first theme (in the key of the tonic), a second theme (in the key of the sub-dominant), and a closing coda. (2) A free development followed by (3) the recapitulation, the first theme (returning this time in the key of the dominant), the second theme (in the key of the tonic), and the coda.

† Unfortunately when the show was revived in the late Seventies with Anthony Quinn instead of Herschel Bernardi, that concept was deleted. So strongly did the composer and lyricist want to defend their *concept*, that they were tempted to enjoin the show from performing. Enjoining a show is an expensive and difficult manœuvre. You must post a bond to stop the show from playing, the bond would reimburse the producers for their loss if they won the arbitration.

so that at the end the trumpet player stood up and blew the rafters off. It was the most exciting thing.

Jerry Robbins didn't like it. He said 'All I want is two minutes' worth of music. Just a couple of tunes and then right into the play.' I told him I'd make it go three and a half. Well, it went 4:35. I had lied to him. We tried in it Philadelphia and he said, 'I don't like it. I don't like it at all.' But it went well and everybody seemed to like it, so we left it in.

He got even with me however when we arrived in New York ... well, you know, you come in the day the show opens about three o'clock and everybody sings a song, and dance number. Everybody kind of loosens up. The band plays a little so they won't play cold opening night. Well, anyway, at three o'clock I walked into the pit. This was the Broadway Theater where the pit is twenty feet below sea level. They had promised me the pit would be raised, but it was three o'clock in the afternoon and the pit hadn't been raised. Now I knew that the overture was going to sound like because we had played it with a pit like that for two previews, and at those two previews – it hadn't sounded. It hadn't gone like it should, so I'd been promised the pit would be raised.

So I walked up to Leland Hayward and he said, 'It sounds fine to me.' I said, 'Leland, you are a wonderful producer, but you don't know the first thing about music. Besides Jerry promised me.' So then I walked up to Robbins who was dancing around the stage. He had no reason to dance around the stage because everybody had been dismissed. But I'm trying to talk to him. I remember him with his little cap. And I grabbed him by the throat. I said 'Jerry, I am going to throw you into the pit. Not only that, when you yell, no one will hear you. Just like no one will hear my music!' And he said 'Oh, baby, I'll fix it.' But the stagehands were all gone. I was a doomed man. I sat there and actually cried.

Then a friend of mine came over to me and said, 'Why are you crying?' I told him I was trying to raise the musicians. He said 'Well, come with me,' and we went down to Twenty-fourth Street and Fifth Avenue where his friend owned a wholesale chair store. I got twenty-four bar stools. So the fiddle players were up on these bar stools playing. Jerry walked up to me after the overture – with the audience screaming and cheering – and he said, 'See, baby?' And I said 'What do you mean, "See, baby?"' They are sitting on twenty-four bar stools!'

The overture is one of the last things to be prepared before opening preview, for songs may be dropped or added, maybe hit songs will be born on the road. And writing it more than once or copying the parts, as well as the rest of the score, is very expensive. Nothing is more maddening for a restless audience than to have to sit through a chorus that will not appear in the show or to wait for the best-known number of the evening that never appears. Luther Henderson recalls:

Orchestrating *Do Re Mi*, I was asked by Jule Styne to write the overture as we went into initial rehearsal, and then again before we opened out of town and then again after the first previews. Before we came into New York, I had written three overtures, all of which were very expensive. *Do Re Mi* was my first experience with overture, and had I had more, I would have gone to his producer and said 'he's asked me to do this, and it's going to cost you a lot of money.' I did not do this with Mr Merrick – for which I think he's never forgiven me. But the point is, an overture should be the summation of the show that's about to begin. If you're going to write the overture before you've tried out or previewed, then you're going to assume that all you've done before is perfect and nothing is going to be taken out.

One of the interesting things I try to do in writing an overture is to use some theme or idea as a focal point [the 'I had a dream' motif in *Gypsy*; the 'cracked face' motif in *Follies*]. It's murderous if that focal point is cut from the show. Then you have a serious problem, my friend!'

UNDERSCORING

As with the overture, the orchestration for music that will be played under dialogue, underscoring, is best left to the very last minute possible. Underscore is the final piece of orchestration, and in many productions copyists are scrambling until the last previews to get it down on paper. The choice of which pieces of which songs are to be used and where they will be inserted is often left solely to the composer. But not always.

Richard Rodgers and Jerome Robbins together elected to use the moving melody 'Something Wonderful' as the music that was heard under the last pages of *The King and I*, the moving scene where the dying monarch passes the crown of a more civilised Siam to his eldest son. The song is heard originally in the first act sung by Lady Thiang, the King's first wife. In that context it refers to Lady Thiang's love for her husband and begs Anna's forbearance. Later, when reintroduced in the second act we feel the song has now become a reference to the burgeoning love relationship between Anna and the King. Finally used in underscoring the King's death, the true meaning of 'Something Wonderful', that this was indeed a remarkable man, is revealed. I believe this example shows the enormous power of reprise and underscoring.

Sweeney Todd is almost continuously underscored, and as

Stephen Sondheim confesses, he had to take the chance that all that music under the dialogue might be distracting to his audience. 'The difference between sung and spoken is a huge difference. It is one of the reasons why there is such trouble making rock work on the stage – the contrast between that kind of singing, which is, you know highly sung, so to speak, and the dialogue. The drop is too much. The same thing is true of underscoring. You might think "Oh, here comes a song", and then you'd be unconsciously waiting for the song, whereas it's just going to go on underscoring.'

EXIT MUSIC

Just as the overture is the first thing audiences hear, the first moments when they will make up their minds about a show, so the exit music is important, because it is the last. It is the flavour that will be left in the public's ear, the one you want them to keep humming as they make their way to the lobby and perhaps buy on cassette or compact disc.

A compilation of the hit tunes, usually played now at a faster tempo to help facilitate clearing the aisles, is desirable even if the musical ends on a sorrowful note. Curtain calls and exit music are generally the last things to be orchestrated.

THE SOUND ENGINEER

Once the score of a musical has been completed, copied and rehearsed, it will fall to the sound engineer to ensure that audiences gain the maximum enjoyment from it. He will see that they understand the words (only if the singers emphasise their diction,) not be deafened by the orchestra, have no dead spots in the auditorium, not be subjected to feedback, and that they receive the emotional high that composer, lyricist, actors, singers, arrangers, orchestrators and orchestra have put in. In a sense these audio people (who prefer to be called sound designers) are the ones who *give us the show*.

Carl Davis, who has composed film scores among other theatre work calls what has happened in the musical theatre a revolution. In his words:

This revolution happened when sound left the theater and we put it in the hands of microphones, electronic instruments and found different ways of thinking about sound. Ways in which the actual acoustic of the theater mattered less. That was the moment when musical theater became different, and a new profession evolved. Now this is important because we are in *his* [the sound engineer's] hands. Conversely, he is in *our* hands. I say that because he cannot bring to the audience what we do not produce. The means by which we make the sound has changed considerably with the introduction of electronic instruments and the advances made in the recording of rock. They have now become the every day vocabulary of sound engineers. For the composer, it means that if you are writing a contemporary work your audience is expecting to hear the sounds they would hear at a rock concert. In opera or theater they are expecting to hear the level of sound that would be made by voices without amplification, in the musical theater, your expectation is very different.

André Bruce who designed the sound for *Les Misérables*, *Miss Saigon* and *Chess*, feels he has first to create a rapport with the director, to understand how *he* wants the show to sound. Bombastic, tender, subtle, brassy, any of these effects can be used at different times and for different numbers. And the art is not an easy one because each theatre presents different problems. Even in these days when blockbuster musicals have been known to transform the insides of theatres, each house presents a different set of problems.

Cost is another thing. As Mr Bruce says, 'the higher the sound level, the bigger the equipment and the more it costs.' Then one has to reinforce the sound coming from the singers. And this can be done with body mikes or fixed stage mikes. Each way has its advantages and disadvantages.

The sound designer can change the total sound of a musical. Andrew Lloyd Webber's *Aspects of Love* is scored for a small chamber orchestra of eighteen, but perhaps because the audience *expects* volume and dimension in the orchestra or because they are in a large theatre, the sound has been expanded to one that is louder than a hundred-piece symphony. The designer need not take all the blame, approval of his levels must have been obtained from composer and director.

As for myself, I know there is no turning back and that sound design is here to stay. I appreciate the fact that I can still clearly hear a body-miked singer with her back turned to the audience and I enjoy the heightened electricity that seems to reach my eardrums as the decibel level rises; it certainly makes the show more alive and vital. But I deplore the fact that what I'm hearing sounds manufactured, (often badly, at that) and humanly impossible, which in turn destroys my belief in the people I am involved with up there on stage. No belief means no empathy or emotion. Instead we are left with excitement and electricity. Perhaps that's the trade-off this technological age has foisted on us.

PREVIEWS: CUTS AND ADDITIONS

Once a show is 'on its feet' the previews will begin. In order to encourage audiences and build up the all-important word of mouth, producers often give discounts to the staunch theatre-lovers who will attend the show that is really a 'work in progress'. The half-price ticket kiosks in Times and Leicester Squares usually do a frantic pre-opening business.

Preview tours, which can last two to three months in various cities, are similar to workshops in that the show will be pulled like taffy, scenes will be cut and songs will be added.

Some producers have found that a show need not open in New York or London to be profitable; it may just be playing previews. At a New York preview of the 1989 revival of *Gypsy*, producer Fran Weisler told me that the show had been 'on the road' for six months, doing terrific business and, miracle of miracles, had already paid off its investors. This particular revival *did* open and to excellent critical notices. But in many cases the Broadway previews can go on as long as the producer likes – in fact, the show may *never* open officially.*

But whether it will open or not, all the creators involved in the show will get their initial chance to see it clearly at the first previews. And they will have to make some soul-searching, ego-swallowing decisions. Everyone involved will have to work seventeen-hour days, trying always to pull what is *best* out of themselves, and being hypercritical of what is *bad* in the show.

---

* John Phillips, lead singer and composer for the phenomenally successful rock group, The Mamas and the Papas, wrote a musical called *Man on the Moon* in 1975. Produced by Andy Warhol and attended by all the 'beautiful people', the work was very successful in the months of previews. As Mr Phillips says: 'my fatal mistake was to open the musical to the attendant critical reviews which were probably the worst received by any show in the history of the theater.'

And they'd better love doing it. Carol Bayer Sager tells a story of what happened to her show *Georgy* [she wrote the lyrics]. She says, 'everyone loved the idea, and then it slowly was taken over by the director, then the actors, and everyone changed the original concept. I never felt it was my show any more.'

Lee Adams, who with Charles Strouse wrote the score for *Bye Bye Birdie* and *Applause* says, 'A musical that is coming toward New York is a juggernaut that is rolling along. But we work well under excruciating pressure. We do a lot of our best work out of town and always add material.'

On The Town was the first major show written by Adolph Green, Betty Comden and Leonard Bernstein. They were all thrilled that seasoned director George Abbott* had chosen to stage it. When it was previewing in Boston, Mr Abbott told his fledgling trio, as Adolph Green recalls, that he loved the score, the book, everything. Then he said, 'There's just one thing. Cut that prologue, that flashback. You don't need it.' Mr Green says that the three collaborators retired from that meeting in a rage and decided to go back and tell their director why they needed the flashback, that it was the whole backbone of the show. 'Once we were back in his office, we explained the basic principle of how it was a beginning, like a prelude, and he said, "O.K. I'll tell you what. You can have either me or the prologue."'

Stories are legion about the legendary *Mr* Abbott, who, because his collaboration so often spells 'hit' has had a long and distinguished theatrical career. He is used to bossing or firing insecure actors, singers and conductors and seems to win every confrontation with librettists or lyricists by sheer clout.

When Irving Berlin's *Call Me Madam* with a book by Lindsay and Crouse – no slouches they – having written *Life With Father, Anything Goes, Red Hot and Blue*, (and in the future) *The Sound of Music* – was in rehearsal, Howard Lindsay was heard to remark, after Mr Abbott had changed several lines without conferring with the librettist, 'Well, I hope

---

* George Abbott (1887–) has been active in the theatre for three quarters of a century. Born in Forestville, New York, his early days were spent acting in plays such as *Dulcy* and *Processional*. Later he turned to writing and directing farces and melodramas such as *Broadway, Boy Meets Girl, Room Service* and *Three Men on a Horse*. His first solo directing effort was *On Your Toes* in 1936. From there he went on to become an almost legendary director of musicals. Among his hits, besides *On the Town* are *The Boys from Syracuse* (1936), *Best Foot Forward* (1941), *Where's Charlie?* (1948), *The Pajama Game* (1954), *Damn Yankees* (1955), *Fiorello* (1959), *Flora the Red Menace* (1965) and *Music Is* (1976).

we still have the same title.' Mr Abbott is reported to have taken great offence and to have given the distinguished Mr Lindsay a dressing down. According to his Dramatists' Guild contract Mr Abbott had no right to alter the text without approval from the author, but Mr Abbott was notorious for taking complete charge of a play and so the librettist grinned and bore it.

I think everyone who has ever been involved in any form of theatre must have had a similar experience. My own happened around the same time as the Bernstein-Comden-Green episode, with my first score. It was scheduled for a week's performances at what is now the Cami Hall on 57th Street in New York. (That was then considered very élitist off-Broadway, and both score and book were outlandish fantasy.) Since we were doing the production on a shoestring budget, I myself had arranged the score for two pianos and percussion and was leading the show from the piano. Imagine my surprise at one of the last rehearsals, when I heard the director (who was also the librettist) interrupt my big ballad on the dominant chord just before its conclusion and insert a long dialogue scene. The song hung in the air and was never completed – even in the second act.

Canny enough in theatre protocol, I never complained until the director and I had our post-rehearsal meeting. And then I blew my top.

'You can't leave my song incomplete and *never* come back to finish it,' I exploded.

'Well, it creates the kind of edge-of-the-seat suspense I want,' he retorted. 'Besides it's too late to change it back, the cast is gone and the show is frozen.'

'Then it's frozen without music,' I fumed, gathering up all the score from the pit. Pages and pages, most of which I had laboriously copied myself.

'All right. We'll put the show on without music, as a straight play,' he said simply, turning his back on me. 'Let me remind you of axiom one of theatre convention. There can be only one boss, and that's the director. Everybody has to learn that or get out,' he yelled as a parting shot while I made my way up the aisle.

That night I paced the floor and by dawn had come to the realisation that by withdrawing my score, I was hurting no one but myself, for my music would then *never* be heard. The director – good or bad – was truly the boss! And so I returned clutching my music for the scheduled rehearsal early the next morning.

'I knew you'd be back. The score is too good for it to be kept in your trunk. Besides I rethought the scene, I think we'll finish the song, and *then* go into the dialogue,' he said, as I breathed a sigh of relief. 'Now, what if we break the music *here*, at this dance scene, put in some dialogue and get the required suspense?' he added. But as I stared him straight in the eye he said, 'Naw, I think we'll leave it as it is.'

Every professional has inscribed on his heart the axiom about the director being the boss, but there is no guarantee that the director will always be in high gear. Working under tremendous pressure to get the show through its previews does not always translate into being inspired. And even the best directors wince at what may be slipshod or second-rate work passed over to get the show opened. As Jerome Robbins says: 'I don't think there's a show I've ever done that I haven't gone to see two or three months later – if I'm lucky and it's running – that I haven't said to myself, "That was only a fill. I wish we could have had more time on it." '

Even more than swallowing hard when seeing a less than perfect section left in preview, is the problem of eliminating songs, often the composer's and lyricist's best efforts, the songs one has always counted on to be crowd pleasers. Mysteriously, they may not seem to be working. Sheldon Harnick, lyricist of *Fiddler on the Roof*, remembers the disastrous opening of that show in Detroit and the elimination of many of the songs in the second act. One of the most successful songs 'in all the auditions we did was "Dear, Sweet Sewing Machine". People loved it. I remember during rehearsal one day as he was staging it, [Jerome] Robbins said, "There's something wrong with this song. I don't know what it is" ... Then we got to the first preview, and Austin Pendelton and Joanna Merlin got to that song. When they finished there was no applause. They did the number O.K., but as Jerry Bock said, there was one applaud. We couldn't believe it. In a situation like that, the first thing you say is the orchestra is too loud. So, the next preview, they took down the orchestra so you could hear the words. Still, one applaud! We never did find out why the number didn't work. But we were running long, and saved five minutes by cutting it.'

If favourite songs are hard to cut, the reader can imagine the sinking feeling involved when one has to cut whole scenes. These cuts may involve changing the concept – a dangerous thing. This is usually where a show may start to lose its identity and begin to become merely a crowd pleaser, which, by pleasing everyone pleases no one. But fortunately a show like *Gypsy* not only was shortened to more manageable length, but gained immediacy by having its opening scene and concept deleted in Philadelphia. Arthur Laurents remembers:

> The kiddie show and the voice from the back of the theater were not the first things you saw. It was supposed to be a rehearsal in a vaudeville house and the first thing you saw was a woman playing a scene. It was supposed to be someone like Ethel Barrymore on tour. There was a painted flat of a fireplace with a girl in a sailor, middy blouse, and some terrible monologue setting the theme of the show. She says, 'I must tell you. I am not your sister, I am your mother.' And it turned out that she was a whore who did it to put the kid through finishing school ... That was the theme of the show – mother and daughter. And you thought 'What is this show you're watching?' and then the blackout would come and you'd see stagehands come on, and the flat would go out and there was Uncle Jocko and the kiddie show. And then you realized you were in a vaudeville house and they had just presented, as they did in those days, a dramatic scene before the next musical number.

Altruistically one thinks pre-preview changes will only occur for the good of the show, but sometimes one is forced, because of psychological problems with actors, to make changes that were never intended. Stephen Sondheim was obliged to cut the counterpoint to 'Small World', which was a song called 'Mama's Talking Soft.'* As he remembers, the two kids are 'on top of a flat looking down and what they are watching is a scene between their mother and this man. They are watching their mother con the man and flirt with him so that he will handle her act, the kids. These are wise children, they are only seven and five at the time, but you see how jaded they are already. They know exactly what's going on. The number looked charming at the run-through. But the seven-year-old girl who played Louise had a fear of heights. She was up there twelve or fifteen feet in the air, and she was trying to be a good

---

*Although the counterpoint song was eliminated from the show its title and motive can still be found in 'Rose's Turn'. It was expedient not to change, reorchestrate or shorten that final tour de force.

girl, but she started to cry, and then got hysterical, so we never tried to do the scene again . . . It would have been truly cruel to fire her because she couldn't get up there, or else to cut the song. So we cut the [counterpoint to the] song . . . It's something that would still be in the show today if that little girl hadn't been afraid of heights.'

PLAY-DOCTORS

Many years ago, after sitting through an extremely stupid musical with a friend of mine, the brilliant costume designer, Helene Pons, I asked her incredulously how professionals, people who make their living in the theatres could possibly see fit to mount such a fiasco. 'Wasn't it obvious on paper, that this story would be boring and laughable by turns?' I asked.

Helene answered in her thick Russian accent and with a European shrug of the shoulders, 'You see, Stephen, they don't know that they don't know.' – a remark I have never forgotten.

I think that has remained true in a large number of cases and that is the reason the majority of musicals disappear so quickly. But the best and most humble theatre people are not afraid to ask for help, often in previews (so as not to lose their basic concept) from their peers.

Play doctors, invariably incognito members of the theatrical community, (lest it be rumoured that the musical is in trouble), are most useful when the play is not seriously ill. Although they will frequently be called in to do actual work and receive a salary for their suggestions, most of the time the doctoring is in the nature of a friendly opinion. But if a musical is truly sick, no amount of doctoring, especially late in the preview run, will repair it. Neil Simon deplores the fact that 'friendly doctoring is on the wane' in present day theatre. 'I read about Moss Hart when I was growing up going out of town to help with someone else's play. Friends would help friends. It doesn't happen very often any more, but I would like to do it a lot if the shows are worth saving.* Mike Nichols did that with me. He came to help out with *Fools*, purely out of friendship.'

---

* In an interview Neil Simon laid to rest the old Broadway enigma of whether or not he did some work on *A Chorus Line*. Yes he did. 'Michael Bennett was a friend of mine,' he explains. 'We had worked on *Promises, Promises*, [for which Mr Simon did the libretto, and Mr Bennett

It has been mentioned earlier that Oscar Hammerstein was Stephen Sondheim's mentor and suggested that his protégé accept the offer to do only the lyrics, and not the complete score of *Gypsy* because of the experience it would afford him. Hammerstein thereafter assumed a godfather role for the project, becoming a kind of benevolent play doctor. Concerning the difficult 'Rose's Turn', Sondheim remembers:

I insisted the number not reach a hand. A woman's having a nervous breakdown should not get applause. To have a mad scene and then have a bow violated everything that I thought I had learned from Oscar Hammerstein, who taught me to be true to character and true to the situation. So I forced Jule to not put an ending on it ... We got to Philadelphia and Oscar Hammerstein came down to see it ... and the most important thing he said was 'You must give Ethel Merman an ending on "Rose's Turn"'. I started to bristle and I said, 'Why?' And he said 'Because the audience is so anxious to applaud her that they are not listening to the scene that follows. Since the scene that follows is what the entire play is about, if you want them to listen, you must let them release themselves. And that is what applause is for. I know it's dishonest but *please*, fellows, put a big ending on that number if you want the rest of the play to play. Or bring down the curtain there. You have to choose one of those two things.' And after taking it under advisement, that's exactly what we did. We put an emotionally fake ending on that song ... As a result of that, the audience bravos and screams and bravos and screams and then they play the last scene and the audience listens.

All the foregoing applies to the best kind of play doctoring, when the play is not desperately ailing and the assistance is in the nature of critical advice. Yet if there is a multimillion dollar musical and it is in real trouble as, let's say, *Shangri-La* was in 1956, a doctor will be called. Although the theatre community had whispered about it for years, Sheldon Harnick has recently gone on record to say that it was he who was 'called

---

the direction.] and he asked me to come down to the Public Theater to see *A Chorus Line* there. Well, it was a knockout; you knew it was going to be a smash. And Michael said, "Come talk to me." We went to a Chinese restaurant, and he said, "You know, it just needs some funny things here and there. Will you do it?" And I said, "Well, it's against the Dramatists' Guild rules to do that." And he said, "What if I got permission?" So I wanted to do it. I was thrilled with the show and it would make me feel good to make a contribution to it, as long as it didn't create trouble. I wrote not an enormous number of lines, and many more lines than he actually used. But I never took credit and I never got money for it.'

in secretly to rewrite lyrics ... They needed someone to do repair work.'*

Similarly, *Grand Hotel*, considered one of the successes of the 1989–90 Broadway season, was in a state of disarray in late 1988. This time, part of the trouble was in the book but the major illness was a tired score. A librettist of some note had to be called in, in this case it was Peter Stone, well known in the theatrical community for doctoring many plays, and Maury Yeston, whose previous score *Nine* had won him a Tony, who added freshness to Wright and Forest's songs. Tommy Tune's directing moved the show into the hit column.

The economics of play doctoring are simple. A contract is made, usually the doctor is entitled to a percentage of the play in proportion to what he adds. This portion usually comes from the original author's percentage. In a discussion before members of the Dramatists' Guild, Mr Stone explained how, with a Guild-approved contract, the librettist, composer and lyricist *always* retained the artistic control of their material, and could not be unseated without their acquiescence, he added: 'Play doctors only come in with the author's consent ... but throwing up your hands and leaving is a form of consent ... When I'm invited out of town to assist on a show, I always ask them to put the author on the phone. If he's gone there's nothing more to be done, but if he's still there, I can ask him, "Are you doing this on your own? Do you want help? If not, nobody's coming."'

The play doctor may choose to accept or more often, as Mr Stone did in *Grand Hotel*, avoid a programme credit. But as David LeVine says, 'Some authors have enormous clout. If Edward Albee goes out and doctors a play, he might have the clout to get billing if he wanted it.'

---

* That show unfortunately, only lasted two and a half weeks, but it was instrumental in bringing Mr Harnick together with Jerry Bock. They wrote their first show together, *The Body Beautiful* in 1958 and followed that with a string of hits including *Fiorello, Fiddler on the Roof* and *She Loves Me*.

PREVIEW AUDIENCES

There are many producers who do not believe in setting a show on its feet out of town. They opt to hold all their previews in New York where they will have to ignore bad word-of-mouth if the show runs into difficulty. These staunch exhibitionists will always tell you that audiences in the boondocks (provinces) are no criterion as to how the show will play in London or New York. There is a great deal to say for this argument, for every time I have been with preview audiences even in large cities like Boston and Philadelphia, the reactions are substantially different from those of Broadway or the West End. The laughs always seem to come in what I assume are the wrong places. Joe Masteroff who provided the libretto for *Cabaret*, an immediate hit in New York, recalls his grim preview days in Boston: 'The reason was that audiences really didn't know what to expect at that point. The name of the show was *Cabaret*, and they expected it to be a normal kind of Broadway musical. Within ten minutes, they had seen these not-so-great-looking chorus girls, and the show seemed to be a little on the grim side. And people began trooping up the aisles. Believe me, we were all very depressed about it!'

FREEZING THE SHOW

Although one can make changes at practically every performance when a show is out of town, before it is exposed to its West End or Broadway opening night, when it gets down to the wire, every show must be frozen. William Hammerstein says:

> Josh Logan always used to tell me, 'Remember, you can make changes right up to the opening night curtain.' Well, he was wrong, because you can throw the actors the wrong clues. Conceptually, I knew what he was trying to tell me: 'Don't let anything go, when you know it's wrong. Fix it. And you can do that right up to the opening.'* Well, you *can*. Up to

---

* Lyricist Carol Bayer Sager who had a flop with *Georgy* and a hit with *They're Playing Our Song* recalls the former's devastating experience. 'The musical director said it was all right, never mind how it sounds in Boston, it will sound wonderful at the Winter Garden [in New York]. It didn't; it sounded the same as it had in Boston.'

a point. But you risk making your actors awfully nervous. If it's Tuesday and your opening is on Thursday, and you ask them to change a line or a piece of business, they get very upset. However, you should continue to adjust up until the moment that you feel it won't throw them off – you have to be very much aware of making the change. Better to make the change *after* the opening of the tryout.

Ethel Merman, professional that she always was, was meticulous about learning her scripts. Once they were mastered, she did not like to make any changes. She felt they threw off her timing. In the last few days before the Broadway opening of *Call Me Madam*, when librettists Howard Lindsay and Russell Crouse asked to insert what they felt was improved dialogue they had just written for one of her scenes, she refused. 'Boys,' she snapped, 'call me Miss Birds Eye of 1950. I am frozen. Not even a new comma!'

12 THE OPENING AND REVIEWS

Working on the Stage. Opening Afternoon. Opening Night. Reviews.

WORKING ON THE STAGE

During the last week, if a show has been doing previews out of town, the cast will get to do the show on its eventual New York or London stage. Because these are metropolises whose audiences may be slightly more sophisticated than those in suburbia, the director usually fine-tunes to what he assumes their taste will be.*

And since theatre sizes vary, the sound, the amplification and body mikes will have to be adjusted as well.

Amplification and Body Mikes

When conducting, Luther Henderson insists upon a week of unchanged material for the orchestra to get used to each other, the cast and the theatre acoustics. 'But,' he adds, 'with the nature of show business, sometimes that is impossible and often two weeks after opening you're still fiddling around with

---

*Although it sounds snobbish, the converse is unfortunately true of musicals that are into long runs. The style is generally broader *not* because the director has guided the cast that way, but because after many performances players have a tendency to emote or go 'over the top'.

269

the sound. Of course the show would have to be a success. If it's a flop, it doesn't matter, you would be closed in that time. But often the critics, public or even the director will say "I can't understand the words", or "the orchestra is awfully loud" and the sound pattern will have to be adjusted from stage and computer. There are so many subtle improvements in acoustical clarity that have been happening recently in theaters all over the world.'

Many of our theatre stalwarts deplore the fact that in order to be financially successful, big musicals – the kind most people want to see – must play in big houses. For, 'a musical', as Burt Bacharach insists, 'must dazzle the senses.' In New York that means theatres like the Gershwin and Minskoff; in London, Drury Lane and the Palace.* And in order to be heard in these large auditoriums, we have in the last quarter century come to accept the fact that all musicals will be amplified. Principals will wear body mikes which will cause certain clinches to be over-amplified – sometimes we even hear the rattle of their jewellery. There will be evenly spaced microphones stuck into the footlights necessitating that singers perform their solos in specified areas of the stage. And there will be dead spots on stage as well which must be avoided.

Although there are a few writers of musicals who take the opposite view, most of today's professionals have welcomed the sound man† as an important part of the production staff and have accepted the sound booth in the same way they accepted the lighting booth a hundred years ago. Terence McNally, an outspoken playwright whose heart is often in the opera house, deplores the building of the big theatre, what he refers to as the 'new monstrosities that keep going up', and says, 'if a voice cannot fill a theater then clearly something is wrong with the size of the house'.‡

But because audiences, often brought up on rock, are accustomed to listening to recordings at a higher decibel level than

---

*The Gershwin Theater, rather exclusively reserved for musicals, is New York's largest legitimate house with a capacity of 1,933. London's Drury Lane seats 2,300.

† Called a necessary evil by some, hailed by others as a blessing to both performers and audiences, Burt Bacharach says the sound man performs one of the most important functions of theatre. 'He must be delicate,' he adds, 'and very careful of the audio level, too. You have older people who go, and you can't beat them and assault their ears with overly loud sound.'

‡ Opera audiences, always purists, are rarely aware that according to Hal Prince, who directs opera as well as musicals, amplification is creeping into most of the world's large opera houses.

was customary a generation ago, there is no way of going back.* And although amplification can flatten the sound of a voice, if well done and unobtrusive it can also intensify our feelings, by allowing a singer to perform a quiet number without strain.

OPENING AFTERNOON

The opening afternoon is the most nerve-racking time in a show's entire life. Cast and orchestra are usually assembled and under the director's supervision and in practice clothes, everybody runs through a number or two, more to warm up than to rehearse. In New York, the cast generally doesn't leave the theatre.

Although it would be hard to apply in New York today, because women generally do their own hair and because of the obligatory six o'clock curtain,† William Hammerstein remembers a theory that allayed the opening night jitters. It originated in the days when he worked with Josh Logan. 'Josh's theory was to keep them busy. Now of course, the girls always want to have the afternoon off to go to the hairdresser. I don't know why they feel their hair should look different on that opening night than on any other, but it makes them feel good to have their hair done. In the days I worked with Josh we always had a last one preview, a matinée on the opening day. And there would be complaints, they'd say, "I don't want to get all exhausted." But you don't get exhausted, you are in a state of high intensity, and if you sit around and worry about – what am I going to do if I forgot the line I forgot the other night? – you make things worse. If you do a performance, you get another one under your belt, and you come out that night and you own the performance. Exhaustion is no danger, performers always seem to rise to the occasion.'

---

*Mr Henderson recalls arranging and orchestrating a review called *Rodgers and Hart* in 1975. 'We did it in a nice small theater, without amplification – it was Burt Shevelove's thing. The cast was hired for their ability to project, and I used a small band, very well muted. The people who came to see it seemed to enjoy it a lot. The critical review summed it up as "a nice show". That's probably one of the most damning things you can have, so we closed in a few weeks.'

†The six o'clock curtain on opening night was established two decades ago so that New York newspaper reviews could be at the Times Square newsstands before midnight and somewhat competitive with the 11:15 television review.

OPENING NIGHT

London, with its more sophisticated and perhaps more tolerant theatregoers has never made the same fuss about 'opening night' as New York has. The West End theatre follows Shakespeare's dictum that the 'play's the thing', and cares little for the Broadway glitter, the photographers and autograph hunters out on the sidewalk, the limousines and taxis spilling out their glamorous passengers, the celebrity and café-society audience dressed to the nines (who formerly thought it was not chic to arrive before the first act was half over), the sophisticates notorious for 'sitting on their hands', frequently leaving after the first act, and the all-powerful *Times* review.

The power of the opening night in America is perhaps best illustrated by what happened to librettist-lyricist Tom Jones on the night of May 3rd, 1960 when *The Fantasticks* made its debut. (By far the longest running show in off-Broadway history, *The Fantasticks* has an enviable and phenomenal record. It is still visible in Greenwich Village at the Sullivan Street Playhouse and is constantly being performed by amateur and professional groups all over the world.)

After the first, unenthusiastic reviews were read, librettist-lyricist Tom Jones remembers heading home and getting 'out of a cab. I vomited my way through Central Park. And I went home and thought I was going to die, really. The next day I managed to get up by noon and eat something which was very hard to do . . . And the afternoon papers were good. The second night, the backers who had read those not-good notices were there . . . there was nobody in the house except a few unhappy backers. Most of them wanted Lore [Noto, the producer], to close the show. It was Thursday night, and the press agent said, "Close it Sunday." And Lore said, "No way," because this had taken the last of his money in savings. He had $3,000. That was it. He had quit his job . . . it committed him. And so we survived. How did we survive? There were two things: theater people spread the word, and the *New York Times* gave us a picture on Sunday. We ran a big ad. There would be twenty people at a show, but they would be Richard Rodgers, Jerome Robbins, Anne Bancroft . . . Cheryl Crawford called at least a hundred people and they came down . . .'

REVIEWS

Very few shows close in London after a single performance but the history of Broadway has been peppered with them. After so-so reviews the majority of American musicals close within a week or two. Londoners are more tolerant, perhaps because many theatregoers read more than one of the daily papers, each of which has a critical review, but not necessarily the next day. And this allows the British public – always of an independent mind – to have many contrasting points of view of any theatrical presentation. New York has two major morning journals and one afternoon one, but only the morning *New York Times* counts.

But I feel the main reason even a second-rate musical can survive for a couple of months in London is because theatre costs are not as astronomically high as in New York. Thus, every show attended does not *have to be* a blockbuster. Audiences will not have blown the entertainment budget for the month on an enjoyable but forgettable evening. And that is why opening night in the West End is not the same matter of life or death it is in New York. As Gretchen Cryer, composer of *I'm Getting My Act Together and Taking it on the Road* says:

> When you talk about reviewers, you're really only talking about Frank Rich of *The New York Times*, and we have to ask what Frank Rich is looking for today. In musicals we know he likes *Sunday in the Park with George*. That's where he thinks the musical theater ought to go. So anybody who's not writing that kind of musical has to be wary, of course. He has a rather narrow view of what musical theater can or ought to be, and I think we all have to make contingency plans for our work if Frank Rich is going to give us a bad review.*

Adverse criticism is one of the hardest things thin-skinned theatre people have to face. But William Hammerstein says they *should* face it. 'You can learn from reviews,' he continues, 'depending on who the critics are. Elliot Norton in Boston was a very instructive critic. My father and Dick [Rodgers] used to have lunch with him every time they had a show up there.

---

*Luckily for the smash hit *The Best Little Whorehouse in Texas*, Richard Eder who was Frank Rich's predecessor on the paper had lost his power by the time the show opened on Broadway. Having received bad off-Broadway criticism, he, as well as all the other reviewers, were not invited to see it again.

And Fred Coe down in Washington. So while you were on the road you could gain something. But if you open on the road to bad reviews, you better take a good look at what you can do. Because there is a tendency to get so deeply involved in your work during the rehearsal period that you don't really see the faults that are inherent. Either you block them out of your mind because you know they are there and you hope you can glide over them with all the wonderful numbers, or you know it's a fault and you hope you can get through the opening night on the road and come to work on it and find a solution.'

'Finding a solution' means that the artist has to believe there *is* a problem. It has often been said that creative people lack the self-confidence of the non-creative. Jerry Herman says that a bad review 'absolutely knocks him out'. He doesn't mind so much if someone he respects, like Walter Kerr, tells him he has done something wrong, but when some of the critics without background tell him he's written a terrible score, he says, 'You need guts, and you need to believe in your heart that you know more about what you are doing than the person who told you you don't.'

Perhaps his sensitivity to both music and lyrics makes Jerry Herman emotional enough to have a thin skin; certainly he has had enough experience with dismissive critics, but Peter Stone, who says, 'I have been writing for the theater long enough to have developed a hard shell,' adds: 'In the very beginning when I went out of town with a show and started listening to members of the audience, I learned that every single individual member of the audience is wrong, but collectively they're always right. Shortly thereafter, by simple association I discovered that critics are members of the audience and individually, are almost always wrong, but collectively they have something to tell you.'

Collectively or individually, even the most knowledgeable critics can be wrong,* cruel or both. The above mentioned

---

* Mr Stone deplores what he calls the 'adversarial relationship', where critics have the last word. In a discussion on the value of criticism, he stated, 'My first musical book was an adaptation of Jean-Paul Sartre, and the review in the *New York Herald Tribune* pointed out that among my sins I had created a line that would have made Sartre roll over in his grave. The fact that he was alive at the time seemed to make no difference. Incensed and young – two qualities I can no longer afford – I sent an angry letter saying that the line was, in fact, *verbatim* from Sartre, feeling secure that this was, indeed, the final word. But an answer was printed in the *Tribune* underneath my own letter: "That may be true, but the play stinks anyway." A very important lesson was learned: don't mess around with anyone with a forum.'

Walter Kerr writing of *Fiddler on the Roof* said 'Too bad. Near Miss.' And according to Sheldon Harnick the *New York Times* critic said, 'Oh, what a show this could have been if they had gotten Ernest Bloch or Leonard Bernstein to write the music instead of Jerry Bock.'

Stephen Sondheim feels that most reviewers are musically ignorant. 'They don't know the difference between orchestrations and arrangements, for example. There's no solution, because the more complex and subtle the music is, for example, the more listening it requires. Generally critics tend to like anything that sounds familiar – which is also true of audiences. Lyrics they think they can deal with, because lyrics are language.* Indeed, they know a little, but not much more. I don't think there's a critic around who's any good on lyrics *at all*.'

Sheldon Harnick feels very much the same way: 'So often the opera that makes a tremendous musical splash its first night is dead a couple of years later. It's already in the audience's ears – they've heard it before and that's why they respond to it.'†

Most composers have little sympathy for a critic's plight, but Stephen Sondheim and composer Burt Bacharach allow that they are aware of the difficulties of the profession. The former contends, 'I consider that I have a very sophisticated ear, but I wouldn't want to write a review of a musical on one sitting.' And the latter goes on to add:

> They have too much to do on the first night. They have to review the sets, the actors, the singing, the clothing *and* the score that they're hearing for the first time. I thought it would be great if the music came out a couple of months before, on a record or cassette, so they would have some familiarity with the work. Listen, I've written things I didn't like the first time – or the second or third time – like a record I'll hear on the air. And I'm in the music business! I didn't like *Hair* the first time I heard the music and I said so publicly. It was a bad mistake to be quoted

---

* The New York theatre critics who awarded the Tony for best musical to *The Music Man* over *West Side Story* will never outlive that ludicrous injustice. One explanation is that an innovative musical like *West Side Story* resisted formula and may not have been understood by them on a single hearing.

† At an interview Mr Harnick recommended Nicholas Slonimsky's book *A Dictionary of Musical Invective* as a way to deal with bad critiques. 'It's a collection of reviews in major papers in Europe and America from Beethoven's time to the 1930s. It's very comforting to read the reviews of *Carmen* where the reviewers are saying, "What is one to make of this absolutely unmelodic trash." They couldn't hear it.'

as saying I didn't like *Hair*. So if I can't discern and separate it the first time, I don't think critics can. I don't think their ears are going to be necessarily better than mine.

Whereas Mr Bacharach is tolerant, Fred Ebb is baffled:

I don't understand their attitudes. I've had shows they didn't like and I really don't understand why. I've had shows that had critical approbation – *The Act* being one, which I thought was a rather sloppy exercise. *The Act* squeaked through on the basis of Liza Minnelli's phenomenal energy . . . If the theater's in difficulty it's all about reviewers who say 'Please take risks.' And shows that do take risks don't have audiences. It's Catch-22. The critics are asking you to do something that doesn't seem possible . . . Their attitude seems to be 'The public be damned.' The shows they're steering you to are boring. Show music isn't being given any weight any more. You spend your whole life learning how to do these things from masters before you, and now there are no rules.

And stoic Marvin Hamlisch accepts critics as a necessary part of theatre. He is quick to point out the score of *A Chorus Line*, which most musicians feel breaks tremendously new ground in an original, yet non-arty, eminently show biz way, did not get across-the-board good reviews for its music. 'The score got killed a few times,' he adds. 'And it hurt. It really did. I had hoped that this would be my "Rhapsody in Blue". What I finally learned is that critics don't know the first time around.'

And so the big question is, should one write for the critics, be shunned at the box office by the public, and perhaps eventually be discovered? The consensus of opinion is an overwhelming no. Perhaps it's best summed up by Tim Rice, lyricist-librettist for *Joseph and the Amazing Technicolor Dreamcoat*, *Jesus Christ Superstar*, *Evita* and *Chess*:

There's hardly a songwriter alive who doesn't care at all about critics' reactions, but I reject the notion of sitting down and writing in a way that's sure to please the critics. It's certainly not my aim, because you can't really please them. Obviously, you're concerned about whether the reviewers will like what you do, but on the whole I've had pretty rotten reviews of nearly everything I do. Yet my shows don't seem to be unpopular with the public.

One day a solution may be found. It may be simply having *two* critics review the musical, a proposal that was espoused by the Dramatists' Guild and advanced to *The New York Times*. The newspaper refused, however, perhaps thinking coverage of new musicals was not important enough to occupy two critics or to pay two salaries. Maybe eventually they'll reconsider the idea.

13

THE RUN

After the Reviews. Waiving Royalties. Staying Fresh. The Closing.

AFTER THE REVIEWS

Once the reviews are in, PR is the byword. Assuming, as is most often the case, the musical has not got panned and has at least received passable reviews, the public relations and advertising chief (usually working through the producer's office) will be called into play to help build up the advance. If the reviews are rave, he will have no problems. News of a hit travels fast, and often by the next morning there will be a line around the block to the box office. Sometimes, if those involved with the show have magic names like Andrew Lloyd Webber or Jerome Robbins or, formerly, Rodgers and Hammerstein,* selling the show to the public will be unnecessary, but even in these cases it is advisable to build up as much advance hoopla

---

* In Richard Rodgers's autobiography, *Musical Stages* he recalls one night after his block-buster hit *Oklahoma!* was launched. Sam Goldwyn called from the theatre and asked the composer to meet him after the performance, and when he saw him, the ebullient little movie producer danced over and planted a kiss on Rodgers's cheek.
'This is such a wonderful show,' he bubbled. 'I just had to see you and give you some advice. You know what you should do next?'
'What?'
'Shoot yourself!'
[The foregoing exchange may give the reader a clue into the real difficulty of dealing with a hit – the frightening realisation of trying to write up to the same level of excellence.]

278

as possible. And the producer's office will have to wring the utmost copy out of each review.

The public is often surprised to see remarkable extracts from reviews of a show that was roundly trounced. I have read reviews that mislead by eliminating all negative references, such as:

> The score is sophomoric, the book even more juvenile and the direction makes no sense whatever. I feel sorry for the cast and _____'s splendid scenery trapped in such a fiasco.

Which becomes:

> 'Splendid scenery.'

If a featured actor's performance is mentioned approvingly, snippets of praise from the critique may be quoted. PR people can sometimes create a full page notice out of these half-truths, and a producer who is already in for a pound may go the whole hog by running the advertisements in all the papers. If the notices are clever enough and there is enough overcall, though it may be touch and go, the show might run.

But even if the critiques are good, there is no guarantee that the show will succeed. Shows like the Sondheim-Lapine *Into the Woods* have been known to have long runs without showing a profit. Economics dictates that on Broadway, at least, three-quarters of a house means playing at a loss. Things are a bit easier in London where shows can muddle through until they find a public or at least hang on by their fingernails until the tourist season rolls round. That season, incidentally, which runs from May to September in the UK is doldrum time on Broadway. Almost any show can make a profit from December through February in New York, but even though all the theatres are air-conditioned, nothing, *absolutely nothing*, opens in June, July or August. What continue on Broadway throughout the summer doldrums are only holdover hits.

WAIVING ROYALTIES

A clever producer may be able to keep a hit running after it has worn out its welcome by announcing a new star's appearance. David Merrick, the cleverest of them all, did just that with his blockbuster, *Hello, Dolly*. After Carol Channing had made the role her own for several years, he featured Ginger Rogers, Ethel Merman and Pearl Bailey (and an all-Black cast), thereby making *Hello, Dolly* the longest running musical of its day. But what happens when business starts to fall off? Producers begin to complain that their 'nut' is too high to assure a profit and they talk about posting the closing notice. The next question put to the creators of the show is, will you waive your royalties? Most professionals would say yes, because they have nothing to gain by closing the show. David LeVine, Executive Director of the Dramatists' Guild, gives the following advice:

> You should say 'Yes' to something reasonable and for a limited period of time. See how a particular proposal works for four or six or eight weeks. If it isn't working, if you are taking a very low royalty while everyone else is getting paid and the producer is making a good profit, you have a second bite at it, an opportunity perhaps to change it for the better ... Also, when you consent to have royalties reduced, you must try very hard to make it a condition that every other royalty recipient, (the director, the choreographer, the producer) must take a cut equal to yours in percentage or amount ... The only participants receiving royalties who you probably will not ask to take a cut are the actors, because if you do that you will lose their run-of-the-play contract. Most actors and actresses who receive a royalty rather than a flat salary are those who you want committed to your particular production.

STAYING FRESH

Generally it's a directorial problem, but one of the hardest things to maintain during a truly long run is freshness. It only seems natural that the urgency of production that originally gripped all the participants of the show should dissipate. Although we expect consistency of quality from restaurants or shoemakers, it seems harder to demand that dependability of inspiration from performers. Luther Henderson's method is to call very frequent rehearsals. He says it takes even more rehearsal if somebody new joins the group, as happened in *Ain't Misbehavin'*, but 'that has a tendency to liven things up and give the show an added freshness.'

William Hammerstein feels similarly about frequent rehearsal. His work as producer, director and stage manager has taught him 'to do everything to sustain the performers enthusiasm. They have to get out there every night as though it's the first night.' He adds:

> It's not easy ... when something's missing that you used to have. And you can't provide new staging. I know that from experience ... when I was stage manager for *Mister Roberts* ... I would go out front at least twice a week to see the whole show. We ran three years, in those days that was a very long time – today shows run ten years. We didn't change the cast as they do today. Anyway in the second year of *Mister Roberts* I became very worried and tried to find those scenes that suffered most from lackadaisical performances. By the way, that never applied to Hank [Henry] Fonda who played Mister Roberts. I don't know how he did it but he would come out every night, and he *was* Mister Roberts. He managed to make it look as though this moment never happened while the others had gotten very routine.
>
> So I took one scene in Mister Roberts' cabin and I said to myself, 'I've got to make them rethink; they're not thinking of the reality of the play.' Casey Walters who was playing the yeoman would say 'Here's your letter, Mister Roberts, I typed it up.' and he would slap the papers down on the table and he'd light a cigarette. Then he'd deliver some more lines and then go out. It became such a routine performance. He was supposed to be in a war, and here it was just Casey Walters doing his job every night. The scene had lost its meaning.
>
> So I had this great idea. I called a rehearsal and discussed all this, and now that they knew what the problem was, they tried it many ways. 'One way,' I said, 'is to change a few things that you're doing as routine. Casey, when you come in, instead of slapping the papers down, hold them for a minute, slap them down later. Don't light that cigarette just because you're saying the line and you know you've got a cue to light the cigarette. Light it earlier – or later – or come in with the cigarette. And everybody agreed with what I was doing.
>
> That night when we got to the scene? Just catastrophe! Nobody could remember the changes and they thought, 'Oh God! What did I say I was going to do here? I can still see Casey. He stopped in his tracks because he couldn't remember anything. Then he slapped down the papers and went through the old routine. And it was just as dull! So as for a solution to keeping things inspired every night, I have never found it. Some actors are able to reapproach the character every night and others become routine. Many performers today have found their solution by not staying

with the show. As a director, that gives you the opportunity to bring in new blood that is going to flow a bit more freely than the old blood.

THE CLOSING

Closing after a substantial run can be a sad time for everyone. Generally the star or stars will have left long ago and may even have opened in a new production. The director will have rehearsed the cast to accommodate their performance to the new starring personality.* But the featured players, the stalwarts, the gypsies will be disbanding. And out of a job.

Addresses will be exchanged backstage, there may even be a proscenium speech by the director, and some moist eyes in the theatre audience as well. In the theatre and especially in musical theatre, relationships flourish quickly, all the intrigues of a close-knit family seem to apply. If the production is going to tour as a unit, many of the cast will already have chosen to stay in the city and new replacements will have been found.

The orchestra will be left behind and, as in previews, pick-up musicians will be hired on the road. Often these are not as good musicians as the Broadway or West End group and the musical director will need much more rehearsal to get a polished performance from them. Generally the musical director will not go on tour with the production, for, since a new show takes so long to be born, he too will be involved in a forthcoming production.

---

*Even though an entirely new set of individuals may be making the tour, most directors try to make the actors fill their predecessors' shoes. Jerome Robbins says: 'Actors can leave their mark on the show, and when they are replaced, or you do another company, they have left something there that you don't want to throw away. Now if you want to go through the process of amending again and restaging a scene with a new actor, you can do it and maybe discover some swell new thing, but we tend to be lazy.' In Mr Robbins's case, one feels it is not laziness, but that he is off and running with a new project.

14 NEW DIRECTIONS

Musical theatre is constantly breaking new ground, although these days it looks to the public at large like two steps forward and one back. For the moment, the formula musical, what is known in Seventh Avenue's garment trade as 'the same as last year – only different –' seems to have the most chance of success in New York or London. These two cities, incidentally, are the only pockets of such creative musical energy in the world, and as we move through the last decade of the twentieth century we witness their output becoming increasingly alike.

But the power shift from one to the other has caused, as Sheridan Morley says, 'a lot of ill feeling in terms of [British and American Actors'] Equity. Rows about the appearance of Sarah Brightman, etc.* How would we British feel if a team of American actors arrived in Stratford and took over Shakespeare? It's understandable that the Americans feel we have invaded the one area in their homeland which was, in fact, their creation. For whatever we say about having its roots in Gilbert and Sullivan, the musical *is* an American invention.'

What caused that switch to the British Isles? How did the creative forces cross the Atlantic, and are they sailing back again, now that a few hits on Broadway seem to have revived the American spirit? Morley, who has written extensively on the British theatre as well as the musical, feels the success of the Beatles pointed the way. He continues:

* See footnote page 232

They made it possible for people to believe that British music could make money abroad. The mechanical change worked in their favour. The coming of cassette the coming of the CD and then the demise of the American musical. Add to that the 'progress' by which bulldozers that have torn up some of the smaller theatres, and, as time marched on, the replacement of the revue form by TV. While *Saturday Night ... Live* was free, Broadway was strangling itself with high ticket prices.

But this season I saw two shows that made me think there is a Broadway musical again. *City of Angels* and *Grand Hotel*. I would not be surprised at all to see that the '90s are not the decade of the British on Broadway but the decade of the Americans back on Broadway. I think Andrew Lloyd Webber and Cameron Mackintosh will be cheering also, because they felt understandably uneasy about what the Americans think of them.

It's obvious Americans are thinking very highly of them and paying very dearly to see the British superhits which are now playing on both sides of the Atlantic: *Cats*, *Aspects of Love*, *Les Misérables*, *The Phantom of the Opera*, and the aforementioned *Miss Saigon*. This only makes us realise more fully that in whatever way the musical is going, both the UK and the US are stumbling into it together.

Now Broadway seems to be having a great deal of success with the déjà vu. Revivals like *Jerome Robbins' Broadway*, *Half a Sixpence* and *Gypsy* are successful in both countries. *Meet Me In St Louis*, an adaptation of a nostalgic movie score that borrows its technique from the West End stage's successful mounting of *Singin' in the Rain*. *Grand Hotel* (an adaptation of the eclectic Thirties movie) and *City of Angels* (about a wise-cracking Thirties Bogart-like detective) are the new entries. London sallies forth with a tremendous multi-themed musical, *Miss Saigon* (the Vietnam War, tolerance, assimilation) while each city, realising the drawing power of rock musicals and rock stars tries to bridge that gap in the musical theatre. Curiously, Sting starred in *The Threepenny Opera* at the Lincoln Center, while Willy Russell's *Blood Brothers* held forth on St Martin's Lane – both used a violently seedy milieu.

Maybe nobody knows where the musical will end up, but lots of people have ideas about where it will *not* spring from. Here's what Stephen Sondheim had to say on the subject:

What's coming up? I can't predict the future, but I do know that what's happened is, obviously, a split between popular and theatrical music. It has widened over the last twenty years because the notion of popular music, which has to do with relentlessness, electric amplification and a kind of insistence, is, I think anti-theatrical; anti-dramatic, to be a little more accurate. I don't think that kind of music can ever define character, because it's essentially always the same, and it must be the same, because that's its quality. It's also a performer's medium; it's the singer, not the song. It's everything that theater isn't. Pop music is swell for rock concerts. Whether they are rock concerts called *Hair* or *Jesus Christ, Superstar*, or rock concerts called 'Rock Concerts' doesn't matter. But when it comes to defining character and telling a story through character, which is after all what playwriting is about, then I think it's useless and can never work.

Jule Styne is like minded, but for a more specific reason.

Rock doesn't come off as well on stage as it does on record, and I'll tell you why. It's not the song but the accompaniment. You can't have that same sound for the girl who died as for the fellow who is getting drunk, or high, or whatever. It's the same pulsating thing. The only way rock can function is if it's in a setting where it belongs. If you're doing a thing of today in a street scene, you play rock. But you can't have a forty-five-year-old man sitting and singing a rock kind of thing. If it doesn't make sense, then don't have anything. Just have the actor sing with a piano or harmonica. But don't have a pulsating thing going on.

Taking a totally opposite viewpoint Carol Bayer Sager, who besides having written lyrics for the hit *They're Playing Our Song* is one of today's most outstandingly successful rock lyricists says:

Rock will grow to become an inevitable force in the theater. It will become more powerful simply because your theatergoer of tomorrow is your rock and roller today. They really have a different sensibility, and they're not going to relate to what our parents related to or what we relate to, because tomorrow's theatergoer has grown up on rock. They're going to have a hard time relating to Sheldon Harnick and Jerry Bock. It'll be easier for them to relate to *Cats*, *Evita* and *Jesus Christ Superstar*. I'm all for newness, for innovation if it's *good*. I'm all for anything that's innovative and breaks ground, as long as it doesn't distract. Or if it distracts, it distracts in the right way that it's supposed to. Then I like it.

Ms Sager's husband, Burt Bacharach, also believes the theatre should be innovative.

The more inventive, the better, all sorts of things are possible. They just cost money. I mean, you could turn the whole theater into part of the stage.* ... You want to touch the audience; you've got to get them involved too. They're used to seeing things that are so incredible on MTV (Music videos). I don't know that you can do a show where somebody just goes from dialogue and opens his mouth and starts to sing, like you could in the past. Credibility, you know. As for rock – well there was *Dreamgirls*. That was more like R & B (Rhythm and Blues) than rock and roll. I can't see rock dominating the theater, but it will certainly have a growing place – and it should have. As for where the theater is heading, I don't know.

That show where 'somebody opens his mouth and starts to sing' was out of fashion for a few years. Librettists were aiming for music to be used only in a performing area (like the movie version of *Cabaret*) or the score to be sung through (like *Aspects of Love*). But musicals seem to be taking their cue from the eclectic world of couture, which permits both the mini and the maxi skirt into fashionable salons. Producers now believe in the co-existence of operatic musicals side by side with the song and dialogue kind.

John Kander who, along with his partner, Fred Ebb, have made their names synonymous with a whole genre of show biz songs: 'New York, New York'; 'Cabaret'; 'City Lights' etc., confesses that he cannot predict the future. In fact, even the current state of the theatre puzzles him, and as a musically eclectic composer (*Flora, the Red Menace, The Happy Time, Cabaret, The Rink*), he deplores being pigeonholed to write a particular kind of show, the Sondheim-intellectual-musical. 'A few years ago I'd have said the theatre is going in all kinds of directions, which was very exciting to me.' Then he adds, 'but somehow or other, I think it's been diminished musically rather than enhanced ... It used to be that composers had the range to do anything. I went to see *Leave it to Jane* ... It was wonderful ... it made me nostalgic for a time I'd never lived in – not because I wanted to write that way, but because I wanted to have the *freedom* to write that way. *Pacific Overtures* was such an intellectual work. Not that there's anything wrong with that, but if that's all you're allowed to do ...'†

* This was actually done in the London presentation of *Starlight Express*. Skaters on prebuilt tracks zoomed through and around the audience seated in the stalls (orchestra). The New York production was not half so enveloping; the tracks were confined to an enlarged stage.

† In 1991 Kander and Ebb were polishing a 'non-intellectual musical' based on the book and movie *The Kiss of the Spider Woman*.

No important force in the theatre is as pessimistic as Stephen Schwartz, who says:

> I don't see any future for the Broadway theater unless it simply becomes . . . a place that houses good work done elsewhere. I think people who write for the theater have to find other places to perfect their material. And then when they get it finished, if someone sees it and says, 'Oh, that's good; I'd like to do that at the Winter Garden', you say, 'Oh, fine, great.' But to try to *plan* a show that goes out of town and opens at the Winter Garden is next to impossible. You have economic pressures. You're spending too much money. You don't have time to work, and you don't have freedom to experiment.

But even Mr Schwartz allows that although he loves pop music and records, he sees his talent as a theatrical one, and intends to keep writing for the musicals. Fortunately he has had enough success, as he says, early in his life (*Godspell, Pippin* and *The Magic Show*, all of which are constantly being restaged and revived), so that he doesn't have to 'worry about feeding my family'. This gives him the opportunity to go from project to project, doing things he's interested in, things that are meaningful to him. And, of course it's out of that 'interest' that his next success will emerge.

From the above it should be obvious that, although nobody can predict its direction, each creator feels passionate about what is important to him in the future direction of musical theatre, and perhaps even more passionately about what is wrong with it. Amazingly, none of them intends to leave it!

From where I sit there seem to be three clearly demarcated schools: (1) The Traditional Musical as practised by Kander and Ebb, Cy Coleman, Jerry Herman, Peter Stone, Marvin Hamlisch, Charles Strouse, Jule Styne. (2) The Intellectual Musical, a small school as led by guru Stephen Sondheim* (his only true disciple seems to be the bloodless William Finn). (3) The Romantic Eclectic Operetta Musical, an even smaller school as practised exclusively by Andrew Lloyd Webber.

---

*Mark Steyn, while being aware of Mr Sondheim's tremendous contributions to the musical, notes that these élitist musicals don't seem to attract the general public or make money. He deplores the fact that the British press ignores Kander and Ebb, Jerry Herman, Cy Coleman and the like whose audiences are far outside the Sondheim coterie. 'This snobbism is sad,' he says, and notes that 'in the last twenty-five years the biggest commercial successes were also highly regarded critically.'

And so we come back full circle to the old dogmatic truths. All the other composers, lyricists and librettists whose names I may have omitted seem to be ineffectual in their attempts to change the form. Each of these, I feel, will continue to flourish side by side by side, well into the next century. None will become obsolete, none is boring. They may well be joined, to a limited extent, by a fully fledged revival of revue and more mixed media musicals in the genre of *Time* and *Chess*.

Somewhere in the middle of the twentieth century, cinema overtook the stage as the primary medium for artistic expression. A couple of decades later, television overtook the movies as the most popular form. Both these marvels left the stage and especially the musical stage behind in their shadow, and the public's entertainment budget was further eroded by a burgeoning recording industry. All of which meant that musicals had to fight hard for a place in the limelight. In the late Sixties they did an about face. Directors with a totally overreaching vision assumed control, originating the ideas and shaping the musical to their vision. In the Eighties they seemed to return the musical to the librettists, composers and lyricists. These artists are still wrestling with the problem. In gigantic theatres or off-off-Broadway; draughty converted churches or posh West End venues; in the suburbs or in the metropolis; making debuts with records or on stages, they are still producing entertainment, even though they don't know if *their* course is the eventual course of their profession. They are creating without waiting for the next Messiah.

And although many of their colleagues have deserted for Hollywood or Eagle Lion, there are still those stalwarts who don't know how to write a score to a click-track, and if they did, wouldn't care to. There are those who prefer the world of 'five-six-seven-EIGHT!' to the electronic world of Nashville or Abbey Road. Add to their number the newcomers born with greasepaint in their veins who donned tap shoes as they outgrew bootees. They are the ones who will point the way.

Richard Rodgers once said that when somebody comes along and writes a musical that becomes a critically accepted smash hit, *he* will become the new leader, the one that everyone will try to emulate. All it takes is one. He or she is out there somewhere writing even now as I write, saying, in the words of Dory Previn, one of our finest songwriters, 'You're gonna hear from me!'

APPENDICES

A LIST OF BROADWAY, OFF-BROADWAY, WEST END AND FRINGE PRODUCERS INTERESTED IN PRESENTING NEW MUSICALS

Here is a basic list of producers who have presented musicals in the last few years. It is up-to-date at the time of this book's going to press. Some of these producers' most recent musical and dramatic productions are listed, but those with no credits following their names and addresses are still producing from time to time; they simply may have been inactive in the last few years.

Each producer's most recent address on record appears under the name. Associate producers are not generally included, nor are producers who don't have individual business addresses where enquiries, scripts or tapes may be sent. The inclusion of their latest shows is intended as a guide to their preference. Some producers want to receive only specific kinds of material, so be aware of what kind of musical you are sending to whom. Others have listed the best way to bring material to their attention. Some have requested all submissions through an agent. In those cases you *must* acquire an agent before you submit, otherwise you will be wasting time and money, for delivery of your work will be refused, or if it should make it through the door, the parcel will be returned to you unopened by the next post. Producers do not want to take a chance on opening work and then being sued for infringement of copyright if they by mere coincidence produce a work similar to one you may have submitted. (See *List of Agents* on page 305) Communication with any of these producers should be clearly marked with the sender's return address and telephone number preferably heading every page and with name and address and phone number on every tape *and* every box in which the tape is sent. In order to save time with those producers who have produced the biggest hits, it might not be amiss to send a one-

291

page letter with a page or two's synopsis of your musical (include a SAE to probe for real interest).

Every producer requires that *all enquiries and submissions be accompanied by a self-addressed, stamped envelope. For overseas mailings a cheque or postal order (in the currency of the country from which the submission will be returned) must be included.*

THE AUTHOR OF THIS BOOK WISHES TO REMIND THE READER THAT NEITHER HE NOR HIS PUBLISHERS TAKE ANY RESPONSIBILITY EITHER FOR LOSS OR THEFT OF MANUSCRIPTS OR TAPES SENT TO THESE PRODUCERS OR THEATRE COMPANIES OR FOR THEIR CONSIDERATION OR RETURN.

Jeffery Ash
Grey Entertainment & Media
875 Third Avenue, NYC
10022

Interested in small musicals.

Emanuel Azenberg
165 West 46th Street, NYC
10036
Biloxi Blues; *Broadway Bound*; *Ain't Misbehavin'*

Accepts scripts and tapes through agents only.

Roger Berlind
10 East 53rd Street, NYC
10021
Stagerlee

Send letter of enquiry before sending the script.

André Bishop
Playwrights Horizons
416 West 42nd Street, NYC
10036
The Perfect Party; *Three Postcards*; *Driving Miss Daisy*; *Laughing Wild*

Waiting time to hear from this organisation is often up to four months. Accepts submissions with SAE.

Ivan Bloch
165 West 46th Street, NYC
10036
The Boys of Winter; *Just So*

Interested in large and small musicals. Send to attention Ivan Bloch; include SAE.

Alexander H. Cohen
Hildy Parks
225 West 44th Street, NYC
10036

Interested in plays and musicals that 'speak to our times' and deal with issues while concurrently entertaining an audience. Submit in person or via an agent.

Leon B. Denmark
The Negro Ensemble
Company
1560 Broadway, NYC 10036
From the Mississippi Delta;
Prince

Accept scripts of dramatic or
comedy nature which explore
black experience and black
life in America and the world.
Will consider musicals with a
strong book. Send scripts
directly to the office of NEC.
Submissions are not
returned.

Lois M. B. Deutchman
23 East 10th Street, NYC
10003
Oil City Symphony.

Nancy E. Diamond
296 Varick Street, Jersey
City, NJ 07302
Funny Feet

Musicals, especially musical
comedies. Send synopsis and
three songs. Do not send
complete script.

Robert Franz
49 High Street
Bethany, Connecticut, 06525
So Long on Lonely Street

Looking for small-scale
musicals and properties that
lend themselves to
commercial development.
Prefer receiving material
through an agent.

James Freydberg
165 West 46th Street, NYC
10036
Burn This; *The Road To
Mecca*

Interested in musicals and
dramatic theatre. Submit by
post only.

Stephen Graham
1560 Broadway, Suite 600
NYC, 10036
The Road to Mecca

Wynn Handeman
American Place Theater
111 West 46th Street, NYC
10036
Neon Psalms; *That Serious
He-Man Ball*; *Splendid
Mummer*

Interested almost exclusively
in works by living Americans.
Innovative, and challenging
work desired. They do not
accept unsolicited
manuscripts, but welcome
plays from writers who have
had full or workshop
productions at professional
theatres. Others may send
synopses and the first 25 pages
of the script. Address
material to Literary
Department, American Place
Theater. Send SAE.

Jane Harmon and Nina Kineally
Jane Harmon Associates
One Lincoln Plaza,
Suite 28–0
NYC 10023
Asinamali; *Driving Miss Daisy*
Submit through an agent or write a letter prior to submitting any material.

Carole Shorenstein Hays
75 Taylor Street, Suite 701
San Francisco, California 94103
They are greatly interested in musicals. Their object is to redress the Broadway revue of the 1940s and 1950s (*Inside USA; Two on the Aisle*) in the contemporary idiom. The impulse is to re-invent rather than revive or restore. Writers and composers with completed material that answers this mandate are encouraged to submit it. Submissions of revue songs should include details on lineage and encumbrances. Send all material to Charlie Willare; The Carole Shorenson Hays Organisation, 234 West 44th Street, Suite 801, NYC 10036.

Mel Howard
311 West 43rd Street, NYC 10036
Black and Blue
Send letter of enquiry before sending the script.

Mary Lea Johnson
Martin Richards
Sam Crothers
The Producers Circle Company
1350 Sixth Avenue, NYC 10019
Rosza
Interested in any theatrical or musical film material. Get in touch with the office *before* sending in material.

Mary Kiel
MK Productions
32 East 57th Street, NYC 10022
Send letter of enquiry before sending the script.

Rocco and Heidi Landesman
1501 Broadway, NYC 10036
Into the Woods
Only interested in material that can succeed on Broadway. *Do not send script*. Send letter of enquiry first.

Will Lieberson
Quaigh Theater
205 West 89th Street, NYC 10024

Send synopsis and cast breakdown before submission of script.

Theodore Mann and Paul Libin

Circle in the Square
1633 Broadway, NYC 10019
The Boys of Autumn; *The Widow Claire*; *Coastal Disturbances*

Produces mostly straight dramatic plays but will look at musicals if they are 'strong on words, ideas, and not spectacle'. They prefer submission through an agent, but will look at synopses accompanied by a dialogue sample and one or two songs on tape.

Jennifer Manocherian

850 7th Avenue, #701, NYC 10019
The Palace of Amateurs

Interested in comedies, musicals, and drama. Send script and tape. Include SAE

Mitchell Maxwell

M. Square Productions
126 Second Avenue, NYC 10003
Blues in the Night

Send letter of enquiry before sending the script.

Lynn Meadow and Barry Grove

The Manhattan Theater Club
453 West 16th Street, NYC 10011
Frankie and Johnny in the Clair de Lune; *The Day Room*; *Woman in Mind*; *Emily*

Interested in musicals if they are small. They have a second stage in which they do finished productions of new work. Submit through an agent, or a letter describing your show – wait for response before sending any material.

Gregory Mosher

Lincoln Center Theater
150 West 65th Street, NYC 10023
Sarafina; *Boy's Life*; *Speed-the-Plow*

They will only accept scripts submitted through an agent *together* with a letter of recommendation from someone in the profession. Agent must send script to Anne Cattaneo, dramaturge.

James M. Nederlander

The Nederlander Company
810 7th Avenue, NYC 10019
Benefactors; *Les Liaisons Dangereuses*; *'Legs' Diamond*

They are looking for musicals, especially star vehicles for large houses. Submission ONLY through agents or professional referral. Musicals must be presented with a demo tape of at least eight completed songs. Do not send one-act plays, synopses or treatments.

Stuart Ostrow

PO Box 188, Pound Ridge, NY 10576

M Butterfly

Submit through an agent or directly. Be patient, it will take him at least 'three or four months to respond'. Send SAE.

Josep Papp and Gail Merrifield

New York Shakespeare Festival

325 LaFayette Street, NYC 10003

The Colored Museum; *Serious Money*; *Wenceslas Square*

Musicals, operas, post to their 'lay' Department. Be patient. It will take three or four months for an answer. Send SAE.

Philip Rose

157 West 57th Street, NYC 10019

Interested in musicals, small and contemporary. Telephone before sending letter.

Gerald Schoenfeld and Bernard Jacobs

The Schubert Organisation

225 West 44th Street, NYC 10036

Social Security; *The Petition*; *Jerome Robbins' Broadway*; *Les Liaisons Dangereuses*; *Chess*

Write letter of enquiry or submit through agent.

Arthur Whitlaw

132 East 38th Street, NYC 10036

Sweet Sue

Interested in musicals with a good plot development and real characters. Accepts submissions only through agents.

John H. Williams

The Program Development Co.

136 East 65th Street, NYC 10021

Stagerlee

Interested in contemporary musicals. Send directly, include SAE.

Eugene V. Wolsk

165 West 46th Street, NYC 10036

Singin' in the Rain

Through agents only. No unsolicited manuscripts accepted.

The following list of British theatre companies and producers interested in producing untried musicals is less specific than the US one. Most of these organisations produce musicals from time to time.

IT IS ESSENTIAL THAT A LETTER OF ENQUIRY DESCRIBING THE MUSICAL, LISTING SIZE OF CAST AND INCLUDING A BRIEF SUMMARY OF THE PLOT BE SENT TO ANY OF THESE PRODUCING COMPANIES LISTED BELOW. *THIS MUST BE ACCOMPANIED BY A STAMPED SELF-ADDRESSED RETURN ENVELOPE.*

The production companies marked with an asterisk are Theatre Clubs which have membership and a membership fee, and necessarily have a limited budget and smaller stage. Although productions are open to the public, Theatre Clubs have the advantage of having a built-in audience of members who generally attend all productions. Since their main source of support comes from their yearly membership fee, they can often mount experimental productions. As such, they make a good sounding-board for future West End production. (One of the small musical hits of the 1990 season was *Noël and Gertie*, first performed at the King's Head Theatre, and later in the West End.) Most of the following organisations produce musicals from time to time.

*Bush Theatre
Shepherd's Bush Green
London W12 8QD

Michael Codron Ltd
Aldwich Theatre Offices
Aldwich
London WC2B 4DF

Compass Theatre Ltd
13 Shorts Gardens
London WC2H 9AT

Ray Cooney Presentations
Duchess Theatre
Catherine Street
London WC2B 5LA

English Stage Company
Royal Court Theatre
Sloane Square
London SW1W 8AS

Façade
11 Lower John Street
London W1R 3PE

Clare Fox and Brian Kirk Ltd
Suite 17, First Floor
26 Charing Cross Road
London WC2H 0DG

John Gale
Strand Theatre
Aldwych
London WC2B 5DL

Greenwich Theatre Ltd
Greenwich Theatre
Crooms Hill
London SE10 8ES

Half Moon Theatre
213 Mile End Road
London E1 4AA

Hampstead Theatre
Swiss Cottage Centre
London NW3 3EX

**Independent Theatrical
Productions**
Monro House
40–42 King Street
Covent Garden
London WC2E 8JS

*King's Head Theatre
115 Upper Street
London N1 1QN

**Knightsbridge Theatrical
Productions**
c/o 2nd Floor
Winchmore House
12–15 Fetter Lane
London EC4A 1JJ

Libby Productions Ltd
Toby Rowland
Prince of Wales Theatre
Coventry Street
London W1V 8AS

**Lyric Theatre
Hammersmith**
King Street
London W6 0QL

Cameron Mackintosh
1 Bedford Square
London
Les Misérables; *The Phantom
of the Opera*; *Miss Saigon*

National Theatre
South Bank
London SE1 9PX

*Orange Tree Theatre
45 Kew Road
Richmond
Surrey TW9 2NQ

Peter Saunders Ltd
Vaudeville Theatre Offices
10 Maiden Lane
London WC2E 7NA

*Soho Poly Theatre
16 Riding House Street
London W1P 7PD

HM Tennent Ltd
Globe Theatre
Shaftsbury Avenue
London W1V 7HD

**Theatre Royal, Stratford
East**
Gerry Raffles Square
Stratford
London E15 1BN

**Tricycle Theatre
Company**
Tricycle Theatre
269 Kilburn High Road
London NW6 7JR

**Triumph Theatre
Productions Ltd**
Suite 4, Waldorf Chambers
11 Aldwych
London WC2B 4DA

**Unicorn Theatre for
Children**
Arts Theatre
6–7 Great Newport Street
London WC2J 7JB

*Warehouse Theatre
62 Dingwall Road
Croydon CR0 2NF

**Michael White
Productions Ltd**
13 Duke Street
St James
London SW1Y 6BD

The Young Vic
66 The Cut
London SE1 8LZ

THEATRICAL AGENTS

An agent's career consists of selling professional work. They have no time or inclination to nurse even the most talented writers or composers along until the work of these artists becomes saleable. Each submission of a script costs them, their secretaries and often a large agency where they may have their offices, much valuable time and often represents a considerable monetary outlay, for it is indeed rare that a work is optioned without many submissions, workshops and auditions. You must remember that any reputable agent will stay with the project from the beginning throughout its life. He will handle radio, television, stage, recording and cinema rights in your country and throughout the world. And there could be many spin-offs that he will be responsible for, from video cassettes to copies of sheet music, piano scores and the possible and eventual printing of the libretto. Of course, the agent stands to make a great deal of money by scooping a percentage of what you may be offered for your work, but remember that the work would probably not see production without a strong agent behind it.

An agent also works for the author's protection, since most

creative people actually *undervalue* their work, the agent acting as a representative of the *true* worth of the project can generally secure a much more advantageous contract than the creative people could possibly achieve. And agents are trained to look out for loopholes or unfavourable clauses in contracts that artists would certainly overlook.

This author believes in agents, but realises that it is not always possible for a newcomer to get an agent to accept his work. I say this in order to help you understand that if an agent rejects your work, it might be for several reasons. Nor does it mean that every agent will react to the same work in the same manner.

Listed below are some reasons an agent might reject handling your work.

1 A particular agent may know better what kinds of properties are being sought by producers at the time you present them with your musical. He also may be aware of a musical on the same subject that had trouble 'getting off the ground'.
2 The agent may specialise only in Broadway, West End, off-Broadway or fringe productions, a category into which your work may not fall. In other words, your work may be too large or too small a project for this particular representative.
3 The agent may have more work than he can handle. A successful musical or play takes many hours of negotiations in dealing with contracts, touring and auxiliary companies and the agent may have called a halt to accepting any new clients at the time you submit your musical.
4 The work may involve too many legal problems, rights to be extricated and untangled, estates to be cleared, which means the pieces of the pie which are represented by royalties may have to be split into too many pieces (this always makes a work more difficult to sell), so the agent will not deem the sale of the work could possibly pay back the effort and expense expended.*
5 The work may be in a form or catering to an audience unfamiliar to a particular agent.†

---

* *Gypsy* was almost stymied by Gypsy Rose Lee's mother; *Ain't Misbehavin'* almost did not open because it had to pay off Fats Waller's heirs; *Funny Girl* took years to work itself loose from Fannie Brice's estate.

† One would not expect a Broadway type agent to have any feeling for, or to be interested in selling a serious, opera-like musical.

6 The work simply may not be professional enough or good enough for a top-flight agent to handle. (This does not mean you need go to an unreputable or shady agency, merely a smaller one where you may be able to get more personal service.) Rod Hall, who handles theatrical works and musical shows for A. P. Watt Literary Agency in London, is only interested in writers who have 'a distinctive style which could only be their own'. He does not make up his mind about accepting a client until they have had a meeting and he has ascertained that (a) the librettist, lyricist or composer has a burning need to write and (b) the chemistry is right between them.

I would caution any of the creators of a musical whose work is rejected by any of the agents listed below against going to one of the many unreputable agents who may advertise in the backs of pulp magazines or telephone directories offering to represent your work. They will usually want *you* to pay something for a critique of your work, after which they will try to hook you into devastating contracts, in which your work is sewn up in perpetuity. No reputable agent charges more than 15 per cent for services.

Check with your local Better Business Bureau, The Dramatists' Guild, The Authors' Guild, BASCA, or ASCAP if you are not sure of the integrity of an agency.

Here then, is a list of theatrical agents in New York City and London who handle dramatic works. Some of them prefer not to handle musicals. *In every case, you must write to them BEFORE submitting your musical. Tell them a little about the subject and ask if they would be interested in seeing a copy of the libretto or hearing a tape of the score BEFORE you send it.**

NEW YORK

Artists Agency
230 West 57th Street 17D
New York, NY 10019
Jeanine Edmunds

Lois Berman
240 West 44th Street
New York, NY 10036

---

* Rod Hall wants his prospective clients to assure him that 'they are serious about making this a full-time career'. He distrusts anyone who wants to dabble in the theatre and would like to have as much information about a prospective client as possible, particularly as to how he or she currently earns a living. He adds 'how not to gain my attention is a letter beginning something like, "now that I've retired, I'm devoting all my attention to writing musicals".'

Coleman–Rosenberg
210 East 58th Street 2F
New York, NY 10022
Deborah Coleman

**Robert A. Freedman
Dramatic Agency**
1501 Broadway, Room 2310
New York, NY 10019
Robert A Freedman
Selma Luttinger

Samuel French Inc.
45 West 25th Street
New York, NY 10010

Graham Agency
311 West 43rd Street
New York, NY 10036
Earl Graham

**International Creative
Management**
40 West 57th Street
New York, NY 10019
Bridget Aschenberg
Sam Cohn
Arlene Donovan
Mitch Douglas
Milton Goldman
Wiley Hausam

The Lantz Office
888 Seventh Avenue
New York, NY 10016
Robert Lantz

Helen Merrill
435 West 23rd Street 1A
New York, NY 10011

**William Morris Agency
Inc.**
1350 Sixth Avenue
New York, NY 10019
Peter Franklin
Geroge Lane
Biff Liff
Gilbert Parker
Esther Sherman
Jerome Talbert

Paramuse Artists
1414 Sixth Avenue
New York, NY 10019
Shirley Bernstein

Flora Roberts Inc.
157 West 57th Street
New York, NY 10019
Flora Roberts
Sarah Douglass

**Rosenstone–Wender
Agency**
3 East 48th Street
New York, NY 10017
Howard Rosenstone

The Shukat Company
340 West 55th Street
New York, NY 10019
Scott Shukat
Peter Shukat

The Tantleff Office
360 West 20th Street 4F
New York, NY 10011
Jack Tantleff

Writers & Artists Agency
70 West 36th Street, Room 501
New York, NY 10018
William Craver

LONDON

A & B Personal Management Ltd
114 Jermyn Street
London SW1Y 6HJ
Bill Ellis

CCA Personal Management Ltd
4 Court Lodge
48 Sloan Square
London SW1W 8AT
Howard Pays

Ray Cooney Plays
Duchess Theatre
Catherine Street
London WC2B 5LA
Ray Cooney
H S Udwin

Samuel French
52 Fitzroy Street
London W1P 6JR
Playscripts Department

Blake Friedman
37 Gower Street
London WC1E 6HH
Conrad Williams

Noel Gay Organisation
24 Denmark Street
London WC2H 9BP
Noel Gay Theatre

Eric Glass Ltd
28 Berkeley Square
London W1X 6HD
Eric Glass

Michael Imison Playwrights Ltd
28 Almeida Street
London N1 1TD
Michael Imison

London Management
235 Regent Street
London W1R 7AG
Apply in writing prior to submission

MLR Ltd
200 Fulham Road
London SW10 9PN
Patricia MacNaughton

William Morris Agency Ltd
31 Soho Square
London W1V 5DG
Send submission direct to New York office

Douglas Rae (Management) Ltd
28 Charing Cross Road
London WC2
Julian Ellison

Sharland Organisation Ltd
9 Marlborough Crescent
Bedford Park
London W4 1HE
Mike Sharland

Unna, Harvey & Stephen Durbridge Ltd
24 Pottery Lane
London W11 4LZ

AP Watt Ltd
20 John Street
London WC1N 2DR
Rod Hall

Warner Chappell Plays Ltd
129 Park Street
London W1Y 3FA
Stewart Newton

DINNER THEATRES INTERESTED IN PRODUCING NEW MUSICALS

Most dinner theatres like to produce revivals of well-known successes, usually light-hearted musical comedies that won't give their audiences indigestion. Composers, lyricists and librettists often feel it is demeaning to be upstaged by a quiche Lorraine or a filet mignon, but the royalties are the same as they would be at a decent off-Broadway or fringe house. Audience attention is rarely divided between food and the show since most dinner theatres serve the meal (usually a buffet) and then present the show. In most of them, only drinks are served during the performances, but even so, this can cause some distraction.

Since most of the audience is in a jolly postprandial mood dinner theatres usually seek out the loud and the familiar. There are, however, a few who accept and produce new works. It is understood, without being repeated in the following cases that a letter of enquiry including a paragraph or two giving the producers an idea of the scope and story of the musical should be sent along with a self-addressed stamped envelope. This may save you time and money, for dinner theatres are quickest to fold their tents and disappear – even in a single season's time. So be wary. Never submit unsolicited tapes and scripts until you get the OK.

Alhambra Dinner Theater
12000 Beach Road
Jacksonville
Florida 33216

The Alhambra is an Equity dinner theatre actively seeking new plays and musicals, producing one a year. The stage is small so musicals should use one set and a maximum cast of eight. Address letter to the attention of Tod Booth.

Barksdale Theater
PO Box 7
Hanover, Va. 23064

The Barksdale is non-Equity, and has dining separate from the theatre. Muriel McCauley will read new or previously produced scripts utilising simple sets. Send letter of enquiry directly to her.

Carousel Dinner Theater
PO Box 427
Ravenna, Ohio 44266

Carousel produces four to six musicals each year. Musicals submitted should have no more than six characters. Submit by letter of enquiry directly to the producer, Prescott F. Griffith.

Circa '21 Dinner Playhouse
PO Box 784–1828 Third Avenue
Rock Island Illinois, 61210

Dennis Hitchcock is looking for small family or children's musicals. Submit letter and if requested, send tape and script.

Country Dinner Playhouse
6570 North Alpine Drive
Hidden Village
Parker, Colorado 80134

Bill McHale, producer for the Country Dinner Playhouse would like a query first. He will then read musicals suitable for theatre-in-the-round with an 18' by 18' stage. Cast should be limited to eighteen. Recent productions, *Evita*; *Show Boat*.

Derby Dinner Theater
525 Mariot Drive
Clarksville, Indiana 47130

Non-Equity production on a 20' by 20' theatre-in-the-round stage. Cast should be no more than nineteen. Productions run six to eight weeks. Recent works: *Ain't Misbehavin'*; *The Sound of Music*.

Firehouse Dinner Theater
514 South 11th Street
Omaha, Nebraska 68102

Interested in musicals or farces. Send letter of enquiry to Richard Mueller. The theatre has a 26' by 30' stage and is an Equity member. Recent productions: *The Rainmaker*; *Guys and Dolls*.

Lake George Dinner Theater
Holiday Inn
PO Box 266
Lake George, NY 12845

David Eastwood, the producer, prefers single-set musicals for this fine Equity playhouse. Send letter of enquiry addressed to him first.

Marriot's Lincolnshire Theater
101 Half Day Road
Lincolnshire, Illinois 60015

Dianne Earley, the artistic director, is looking for previously unproduced musicals suitable for a 24' by 24' arena stage in an 870-seat theatre. Cast could have as many as twenty-five. Equity. Recent productions: *Baby*; *A Chorus Line*.

Mission Hills Dinner Theater
9420 Reseda Blvd. #412
Northridge, California 91324

Interested in original never-before-produced musicals. The stage is 30' by 25'. Write letter of enquiry to Edmund Gaynes.

Neil's New Yorker Dinner Theater
Route 46
Mountain Lakes, New Jersey 07046

This theater has a large stage but limited fly space. Sets should be modest and cast limited to twelve. Write letter of enquiry to Bell Productions, c/o Brenda Killip, 203 Boonton Ave, Boonton, New Jersey.

Stanly Hotel Theater
333 Wonderview Road
Esters Park, Colorado 80517

Non-Equity. Send letter of enquiry to Melody Page who is interested in 'non-typical dinner theatre musicals'. The stage is 50' by 40'.

Upstairs Dinner Theater
221 S. 19th Street
Omaha, Nebraska 68102

Deborah Denenberg will consider new scripts for musical comedies only. The cast must be fourteen or less. Non-Equity. Recent productions: *Joseph and the Amazing Technicolor Dreamcoat*; *Catch Me If You Can*.

West End Dinner Theater
4615 Duke Street
Alexandria, Va. 22304

Director James Matthews wants family-style musicals. His theatre has a 40' by 50' stage and can accommodate multiple sets and twenty to twenty-five cast members, but there is no fly space. Send letter of enquiry before sending tape and script.

SOURCES OF SUPPORT

Many organisations are active in aiding composers, lyricists and librettists by giving them a place to work uninterruptedly. Other groups sponsor conferences and festivals. Sometimes the creators of a musical may be better served by living and learning about their respective crafts in an academic setting – these are called residencies. There are foundations that sponsor workshops and those who give awards of cash to worthy musical projects. And there are also fellowships and grants that provide the means for study of a certain culture or subject that may be developed into a musical. Additionally there is emergency assistance available to members of The Dramatists' Guild, PEN International and BAFTRA. These listings follow, listed alphabetically within each range of assistance.

Artist Colonies

Act I Creativity Center
457 Lucy Road
Lake Ozark, Missouri 65049
Charlotte Plotsky,
Administrator

Act I offers a one-week to one-month stay for four to eight adults at a time in an air-conditioned private home on a lake front. Residents have their own rooms and all meals are provided Mon–Sat a.m. Admission fees based on ability to pay. Facilities are open all year round.
Eligibility: Composers, lyricists, librettists.
Application: Write to D. G. Plotsky #1201
4550 Warwick Blvd.
Kansas City, Missouri 64111
$10 Fee upon application.

Deadline: One month prior to desired residence.

Chateau de Lesvault
Onlay
58370 Villapourçon
France

Five rooms available October to May at classical style French country residence. Cost: 3600 French francs per month for room, board and utilities.
Eligibility: Creative artists working on a project.
Application: By letter at least two months in advance of intended stay.

Dorland Mountain Arts Colony
Box 6
Temecula, California 02390

Four to six people at a time are accommodated in individual cottages without electricity for $150 monthly for one or two months. Pianos and typewriters are provided. Residents take care of their own meals.
Eligibility: Playwrights and composers.
Application: Form, resumé and samples of work.
Deadline: March 1 and September 1. Notification: in eight weeks.

Dorset Colony House
Box 519
Dorset, Vermont 05251
John Nassivera, Director

Colony House is open from September to May as a residence for writers who stay from one week to two months. Each writer is provided with a room and desk. Public rooms include library, sitting room, large dining room and a large kitchen. There is a voluntary fee of $50 per week.
Eligibility: Generally 'produced' playwrights, composers, librettists and lyricists, but all applications are considered.
Application: Letter of enquiry with resumé and brief description of work-in-progress.
Deadline. None: Notification: in four weeks.

William Flanagan Memorial Center
c/o Edward Albee Foundation
14 Harrison Street
New York, NY 10013
David Briggs, Foundation Secretary

Residence open from June to October in Montauk, LI. Residencies last for one month. Residencies are free of charge to artists with talent and need.
Eligibility: Lyricists and librettists. There is limited space for composers.
Application: Write for two application forms, answer with two recommendations and letter of intent. Applications will be accepted after January 1.
Deadline: April 1. Notification: May 15.

Hambidge Center for the Creative Arts and Sciences
PO Box 339
Rabun Gap, Ga. 30568
Ray Pierotti, Executive Director

The centre is located in six hundred acres of wooded

slopes, mountain meadows and streams. It is listed in the National Register of Historic Places. Fellowships of two weeks to two months are awarded to individuals engaged in all areas of the arts, humanities and sciences for the purpose of solitude and pursuit of creative excellence in their profession. Those accepted are given a private cottage equipped with a kitchen, sleeping and bathing facilities and a work/studio area. The centre is open May–October.

Eligibility: Playwrights, poets, composers, lyricists, librettists and visual artists. Acceptance by admission committee depending on space available.
Application: Send for forms.
Deadline: None. Notification: five to eight weeks.

MacDowell Colony

100 High Street
Peterborough, New Hampshire 03458
Christopher Barnes, Resident Director

The colony provides isolated studios, board and room in a semi-rural woodland setting for writers, visual artists, composers and film/video artists. The colony is open all year round: residencies average six weeks. Fees are set by the artist.

Eligibility: Playwrights, librettists, composers, etc.
Application: Write to the above for current forms.
Deadline: Request forms eight months before season desired.

Palenville Interarts Colony

PO Box 59, Woodstock Avenue
Palenville, NY 12463
Joanna Sherman, Artistic Director

A 110-acre estate providing two-to-eight week residencies between June 1 and Sept. 30 for performing, visual and literary artists. Private accommodations and separate working quarters; dance studios; active theatre space. A residency fee of $175 per week is suggested: some partial grants are available.
Eligibility: Applicants should be semi-professional or must demonstrate a high level of artistic ability.
Application: Write or call for form: work sample will be requested.
Deadline: April 1.
Notification: less than four weeks after April 1.

Ragdale Foundation

1260 N. Greenbay Road
Lake Forest, Illinois 60045
Jill Harris, Director

Foundation provides private rooms on a year-round basis to playwrights, librettists, lyricists and composers for two weeks to two months. Meals are provided. Fee is $70 per week; financial assistance is sometimes available upon statement of need.
Application: Form, samples of work and references.
Deadline: None, but it is advisable to apply three to six months in advance.

Shenandoah Valley Playwrights' Retreat
Shenan Arts Inc.
Route 5, Box 167–F
Staunton, Virginia 24401
Robert Graham Small, Director

This retreat exists to assist writers in the development of their scripts through an intensive workshop programme with actors, directors and dramatists which culminates in staged readings. Annual three-week August workshop openings for writers who compete for fellowships.
Eligibility: Playwrights and librettists only.
Application: Two copies (typed and bound) of a project you wish to work on, a personal statement as to your background as a writer.
Deadline: Postmarked by April 1. Notification: by June 1.

Virginia Center for the Creative Arts
Mt San Angelo
Sweet Briar, Virginia 24595

Residential fellowships granted for one- to three-month periods include room, board and private studio. Located on 445-acre estate near Sweet Briar College; open year round. Daily fee is $20.
Eligibility: Playwrights, composers, lyricists and librettists who have demonstrated professional achievement.
Application: Letter of enquiry with sample of work, resumé, and $15 filing fee.
Deadline: January 25 (May–Sept.), May 25 (Sept.–Jan.), Sept. 25 (Jan.–May). Notification: 8 weeks after deadline.

Helen Wurlitzer Foundation
PO Box 545
Taos, NM 87571
Henry Sauerwein, Director

Open from April 1 to September 30 the Foundation provides space for all creative artists in residencies of no more than six months (the usual stay is three months). Residency is

rent and utility free, but residents must provide their own food and maintain their accommodation.
Eligibility: Creative persons in all media. Write for information.

Residencies

Atlantic Center for the Arts
1414 Art Center Avenue
New Smyrna Beach, Florida 32069

The Atlantic Center for the Arts offers five residencies, three weeks long, at which nationally and internationally prominent artists from different disciplines come to the Center to conduct interdisciplinary workshops, lecture, criticise works-in-progress, give readings and recitals, exhibit their work and develop interdisciplinary projects. The facility is air-conditioned and accessible to the handicapped. The three-week session is $200 and residents must provide their own transportation, lodging and food. (The ACA will help locate lodging.)
Eligibility: Visual artists, performing artists and writers (composers, librettists and lyricists). Deadlines and application procedures depend on the particular residency. Write to the above address for details.

Banff Center School of Fine Arts
Box 120 Banff
Alberta, Canada TOL OCO
John Metcalf, Artistic Head

Musical theatre programme – Residence for composers and librettists. Writers attend rehearsals and workshop productions. Room and board provided. Limited scholarships available. Candidates encouraged to seek other sources for travel.
Application: Send resumé, score and cassette tape.
Notification: Six weeks.

Belagio Study and Conference Center
Rockefeller Foundation
1133 Sixth Avenue
New York, NY 10036

Four- to five-week residencies for playwrights, composers, lyricists and librettists at Lake Como, Italy. Free room and board for artist and spouse.
sheet and details.
Deadline: Applications considered five times a year. Apply a year or more in advance.

The Corporation of Yaddo
Box 395
Saratoga Springs, NY 12866

Yaddo provides a flexible schedule, from two weeks to two months.

Eligibility: Playwrights, librettists, lyricists and composers.
Application: Samples of work and letters of reference; $10 fee.
Deadline: Jan. 15 and Aug. 1. Notification: six weeks after deadline.

Hawthornden Castle International Retreat for Writers
Lasswade, Midlothian
Scotland EH18 1EG

Up to six weeks in a remotely situated castle amid wild romantic scenery, a half-hour bus journey from Edinburgh. Five fellows per session accommodated in study-bedrooms; daytime silence rule, communal breakfast and evening meal.
Eligibility: Dramatists, librettists, novelists, poets and other creative writers who have published at least one book or have had a play professionally performed.
Fees: Residency is free; no financial aid for travel or any other expense.
Dates: Four six-week sessions from February to July and September to December.
Application: Letter of enquiry.
Deadline: End of September. Notification: three months.

Montalvo Center for the Arts
Box 158
Saratoga, Calif. 95071
Elizabeth Challener,
Executive Director

175-acre estate close to San Francisco. Open all year round to the public as an arts centre and available for three-month residencies to five playwrights/librettists and/or composers. Cost is $100 per month ($115 per couple) for an apartment. Limited financial assistance is available.
Eligibility: Playwrights, librettists and composers with evidence of professional activity and recognition.
Application: Form, resumé, sample of work and references.
Deadline: None. Notification: one month after all material is received.

Theater in the Works
112 Fine Arts Center
University of Massachussetts
Amherst, Mass 01003
Virginia Scott, Resident
Dramaturge

Four playwrights are invited to be in residence for two weeks in July. Each playwright spends the first week working with a director and a dramaturge; the second week is spent working with a

professional company. Two book-in-hand performances are given at the end of the second week before an audience invited to stay and discuss the play with the playwright. Each playwright receives a $650 stipend, housing and travel.
Eligibility: Playwrights, composers, librettists, lyricists. The works submitted for development should have had no substantial professional productions and should still be in progress.
Deadline: Scripts should be submitted after January 1 and before March 15.
Notification: May 15.

Tyrone Guthrie Centre
Annaghmakerrig, Newbliss
County Monaghan, Ireland
Bernard Loughlin, Resident
Director
The centre offers residencies from one week to three months in a country house for all artists including playwrights, composers, lyricists and librettists who have had work published or produced. Each resident has a private apartment within the house. There is a music and rehearsal room available.
Eligibility: Cost is 1000 Irish Pounds per month for artists from abroad.

Application: Forms available; submit sample of work, resumé and letter of intent. Particular consideration given to clear outline of project to be undertaken.
Deadline: None. Notification: one month.

Conferences and Festivals

Eugene O'Neill Theater Center National Music Theater Conference
305 Great Neck Road
Waterford, Connecticut
06385
Pauline Haupt, Artistic
Director
Open to composers, librettists, lyricists. Four-week development period for new music theatre works of all genres, some presented as staged readings, others developed privately. Creative artists receive stipend, travel from New York City, room and board.
Eligibility: US Citizenship; projects to be worked upon or presented will only be accepted if the rights have been cleared; unproduced works only.
Application: Send for detailed guidelines and form.
Deadline: February 1 (subject to change) for summer and early autumn.

Women in Theater Festival

Watermelon Studio Inc.
64 Wyman Street
Jamaica Plain, Mass 02131
Sophie Parker, Festival
Director

The Women in Theater Festival is an annual event which showcases women performers and artists in a series of performances, workshops, play readings and panel discussions. Founded in 1984, the Festival came into being out of a need to introduce the general public to works created by women in the fields of dance, music and the visual arts. Programming now ranges from contemporary drama, music and comedy to post-modern dance, abstract art and multimedia performance art. Festival artists are selected by a committee which meets the autumn prior to the next year's festival, and artists and companies selected are contacted by November. The Festival takes place in March each year in association with Boston and Massachussetts performing arts centres and universities.
Application: Send letter of enquiry to the above address.

Workshops

ASCAP Musical Theater Workshop

1 Lincoln Plaza
New York, NY 10023
Charles Strouse, director

Participants present selections from their works in progress to panels of well-known professionals working in all aspects of theatre. *Eligibility*: Any theatre composer or lyricist able to attend ten Monday sessions. *Application*: Send a cassette including four theatre songs plus a resumé of theatre and musical background to Bernice Cohen, director of musical theatre activities.

BMI–Lehman Engel Musical Theater Workshop

320 West 57th Street
New York, NY 10019
Norma Grossman, Director

Series of workshops to refresh and stimulate professional writers as well as encourage and develop new creative talent for the contemporary theater.
Composers'/lyricists' workshops – September to May. Two-hour weekly sessions.
Eligibility: Composers and lyricists.

Application: Composers:
Letter of enquiry and three
contrasting compositions on
cassette.
Lyricists: Letter of enquiry
and three contrasting lyrics,
comedy, ballad, other.
Composer/lyricists: Letter of
enquiry and three contrasting
songs, comedy, up-tempo,
ballad.
Provide short setup for each
song or lyric.
Interviews held prior to
Labor Day (early September).
Deadline: August 1.

Librettists Workshop –
Programme analyses and
discusses current as well as
past musicals. Students are
encouraged to join forces with
the composer/lyricist
workshops for actual
collaboration on a musical.
Specific assignment to solve
musical theatre problems.
Eligibility: Writers of all
genres are encouraged to
apply.
Application: Excerpts from
works published, produced
or in progress. Must include
at least one sample of
humorous writing.

Broadway Tomorrow
191 Claremont Avenue, Suite
53
New York, NY 10027
Elyse Curtis, Artistic
Director

New musicals are given initial
audience exposure and
developed in full productions
through concerts and
readings of librettos with the
writer and composer
involved.
Eligibility: Composers,
lyricists, librettists, residents
of metropolitan New York
area or able to spend time in
the city.
Application: Submit audio
cassette of music script,
synopsis, cast breakdown,
resumé, reviews if any and
acknowledgement postcard.
Deadline: None.

**Lehman Engel Musical
Theater Workshop**
1605 North Cahuenga Blvd.,
#216
Hollywood, California 90028
John Sparks, co-director

This is a workshop based on
the curriculum developed by
Lehman Engel. The first year
is spent doing music, lyric
and book writing
assignments. If, at the end of
the first year, the individual
has completed the
assignments and the directors
of the workshop feel he or she
can make a contribution to the
general workshop the writers
can work on their own
projects and bring them in to
sessions as often as they wish.
The workshop meets every
fifth week. Monday to

Thursday evenings from September to May. There is a $100 membership fee.
Eligibility: Composers, lyricists, librettists.
Application: Write for application.
Deadline: August 1.
Notification: September.

Musical Theater Works

Clinton Wilder Development Readings
440 LaFayette Street
New York, NY 10003
Mark Herko, associate artistic director

A year-round developmental programme consisting of a series of informal and staged readings where the authors work closely with the Musical Theater Works staff members and develop material.
Eligibility: Previously unproduced American works of composers, lyricists and librettists.
Application: Submit full-length musical with complete book and cassette of score. Casts of ten or fewer are preferred, but larger shows are not excluded.
Deadline: None. Notification: two months.

The New Dramatists Composer/Librettist Studio

424 West 44th Street
New York, NY 10036
Jean Passanante, Artistic Director

A three-week workshop in which composers work with members of the New Dramatists on a series of collaborative exercises designed to explore the composer/librettist relationship. The resulting pieces will be rehearsed with singers and presented in an open recital. $600 stipend, travel expenses and housing if needed are provided.
Eligibility: Composers.
Application: Send resumé, cover letter, and tape of your work including material written for the voice.
Deadline: Early June.
Notification: early September.

New Musicals Project

Colombia College
72E 11th Street
Chicago, Illinois 60605
Sheldon Patinkin, artistic director

A year-round workshop with directors and dramaturge to help material grow to production level. Possible staged readings or productions. Salary provided.

Material must be original or in the public domain and not previously produced.
Application: Outline, treatment of script with examples of music, authors' bios and history of the project.
Deadline: None. Notification: two to three weeks.

New Musical Voices
Theatre Royal
Royal Parade
Plymouth
Devon PL1 2TR

A series of weekend workshops for lyricists and composers. Each workshop is led by an experienced and professional composer and lyricists. Members are encouraged to discuss, experiment or simply observe the creative process. Workshops coincide with a series of talks and demonstrations that provide an insight into the production and performance of musical theatre.
Application: Contact the Theatre Royal box office for information and enrolment.

New Voices at Greene Street
Double Image Theater
445 West 59th Street
New York, NY 10019
Brian Chavanne, coordinator

New Voices at Greene Street presents eighteen staged readings each season at the Greene Street Café open to the public and free of charge. It is designed to nurture and expose new writers, librettists and composers to the theatrical community. Moderated discussions with the playwrights, cast and audience help to promote more informed and interested theatregoers.

Fellowships and Grants

American–Scandinavian Foundation
127 East 73rd Street
New York, NY 10021
Grants of $2,000 for short visits. Fellowships of $8,000 for a full academic year for graduate study in Denmark, Finland, Norway, Ireland and Sweden.
Eligibility: US citizens and permanent residents who have completed undergraduate study by the time their overseas programme begins. Also awards to Scandinavians for study in the US.
Application: Write to the Exchange Division, ASF address above.
Deadline: November 1.

Artists Foundation
8 Park Plaza
Boston, Massachussetts
02116

Annual programme of unrestricted fellowships of $9,000 and a $500 finalist award on the basis of excellence of work submitted for review. Categories include Music Composition, Playwriting, Fiction, Non-Fiction and Poetry.
Eligibility: Eighteen years of age or older. Massachusetts resident for six months or longer prior to deadline. No registered students.
Application: Form obtainable from the above address directed to Fellowship Department.
Deadline: The first week in October.

Bush Arts Fellowship
E900 First National Bank Bldg.
St Paul, Minnesota 55101
Sally Dixon, Programme Director

Annual fellowship, up to fifteen grants of $24,000 plus $6,240 for production and travel.
Eligibility: Twenty-five years or older. Resident of Minnesota, South Dakota or North Dakota for twelve of the last thirty-six months. Playwrights, librettists, fiction and non-fiction writers, composers and individuals practising the visual arts and choreographers. Please check with the foundation for other eligibility requirements.
Deadline: Late October.
Notification: five months.

City of Atlanta Bureau of Cultural Affairs
236 Forsyth Street
Atlanta, Georgia 30303

Semi-annual programme of individual grants ($500–$2,500) and annual fellowships ($8,000).
Eligibility: Playwrights, composers, lyricists and librettists residing in Atlanta and demonstrating artistic ability.
Application: Send for form.
Deadline: October, November, May.
Notification: Three months.

John Simon Guggenheim Foundation
90 Park Avenue
New York, NY 11016

Eligibility: Individuals who have already demonstrated exceptional capacity for productive scholarship or exceptional creative ability in the arts including playwrights, librettists and composers. US or Canadian citizens or permanent residents or citizens or residents or citizens or permanent residents of Latin America or the Caribbean. *Application*: Send for form. *Deadline*: October 1. Notification: March of the following year.

Kleban Foundation
The Dramatists' Guild
234 West 44th Street,
New York, NY 10036

This foundation was set up in memory of the late lyricist of *A Chorus Line*. Current amount of grant is unknown but in 1989, grants were $150,000 for lyricists and librettists working in the artistic form known as the 'American musical'. Paid in three yearly instalments of $50,000.
Eligibility: Lyricists or librettists who *haven't* had shows on Broadway in the past two years.
Application: Letter describing intentions, 5–8 typewritten pages of lyrics or two acts of a book. Cassettes optional. No submissions will be returned.
Deadline: September 30.

National Institute for Opera and Music Theater
John F. Kennedy Center
Washington, DC 20566
Maria I. Thompson, program manager

Grants to individuals and collaborative teams, focus on career-entry-level.
Application: For late autumn deadlines. $20 application fee.

New York Foundation for the Arts
5 Beekman Place
New York, NY 10038

Artist Fellowship Program – a fellowship of $7,000 offered to playwrights and composers who have had two years of residency in New York and who demonstrate professional accomplishment and commitment.
Application: Write for brochure and form. Applications accepted from June 1.
Deadline: September 5.
Notification: eight months.

Theater Communications Group
355 Lexington Avenue
New York, NY 10017
Peter Zeisler, director

Rehearsal Observerships – Travel monies available biannually to enable writers whose works are receiving full productions at TCG constituent theatres to be in residence during a minimum of two consecutive weeks of rehearsal.
Eligibility: Playwrights,

composers, lyricists, librettists, translators. TCG artistic directors may nominate freelance artists whose careers would benefit from broader exposure in the field to aid their artistic growth. Up to $2,000 will be awarded for each observership.
Application: Only by participating TCG theaters.
Deadline: September 15 and February 15.

Emergency Financial Assistance

The Authors' League Fund
The Dramatists' Guild
Fund
234 West 44th Street
New York, NY 10036
Susan Dury, administrator
A year-round programme of interest-free loans with flexible repayment plans. Loans are made for immediate temporary need (rent, medical expenses, etc.).
Eligibility: Produced or published playwrights, composers, lyricists or librettists.
Application: Form accompanied by documentation of production or publication.
Deadline: None. Notification: two to four weeks.

Pen American Center
568 Broadway
New York, NY 10012
Christine Friedlander, coordinator
PEN writers' fund provides up to $1,000 in emergency grants and loans. PEN fund for writers and editors with AIDS is administered under PEN Writers' fund with the same guidelines.
Eligibility: All produced and published writers and librettists.
Deadline: None.

PRIZES

The Vivian Ellis Prize

This is the most prestigious musical prize in Britain. Named for the composer of *Mr Cinders* and *Bless the Bride* the winner receives £2,000 cash payment as well as a production of the work selected. The prize is awarded by a distinguished panel of British theatre notables including Vivian Ellis, Don Black, Dan Crawford, Ian Horsbrugh, Cameron Mackintosh, Tim Rice, Jonathan Simon, Mark Steyn and Wendy Toye. Details follow:

1 Entrants are required to submit the synopsis of a musical, either on an original theme or based on existing work. Any style will be considered from operetta to rock opera. The synopsis should illustrate how the story would be broken down into scenes and where the musical numbers would come.

2 Entrants must submit the book to an act including all dialogue and lyrics.

3 Three musical pieces, preferably of contrasting character, must be submitted. Two from the act submitted and one from another.

4 The musical must not have been previously published or professionally performed in public.

5 If an already existing work is used copyright permission must be obtained.

6 Entrants accept that cassettes of their work will be made for circulation to judges.

7 The competition is open to persons normally resident in the UK and Republic of Ireland for at least the past three years. THEY MUST BE UNDER THE AGE OF THIRTY-ONE.

8 Each entry must be accompanied by a completed and signed application form giving the details of all the collaborators.

9 There is a fee of £5 per entry to cover costs. A cheque to the Performing Rights Society should be sent with the entry.

10 Extracts from the selected works will be performed at the Guildhall School of Music in London. Tel: 071-580-5544 ext 8310

11 The workshop will be held before an invited audience and any part of the proceedings may be broadcast live or

recorded, and a video may be made.

12 The workshops are held at the Guildhall School of Music in London and all entrants must be available to attend.

13 Entrants selected must agree to promote the Vivian Ellis Prize in publicity and literature and programmes relating to the subsequent performances of their works.

14 Acceptance or rejection of all entries is at the discretion of the administration.

15 All material will be returned to the entrants after the competition. All items should be clearly labelled with the name and the address and phone number of the entrant.

16 Enquiries should be sent to:

SUSAN DOLTON,
Administrator
THE VIVIAN ELLIS PRIZE
Performing Rights Society
29/33 Berners Street
London W1P 4AA

'New Musical Voices'

Composers and lyricists are invited to collaborate and submit ideas for a piece of music theatre of no more than forty minutes duration. The idea should involve no more than ten characters and three musical instruments.

The competition takes place bi-annually. Submissions should be delivered to The Theatre Royal, Plymouth (Tel: 0752 223929) and marked 'New Musical Voices' by 31 March.

Six entries chosen to be further developed and informally rehearsed with a professional director. From these, three will be chosen for production. Each piece chosen will receive a fee of £200.00.

Quest for New Musicals

The UK's first Festival of Musicals will take place in the heart of the English Peak District at Buxton Opera House over Easter 1992. Eight new musicals, chosen by an expert panel of judges and members of the theatre-going public from entries for the Quest for New Musicals competition, will be selected for a professional workshops showcase. Further details are available from The Quest Secretary, Buxton Opera House, Water Street, Buxton, Derbyshire SK17 6XN.

PERMISSIONS

Page 64: 'Good Thing Going' (Stephen Sondheim). Copyright © Revelation Music Publ. Corp.

Page 65: 'Ol' Man River' (Music by Jerome Kern and lyrics by Oscar Hammerstein II). Copyright © 1927 Polygram International Publishing, Inc., copyright renewed. International Copyright Secured. All rights reserved. Used by permission.

Page 67: 'All I need is the Girl' (Sondheim/Styne). Copyright © 1936 by Chappell & Co. Corp. Reproduced by permission of Warner Chappell Music Ltd.

Page 70 ftn.: 'It's De-Lovely' (Cole Porter). Copyright © 1936 by Chappell & Co., Inc. Copyright renewed; assigned to Robert H Montgomery, Trustee of the Cole Porter Musical and Literary Property Trusts. Chappell & Co., Inc., owner of the publication and allied rights throughout the world. International Copyright Secured. ALL RIGHTS RESERVED. Used by permission.

Page 83: 'I've Grown Accustomed to her Face' (Lerner/Loewe). Copyright © Chappell Music Ltd. Reproduced by permission of Chappell Music Ltd.

Page 83: 'The Party's Over' (Comden/Green/Styne). Copyright © Stratford Music Corp. Reproduced by permission of Chappell Music Ltd.

Page 156: 'Send in the Clowns' (Stephen Sondheim). Copyright © Revelation Music Corp. Reproduced by permission of Warner Chappell Music Ltd.

Pages 171 & 172: 'The Surrey with the Fringe on Top' (Music by Jerome Kern and lyrics by Oscar Hammerstein II). Copyright © 1943 by Williamson Music Co. Copyright renewed. Used by permission.

Page 177: 'I'm an Ordinary Man' (Lerner/Loewe). Copyright © Chappell Music Publ. Corp. Reproduced by permission of Warner Chappell Music Ltd.

Page 178: 'Ice Cream' (Bock/Harnick). Copyright © Carlin Music Corporation. Used by kind permission of Carlin Music Corporation, 14 New Burlington Street, London, W1X 2LR.

Pages 179–80: 'A Little Priest' (Stephen Sondheim). Copyright © Revelation Music Corp., reproduced by permission of Warner Chappell Music Ltd.

Page 192: 'Meeskite' (Kander/Ebb). Used by kind permission of Carlin Music Corporation, 14 New Burlington Street, London, W1X 2LR.

Page 196: 'The Physician (But he never said he loved me)' (Cole Porter). Copyright © 1933 by Cole Porter. Renewed by Warner Brothers Inc. International Copyright secured. All rights reserved. Used by permission.

Page 197: 'That is the End of the News' (Noël Coward). Copyright © Chappell Music Ltd. Reproduced by permission of Chappell Music Ltd.

Pages 198–9: 'To Keep my Love Alive' (Rodgers & Hart). Copyright © Harms Inc. Reproduced by permission of Chappell Music Ltd.

Page 203: 'You Are Love' (Music by Jerome Kern and lyrics by Oscar Hammerstein II). Copyright © 1928 PolyGram International Publishing Inc. Copyright renewed. International Copyright secured. All rights reserved. Used by permission.

Page 204: 'So in Love' (Cole Porter). Copyright © by Chappell & Co., Inc. Copyright renewed; Assigned to Robert H Montgomery, Trustee of the Cole Porter Musical and Literary Property Trusts. Chappell & Co., Inc., owner of publication and allied rights throughout the world. International copyright secured. All rights reserved. Used by permission.

Page 205: 'Hello, Young Lovers' (Rodgers/Hammerstein). Copyright © 1951 by Richard Rodgers and Oscar Hammerstein II. Copyright renewed Williamson Music Co., owner of publication and allied rights.

Page 214: 'Cocktail Counterpoint' (Jerry Herman). Copyright © E H Morris & Co Inc. Reproduced by permission of Chappell Music Ltd.

BIBLIOGRAPHY

Abbott, George, *Mister Abbott*, Random House: New York 1963

Atkinson, Brooks, *Broadway*, Macmillan: New York 1970

Baillet, Whitney, *Alec Wilder and His Friends*, Houghton-Mifflin: Boston 1974

Bergreen, Laurence, *As Thousands Cheer: The Life of Irving Berlin*, Hodder & Stoughton: London 1990

Billington, Michael, *Performing Arts*, QED: London 1980

Boardman, Gerald, *American Musical Theatre*, Oxford University Press: New York, 1986
  American Musical Revue, Oxford University Press: New York 1985
  Jerome Kern, Oxford University Press, New York 1980

Bowers, Dwight Blocker, *American Musical Theater*, Smithsonian: Washington, D.C. 1989

Brahms, Caryl (with Ned Sherrin,) *Song By Song*, Ross Anderson, Egerton, Bolton 1984

Castle, Charles, *Noel*, Abacus: London 1984

Citron, Stephen, Songwriting: *A Complete Guide to the Craft*, Morrow: New York 1985

Cohen, David (with Ben Greenwood) *The Buskers*, David & Charles: London 1981

Coward, Noël, *Autobiography*, Methuen: London 1986
  The Lyrics of Noël Coward, Overlook: Woodstock, New York 1983
  Collected Verse, Methuen: London 1987

Damase, Jacques, *Les Folies du Music-Hall*, Spring Books: London 1960

Dietz, Howard, *Dancing in the Dark*: New York 1974

Edwards, Anne, *Matriarch: Queen Mary and the House of Windsor*, Hodder & Stoughton: London 1981
  Early Reagan, Hodder & Stoughton: London 1987

Engel, Lehman, *Words With Music*, Schirmer-Macmillan: London 1972
  Getting Started in the Theater, Collier-Macmillan: London 1975

The American Musical Theater, Collier-Macmillan: New York 1975

Their Words are Music, Crown: New York 1975

Fordin, Hugh, *Getting to Know Him: Biography of Oscar Hammerstein II*, Ungar: New York 1977

The World of Entertainment, Doubleday: Garden City NY 1975

Gershwin, Ira, *Lyrics on Several Occasions*, Viking: New York 1973

Gottfried, Martin, *Broadway Musicals*, Abrams: New York 1979

Green, Benny, ed., *A Hymn to Him: The Lyrics of Alan Jay Lerner*, Pavilion-Michael Joseph: London 1987

Let's Face the Music, Pavilion-Michael Joseph: London 1989

Green, Stanley, *Encyclopedia of the Musical Theater*, Da Capo: New York 1984

Guernsey, Otis E., *Broadway Song and Story*, Dodd-Mead: New York 1985

Hammerstein, Oscar, *Lyrics*, Hal Leonard: Milwaukee 1985

Hart, Dorothy, *Thou Swell, Thou Witty: The Lyrics of Lorenz Hart*, Harper and Row: New York 1976

Hart, Moss, *Act One*, Random House: New York 1959

Higham, Charles, *Ziegfeld*, Regnery: Chicago 1972

Hirsch, Foster, *Harold Prince and the American Musical Theatre*, Cambridge University Press: Cambridge 1989

Jablonski, Edward, *Gershwin*, Simon & Schuster: London 1988

Kasha, Al (with Joel Hirshorn), *Notes On Broadway*, Contemporary: Chicago 1985

Kendall, Alan, *George Gershwin*, Harrap: London 1987

Kimball, Robert, ed., *The Complete Lyrics of Cole Porter*, Knopf: New York 1983

(with Dorothy Hart), *The Complete Lyrics of Lorenz Hart*, Knopf: New York 1986

(with Alfred Simon), *The Gershwins*, Atheneum: New York 1975

Krasker, Tommy (with Robert Kimball), *Catalogue of the American Musical*, National Institute for Opera and Musical Theater: Washington DC 1988

Kreuger, Miles, *Show Boat*, Oxford University Press: New York 1977

Lees, Gene, *The Singers and the Song*, Oxford University Press: New York 1987

A Modern Rhyming Dictionary, Cherry Lane Books: Greenwich CT 1981

Lerner, Alan Jay, *The Street Where I Live*, Norton: New York 1978

The Musical Theatre, Collins: London 1986

Logan, Joshua, *Josh*, Delacorte Press: New York 1976

Martin, George, ed., *Making Music*, Pan Books: London 1986

Morley Sheridan, *Spread a Little Happiness*, Thames and Hudson: London 1987

Gertrude Lawrence, McGraw-Hill: New York 1981

Shooting Stars, Quartet Books: London 1983

Payn, Graham ed. (with Sheridan Morley), *The Noël Coward Diaries*, Macmillan: London 1982

Raymond, Jack, *Show Music on Record*, Ungar: New York 1982

Richards, Stanley, ed., *Great Musicals of the American Tradition*, :

Schwartz, Charles, *Cole Porter*, Dial Press: New York 1977

Stevacre, Tony, *The Songwriters*, BBC: London 1985

Wilder, Alec, *American Popular Song*, Oxford University Press: New York 1972?

Zadan, Craig, *Sondheim & Company*, Harper & Row: New York 1986

INDEX

329